THE STORMY SEARCH FOR THE SELF

THE STORMY SEARCH FOR THE SELF

A Guide to Personal Growth
through Transformational Crisis

CHRISTINA GROF
and
STANISLAV GROF, M.D.

JEREMY P. TARCHER, INC.
Los Angeles

Library of Congress Cataloging in Publication Data

Grof, Christina.
    The stormy search for the self : a guide to personal growth
through transformational crisis / Christina Grof and Stanislav Grof.
        p.   cm.
    Includes bibliographical references.
    1. Spiritual life.   2. Psychiatric emergencies.   I. Grof,
Stanislav, 1931–   . II. Title.
    BL624.G76   1990
    291.4'2—dc20   89-29259
    ISBN 0-87477-553-1   CIP

Jeremy P. Tarcher, Inc.
5858 Wilshire Blvd., Suite 200
Los Angeles, CA 90036

Distributed by St. Martin's Press, New York

Design by Tanya Maiboroda

Manufactured in the United States of America
10 9 8 7 6 5 4 3 2 1

First Edition

CONTENTS

ACKNOWLEDGMENTS

As we have taken the personal and professional steps that have resulted in the writing of this book, we have been deeply affected by some very special and significant people. We would like to offer our gratitude to them for all they have given us.

First of all, thank you to our families for loving and supporting us during our many detours and diversions, and especially to our beloved children, Nathaniel and Sarah Healy, who play such essential roles in our lives and constantly bring us new hope, outrageous humor, and great happiness.

We have had the good fortune to encounter a number of teachers and other sources of inspiration who have offered us friendship and direction: our deep gratitude goes to the late Swami Muktananda Paramahansa, former head of the Siddha Yoga lineage, for his far-reaching influence in our lives; to the late Joseph Campbell, our beloved friend, matchmaker, and guide; to John Perry and Julian Silverman, for their pioneering work and their encouragement as we confronted some of the social and professional barriers that they know all too well; to Anne and Jim Armstrong, Angeles Arrien, Sandra and Michael Harner, Dora Kalff, Jack and Liana Kornfield, Father Thomas Matus, Brother David Steindl-Rast, Frances Vaughan, and Roger Walsh, our colleagues and dear friends in the transpersonal world, who through their personal explorations, teaching, and ways of being have helped to show us our own possibilities.

Thank you to the many gifted people who are involved in Holotropic Breathwork™ for their continuing enthusiasm and for the courage to undertake their own personal transformation and to Jacquelyn Small and Gregory Zelonka for their support of our work.

We offer our appreciation and respect to Jeremy Tarcher for gently nudging us until we wrote this book, and our sincere thanks to our editor, Dan Joy.

Our deep gratitude goes to Rod Allison, Sam Freeman, Betty Monaghan, Noelle Nichols, Mickey Reny, Nette Whitmore, and the other members of the loving staff at the former Brightside chemical-dependency treatment center in Carmel, California. We were enveloped by their patience, compassion, understanding, and humor during our darkest hour, as they helped us to transform our crisis into a miraculous opportunity for healing and expansion.

A special thank you to Margaret Stevens for her honest, willing, and sensitive assistance during the formulation of this project. Our gratitude goes to the staff and volunteers of the Spiritual Emergence Network, and especially to those who have served as its coordinators: Rita Rohen, Charles Lonsdale, Megan Nolan, Nicola Kester, and Jeneane Prevatt. Their valuable contributions and personal commitment, in spite of many hurdles, have provided countless numbers of people with much-needed help. And finally, thank you to the many individuals who, over the years, have told us very personal stories of their involvement with spiritual emergencies. Without them, we would not have written this book.

AUTHORS' NOTE

We dedicate this book with love and respect to the memory of Richard Price, the cofounder of the Esalen Institute in Big Sur, California, a gentle, compassionate Gestalt practitioner and teacher, a caring husband and father, and a remarkable human being. During our early interest in the area of spiritual emergency, Dick offered us his vital enthusiasm, invaluable support, clear vision, and loyal friendship as we pursued what seemed at times a lonely and sometimes unpopular path.

Dick knew the vicissitudes of the spiritual journey from his own experience, having personally lived through two transformative crises. During the first, which occurred when he was a young man, he was hospitalized for many months and received heavy tranquilizing medication, electroshock therapy, and over sixty-seven insulin coma treatments. The second episode occurred a number of years later and was handled very differently by people who had some understanding of the process and were willing to support him.

For many years, Dick was dedicated to the idea that experiences such as his are in reality opportunities for growth, healing, and expansion. He had seen and felt the violent intrusions that often accompany professional interventions, and worked to provide alternatives to traditional modes of treatment until his tragic death during a hiking accident in 1985. His commitment to these ideas was an inspiration to us, and his support during the creation of the Spiritual Emergence Network was essential to its existence. In writing this volume, we hope to provide useful ideas, information, and suggestions that will assist in the realization of some of the dreams that we shared with our dear friend Dick Price.

Christina and Stanislav Grof
Mill Valley, California
February 1990

INTRODUCTION

Spiritual development is an innate evolutionary capacity of all human beings. It is a movement toward wholeness, the discovery of one's true potential. And it is as common and as natural as birth, physical growth, and death—an integral part of our existence. For centuries, entire cultures have treated inner transformation as a necessary and desirable aspect of life. Many societies have developed sophisticated rituals and meditative practices as ways to invite and encourage spiritual growth. Humanity has stored the treasure of the emotions, visions, and insights involved in the process of awakening in paintings, poetry, novels, and music, and in descriptions provided by mystics and prophets. Some of the most beautiful and valued contributions to the world of art and architecture celebrate the mystical realms.

For some individuals, however, the transformational journey of spiritual development becomes a "spiritual emergency," a crisis in which the changes within are so rapid and the inner states so demanding that, temporarily, these people may find it difficult to operate fully in everyday reality. In our time, these individuals are rarely treated as if they are on the edge of inner growth. Rather, they are almost always viewed through the lens of disease and treated with technologies that obscure the potential benefits these experiences can offer.

In a supportive environment, and with proper understanding, these difficult states of mind can be extremely beneficial, often leading to physical and emotional healing, profound insights, creative activity, and permanent personality changes for the better. When we coined the term *spiritual emergency*, we sought to emphasize both the danger and opportunity inherent in such states. The phrase is, of course, a play on words, referring both to the crisis, or "emergency," that can accompany transformation, and to the idea of "emergence," suggesting the tremendous opportunity such experiences may offer for personal growth and the development of new levels of awareness.

The Stormy Search for the Self is for people whose lives are touched by spiritual emergency. It is for those who are actually experiencing or have experienced such a crisis, for their families and friends, and for the counselors, clergy, psychologists, psychiatrists, and therapists who might become involved in this extraordinary but completely natural process.

It is also a guide for anyone who is involved in personal transformation. Although these pages focus specifically on the difficult aspects of spiritual crisis, the lessons contained here are also applicable to those whose emergence, though relatively gentle, is nevertheless bewildering and, at times, uncomfortable. Those who have had this kind of experience may benefit from the suggestions given here as to how to better cooperate with and gain from this important process.

Throughout history, people in intense spiritual crises were acknowledged by many cultures as blessed; they were thought to be in direct communication with the sacred realms and divine beings. Their societies supported them through these crucial episodes, offering sanctuary and suspending the usual demands. Respected members of their communities had been through their own emergencies, could recognize and understand a similar process in others, and, as a result, were able to honor the expression of the creative, mystical impulse. The often colorful and dramatic experiences were nourished with the trust that these individuals would eventually return to the community with greater wisdom and an enhanced capacity to conduct themselves in the world, to their own benefit as well as that of society.

With the advent of modern science and the industrial age, this tolerant and even nurturing attitude changed drastically. The notion of acceptable reality was narrowed to include only those aspects of existence that are material, tangible, and measurable. Spirituality in any form was exiled from the modern scientific worldview. Western cultures adopted a restricted and rigid interpretation of what is "normal" in human experience and behavior and rarely accepted those who sought to go beyond these limits.

Psychiatry found biological explanations for certain mental disorders in the form of infections, tumors, chemical imbalances, and other afflictions of the brain or body. It also discovered powerful ways of controlling symptoms of various conditions for which the causes remained unknown, including the manifestations of spiritual crises. As a result of these successes, psychiatry became firmly established as a medical discipline, and the term *mental disease* was extended to include many states that, strictly speaking, were natural conditions that could not be linked to biological causes. The process of spiritual emergence in general, along with its more dramatic manifestations, came to be viewed as an illness, and those who demonstrated signs of what had been previously thought of as inner transformation and growth were in most cases now considered to be sick.

Consequently, many people who have emotional or psychosomatic symptoms are automatically classified as having a medical problem, and their difficulties are seen as diseases of unknown origin, although clinical and laboratory tests do not offer any supportive evidence for such an approach. Most nonordinary states of consciousness are considered pathological and are treated with traditional psychiatric methods such as suppressive medication and hospitalization. As a result of this bias, many people who are involved in the natural healing process of spiritual emergence are automatically put in the same category as those with true mental illness—especially if their experiences are causing a crisis in their lives or are creating difficulties for their families.

This interpretation is further fueled by the fact that much of our culture does not recognize the significance and value of the mystical domains within human beings. The spiritual elements inherent in personal transformation seem alien and threatening to those who are unfamiliar with them.

In the last couple of decades, however, this situation has been changing rapidly. Spirituality has been reintroduced into the mainstream culture through renewed interest in sacred systems such as those found in Eastern religions, Western mystical literature, and Native American traditions. Numerous people are experimenting with meditation and other forms of spiritual practice; others are involved in self-exploration using various new therapies. Through these methods, they are discovering new dimensions and possibilities within themselves. At the same time, revolutionary developments in many disciplines are rapidly closing the gap between science and spirituality, and modern physicists and researchers in other fields are moving toward a worldview similar to that described by the mystics.

Along with the renewed interest in mysticism, we are seeing another phenomenon: growing numbers of people are having spiritual and paranormal experiences and are willing to talk more openly about them. A survey by the Gallup Organization showed that 43 percent of the people polled admitted to having had unusual spiritual experiences, and 95 percent said that they believed in God or a universal spirit. From our own observations, it appears that coinciding with this expanded interest is a growing incidence of difficulties related to the transformation process.

We became deeply aware of this apparent increase in spiritual emergencies as we traveled around the world in the past decade, presenting workshops and lectures in which we talked about our personal experiences and our alternative understanding of some states that have automatically been labeled as psychotic. We were amazed to find many people who resonated with various elements of our stories. Some had been through transformative experiences and felt more fulfilled as a result.

Many others had had similar experiences but told us tragic stories of families and professionals who misunderstood them, of hospital commitments, unnecessary tranquilizers, and stigmatizing psychiatric labels. Often, a process that had originally begun as healing and transformative had been interrupted and even complicated by psychiatric intervention.

We have also met creative, compassionate, and innovative mental-health professionals—psychiatrists, psychologists, and others—who are looking for or are already providing alternatives for their patients. Many have expressed their frustration at not being able to pursue their ideas and approaches within their hospitals or clinics, largely due to their organizations' rigid adherence to the medical model, traditional administrative policy, and bureaucratic restrictions. They have told us of their professional loneliness and their desire to connect with like-minded people in their field.

As more and more people face spiritual emergencies, a growing number are becoming dissatisfied with the application of traditional psychiatric treatment during such events. Just as in recent years potential parents have actively pressured medical professionals to return to a sense of the time-honored reverence for birth and its dynamics, people involved in a transformational crisis are beginning to demand that professionals recognize their difficulties for what they are: challenging stages in a potentially life-changing process.

Consequently, it is crucial to address the issues surrounding spiritual emergence and spiritual emergency, to increase the understanding of the various states involved, and to formulate new treatment strategies that will help people live through and gain from them. We became deeply interested in the interface between spiritual development and psychological health largely because of our extensive personal exposure to it. Stan's curiosity about alternative approaches to the treatment of psychosis developed over three decades of research as a clinical psychiatrist into the therapeutic potential of nonordinary states of consciousness. As he worked with traditional models, he began to realize that the current scientific understanding of the human psyche was too limited and that many of the states that psychiatry automatically categorizes as symptoms of mental disease are actually important and necessary components of a profound healing process.

Christina's exposure to spiritual emergency began with a powerful spontaneous spiritual awakening during the birth of her first child. This experience was followed by years of difficult and demanding mental, emotional, and physical states. She discovered that these manifestations closely resembled what Yogic literature describes as the "Kundalini awakening." Our life together at the time of Christina's almost daily involvement in the transformational process forced us to learn many of the lessons that constitute the core of this book. To more completely reflect our personal involvement in this area, we have told our own stories in detail in two prologues.

This book is composed of three major sections, each addressing a different aspect of spiritual emergency. In Part One, we define the idea of spiritual emergency, clarify some of the concepts that underlie it, and describe how it feels and which forms it takes. The first chapter—entitled "What Is Spiritual Emergency?"—discusses the elements that characterize a crisis of transformation. How does this phenomenon differ from mental disease on the one hand and spiritual emergence on the other?

In the following two chapters, we explore the inner world of a person in a spiritual emergency. "The Dark Night of the Soul" describes the "negative" experiences that can occur during a spiritual crisis, and "Encountering the Divine" discusses "positive" states of mind.

Chapter 4, "Varieties of Spiritual Emergency," identifies ten important varieties of transformative crisis, discussing the qualities, characteristics, and specific challenges of each. Chapter 5, "Addiction As Spiritual Emergency," explores the idea that alcoholism, drug dependency, and other addictions can also be seen as spiritual emergencies that offer the same potential for beneficial inner development as other forms of transformative crises.

Part Two outlines many of the ancient and modern maps of the spiritual journey. Chapter 6, "Spiritual Lessons from the Past," looks at cultures that had high regard for spiritual experiences and acknowledged their healing power and transformative value. In Chapter 7, "Modern Maps of Consciousness," we review some of the developments in modern consciousness research and the new understanding of the human psyche that it has generated.

Part Three offers practical suggestions for those who are going through a spiritual emergency, as well as for those close to them. Chapter 8, "Strategies for Everyday Life," addresses the difficulties in trying to strike a balance between the requirements of an intense, dramatic inner process and the daily demands of the external world. In Chapter 9, "Guidelines for Family and Friends," we offer suggestions for concerned friends and relatives, discussing how they can best relate to the person in crisis and what they can do for themselves.

Chapter 10, "Who Can Help and How?," provides guidelines for finding support from such resources as sympathetic therapists, health professionals, spiritual teachers and communities, and self-help groups.

Concluding this section is "The Homecoming," a discussion of existence after spiritual emergency, offering recommendations for utilizing the rewards that come with inner growth to enhance one's life.

The epilogue, "Spiritual Emergence and the Global Crisis," addresses the relevance of spiritual emergency for the current global situation. People who go through a transformative process often develop an increased tolerance for others, a greater capacity for synergy, an ecological awareness, and a reverence for life. The apparent increase in the number of spiritual emergencies worldwide provides hope that this dynamic inner awakening, if properly understood and supported, can help to alleviate a multitude of problems now facing the global community.

Of the three appendices, the first focuses on the history and services of the Spiritual Emergence Network, the second outlines a vision of residential care centers for those in spiritual emergency, and the third offers special comments for mental-health professionals.

This book tries to present a balanced and comprehensive picture of spiritual emergency: some of the sections offer practical guidelines; others, theoretical understanding. Those who are having problems related to an inner transformation process, as well as the people surrounding them, may find it helpful to read the practical section (Part Three) first.

The kinds of intense transformative states of mind that are described in this book are more challenging and difficult than those that one ordinarily finds during the process of growth and transformation. If you participate in spiritual practice or other forms of deep inner exploration, you will not necessarily have a disruptive spiritual emergency. In fact, most people do not. We are well aware that for many people, this process is relatively easy and gentle. However, it is important to focus here on the critical aspects of transformation.

In discussing alternative approaches to the states associated with transformation, we are not proposing that they replace medical or psychiatric considerations. We want to emphasize that true mental diseases exist and require psychiatric treatment and care. While we firmly believe that *some* of the people who are labeled as psychotic are really undergoing difficult stages of spiritual opening, we are by no means implying that all psychoses are really transformative crises. The reader should be cautioned against taking such a generalized attitude. In Chapter 1 as well as in the appendix for professionals we discuss ways to distinguish between spiritual emergency and states that require traditional psychiatric or medical treatment.

There are many professionals in the psychiatric community who offer humane, loving, and comprehensive care for their patients. When we talk generally about traditional psychiatric approaches and the need for change in the field, we by no means intend to demean those individuals working in that context who have moved past the limitations and expectations of conventional routines in order to treat their clients more effectively. Valuable personal healing can and does take place in many hospitals and clinics; however, this is often due to exceptional individuals whose presence and influence cannot be ignored. One of our hopes in writing *The Stormy Search for the Self* is to encourage these creative professionals and help to expand their number.

This book has been a joint project unlike any we have ever shared. We have not only greatly enjoyed the process of writing it but also relished the experience of working together in exploring a meaningful area of our own personal and professional lives. We are two very different people from two divergent backgrounds. The writing was divided accordingly to allow each of us to draw from our own greatest strengths.

Christina has concentrated on the descriptive and practical chapters in the first and last sections, the chapter on addiction, and the appendices on the Spiritual Emergence Network and the residential care center; Stan has focused on the historical and anthropological insights, clinical issues, and scientific considerations of the middle segment, as well as the epilogue on the global crisis and the appendix for professionals.

We have tried to write the book we wish had been available during our own involvement with spiritual emergency. We hope that this volume will reassure, inform, and inspire those who are affected by the process of transformation, helping them to change these crises into opportunities for healing.

THE UNINVITED GUEST: CHRISTINA'S STORY

The Guest is inside you, and also inside me;
you know the sprout is hidden inside the seed.
We are all struggling; none of us has gone far.
Let your arrogance go, and look around inside.

The blue sky opens out farther and farther.
the daily sense of failure goes away,
the damage I have done to myself fades,
a million suns come forward with light,
when I sit firmly in that world.
KABIR, *The Kabir Book*

My own transformative journey is the primary reason for my intense interest and involvement in the area of spiritual emergency. For many years, I was immersed in a dramatic and challenging awakening that I felt had come uninvited into my existence; as this process continued, it changed my life and profoundly affected both Stan and me. Having lived daily with the intricacies of my adventure, we both learned many lessons, which have been helpful to others, and which have formed the core of the work that led to this volume, as well as to our first book in this field, *Spiritual Emergency: When Personal Transformation Becomes a Crisis*.

This is the case history of a spiritual emergency that we know the best. I have discovered that when I tell my own story, many people resonate with it, finding it helpful to know that they are not alone; perhaps the details vary, but the general dynamics seem to be common to many of us. As you read it, perhaps some of the themes that I describe will be familiar to you, either from your own life or the life of someone close to you. Be aware that I am describing my own spiritual emergency and that it is probably more colorful and dramatic than most. This is not the way it is for everyone.

Even though my journey was for many years turbulent and chaotic, I have moved through the overwhelmingly difficult stages to a clearer, more integrated way of existing than I have ever known. Once-jarring energies have become smooth and flowing, and the chaos of years past has been transformed into creativity. Numerous emotional issues that used to restrict me have been removed, and many of my former fears have been swept away. As a result of living through the challenges, I feel happier and more peaceful than ever before.

I spent most of my childhood in suburban Honolulu. From all appearances, I was like many young girls who grew up during the forties and fifties. Along with others of my generation, I concentrated on being a "good girl," relying on conventional values, doing what was expected of me, and remaining very much in control of myself. When I was not in school, I spent much of my time outdoors—swimming, surfing, and horseback riding. When I was ten, I learned about the Episcopal church near our house and developed a passion for Jesus. A couple of years later, I was confirmed into the church.

I loved the soft, sparkling celebration of birth at Christmas; it was a time of magic and poignancy. But the power of the events around Easter captivated me the most. To me, Jesus was not some historical figure who lived two thousand years ago. His death and resurrection were vivid experiences in which I could participate. He was real, present, and available to me here and now.

As I grew older, my connection with formalized religion faded and I discovered the same passionate feelings that I had had in church as I explored art, literature, and mythology. In college, I studied with the great mythologist Joseph Campbell and was excited to find the themes of death and rebirth appearing repeatedly in the myths of many cultures. In spite of my mind-expanding studies, though, my personal worldview was limited and fearful. I was afraid of many elements in life, and I was terrified of death. I believed that we walk through this world only once. We are born, we do as much as we can before death catches up with us, and then we die.

June 1964

Days after graduating from college, I married a high-school teacher whom I had met in Hawaii. We lived in Honolulu, where I taught art and creative writing. Having always enjoyed physical movement, I practiced gymnastics and joined a weekly Hatha Yoga class for exercise. I maintained a fairly traditional outlook on life and thought that my feelings of well-contained unhappiness were simply to be accepted as part of existence. And yet, deep down, I felt an unspecific inner yearning.

After four years, we decided to start a family and I immediately became pregnant with our first child. During the nine months of pregnancy, I combined Hatha Yoga stretches with the techniques I learned in classes of Lamaze childbirth preparation. I loved being pregnant, feeling that I was participating in a miracle, and eagerly anticipated the arrival of our baby.

September 28, 1968

Lying on the delivery table, I glanced up at the immense surgical lamp and the kind, curious faces of the doctor, the assisting intern and nurses, and my husband. After only a few hours of labor, my son was suddenly and rapidly making his way into the world as I enthusiastically cooperated. As the people around me encouraged me to "push . . . push . . . nice and hard, remember to breathe . . . ," I felt an abrupt snap somewhere inside of me as powerful and unfamiliar energies were released unexpectedly and began streaming through my body. I started to shake uncontrollably. Enormous electrical tremors coursed from my toes up my legs and spine to the top of my head. Brilliant mosaics of white light exploded in my head, and instead of continuing the Lamaze panting, I felt strange, involuntary breathing rhythms taking over.

It was as though I had just been hit by some miraculous but frightening force, and I was both excited and terrified; the shaking, the visions, and the spontaneous breathing were certainly not what I had expected from all of my months of preparation. As soon as my son was delivered, I was given two shots of morphine, which stopped the whole process. Soon, the wonder faded and I became embarrassed and fearful. I was a restrained, well-mannered woman who had a strong sense of authority over my life, and now I had completely lost control. Very quickly, I pulled myself together.

November 2, 1970

Two years after Nathaniel's birth, a similar experience happened during the final stages of my daughter Sarah's delivery. The experiences were even more forceful than the previous time, and I was given a large injection of tranquilizers, which confirmed my feeling that whatever was going on was somehow a sign of illness.

Afterward, I did what I could to repress and forget what I considered to be an inappropriate and humiliating occurrence. I loved being a mother and spent almost all my time with my children. I continued to study Hatha Yoga to keep in shape, becoming quite adept at performing complex physical exercises.

One day, someone in my advanced yoga class mentioned, with some excitement, that there was a guru from India coming to Honolulu who was offering a three-day retreat in which there would be chanting and meditation, interspersed with spiritual discourses. My marriage was disintegrating as the result of years of differences and unhappiness. I wanted a weekend away from home, and although I was not particularly interested, I signed up for the retreat, having no idea what I was getting into.

July 1974

The guru was known as Swami Muktananda, "Baba" to his followers. Originally from South India, he began his fervent spiritual search when he was fifteen, which eventually led him to his master, Bhagawan Nityananda. After years of intense meditation practice under his teacher's guidance, he attained self-realization. He became an acknowledged *shaktipat* master—one who is able, through a look, a touch, or a word, to awaken spiritual impulses and energies in people, beginning a process of spiritual development. During his later life, Muktananda made many trips to the West, where he initiated thousands of people through *shaktipat* into his tradition of Siddha Yoga, as well as lecturing and writing widely on meditation, yoga, the mind, and other spiritual topics.

The best way of describing my meeting with Muktananda is to say that it was like falling deeply in love or meeting a soul mate. My contact with him completely altered the course of my life. Although I knew little about Muktananda and his world, on the second day of the retreat I received *shaktipat*, entirely unexpectedly. During a meditation period, he first looked at me and then, with some force, slapped me several times on the forehead with his hand. The impact of that seemingly simple event blew the lid off the experiences, emotions, and energies I had been holding down since Sarah's birth.

Suddenly I felt as though I had been plugged into a high-voltage socket as I started to shake uncontrollably. My breathing fell into an automatic, rapid rhythm that seemed beyond my control, and a multitude of visions flooded my consciousness. I wept as I felt myself being born; I experienced death; I plunged into pain and ecstasy, strength and gentleness, love and fear, depths and heights. I was on an experiential roller coaster, and I knew I could no longer contain it. The genie was out of the bottle.

During the next few months, my whole life changed. My neat, restricted worldview was shattered, and I began to discover new possibilities within myself as my meditation experiences continued. Coincidentally, everything that I thought I was or had disappeared in rapid succession: the marriage ended, and with it went my status, money, even my credit cards. I felt as though my life had been switched into rapid motion, that many things that would have happened in time were suddenly accelerated. I was increasingly impelled by some unknown inner force to meditate and practice yoga, and I recognized Muktananda as my spiritual teacher. My preoccupation with new spiritual pursuits resulted in increasingly ineffective work, and I soon left my job. Many of my friends and family withdrew, bewildered by my new interests and upset by the failed marriage.

I had begun to have what I called anxiety attacks—shots of driving energy that sometimes made it difficult to concentrate on daily tasks. I was consumed with a mixture of panic, fear, and anger. Yet, at the same time I was aware of a gentle, deep connection with a new spirituality, an unfamiliar source inside me that was expansive, joyful, and peaceful. I no longer knew who I was or where I was going, my identity in the world was gone, and I did not feel in control of my life anymore.

May 1975

These events were intensified by an automobile accident in which I once again looked directly at death. In the flurry of activity and the crashing of metal and glass, I saw my life pass before me as though it were a movie. I was certain that I was dying. Suddenly I seemed to pass through an opaque curtain of death into a deep feeling of connection with everything in the universe. I sensed that I was part of some intricate, unified network that was all-inclusive and eternal, and I felt that in that place I would continue to exist in some form forever. My belief in the finality of death was undermined by an event that was so real it could not be denied, and I could no longer believe that death was the end of everything.

After a period of profound elation as a result of my discoveries, I came crashing down, drawn out of my new awarenesses by an increase in driving physical energies and forceful emotions—the electrical tremors, anxiety, and fear that had become part of my daily life. I had been rapidly propelled out of my safe, known reality into something that included death, birth, rebirth, spirituality, and many new physical and emotional feelings. I was frightened and lonely, and, since I had never heard of these experiences happening to anyone else, the only way I could understand my sudden departure from normalcy was to assume that I was becoming insane. I felt crazy and began to picture myself spending the rest of my life in a state mental institution.

Summer 1975

In June, our divorce was finalized and I sadly and fearfully ventured into an unknown solitary life. I decided to travel to the East Coast to see some friends and to find some new direction. There, I suddenly felt inspired to call Joseph Campbell, who had remained a friend in the years since college. We met in a small Italian restaurant in New York City, and I poured out my confusion. Joe listened intently and compassionately and, after thinking for a while, said, "I have a friend in California, at a place called Esalen, who knows about these things. His name is Stan Grof. Why don't you go to see him?"

I followed my mentor's advice, and that meeting in Big Sur, California, began a personal and professional relationship that has existed ever since. After hearing my story, Stan gave me his newly published first book, *Realms of the Human Unconscious*, and said, "Read the sections about the death-rebirth process and transpersonal experiences and see if any of the material makes sense."

I took the book and read it. I was amazed. It was based on Stan's twenty years of research with LSD and described the model of the human mind that had emerged from the detailed records he had kept of people's experiences during more than four thousand sessions. Even though I knew little about drugs and had certainly not explored LSD, the descriptions I was reading exactly matched many of my spontaneous experiences of birth, death, rebirth, and spirituality as well as the wide range of emotions and physical sensations. It was a revelation to suddenly have guidelines that helped me understand what had been happening to me.

What was just as important as Stan's insights was his strategy. He was saying that although these experiences can often be dramatic, arduous, disorganizing, and frightening, it is important to stay with the process and move through it. Also, if these experiences are properly supported, confronted, and integrated, they can be transformative, therapeutic, healing—perhaps even evolutionary.

This was just what I needed to hear. At a time when I felt absolutely, irrevocably lost, fearing for my sanity, my attitude suddenly changed. I was no longer convinced that I was crazy. Perhaps this really was simply a difficult stage in a process that would ultimately transform me from a limited, unhappy, isolated individual into a fulfilled, creative, serene human being.

October 1975

Stan and I began our life together in California, and although I was warmed and excited by the glow of a new and nourishing relationship, the inner chaos grew. I was constantly propelled by the now-familiar energies. Intense electrical tremors continued to hurtle through my body, causing increasingly violent shaking and involuntary rapid breathing. Constant physical pain became a daily reality, expressing itself through tensions in my legs, lower back, shoulders, and neck, and I was plagued by excruciating headaches, especially behind my eyes. I began to have spontaneous visions of all kinds, some of them coming from what appeared to be other historical times and places.

A new phenomenon began to dominate my reality. Astounding coincidences began to occur regularly in my life. I would talk about someone from my past and that afternoon receive an important letter or telephone call from that person. Or I would draw something that I had seen in a vision and the next day, while leafing through a book, unexpectedly come upon the same image. When these unusual occurrences started happening, I was fascinated. But soon they appeared constantly, and I felt oppressed by their content: many of them had to do with difficult family problems, death, loss, and grief. My former husband had legally obtained physical custody of our children, and the pain of losing them was unbearable. My reliable cause-and-effect world was no longer available; again, I felt out of control as I watched something else run my life.

May 11, 1976

Waking up on this morning, I found that I could no longer hang on to my familiar daily reality, and I slid into five days and nights of dark and fearsome experiences. As I sank helplessly into the inner turmoil, I thought desperately, This is the final step. I have lost everything else in my life, and now I am losing my mind.

Stan, on the other hand, had a very different point of view. Because of his work with LSD, he was familiar with the sometimes dramatic manifestations of the process of personal transformation, and he recognized my episode as such. It was happening spontaneously, without a chemical catalyst, and yet the range of the experiences was similar. With gentle enthusiasm, Stan told me he felt that this was not irreversible psychosis, but instead a very important step in my spiritual journey. We called it a "spiritual emergency."

He assured me that I was involved in a cleansing process, that old, trapped emotions, memories, and experiences that were causing problems in my life were being released. Rather than sickness, this was a step toward healing. Even though it was painful at the time, Stan told me that I would eventually emerge with a new sense of clarity, freedom, and peace. Suggesting that this was a propitious opportunity to radically develop myself, he encouraged me to face whatever came up: "The worst thing you can do is to resist what is happening; that will only make it more difficult. The best thing is to go completely into whatever comes up, fully experiencing it and moving through it."

With a great deal of support from Stan, I was finally able to allow the experiences and emotions to move through me relatively unobstructed. It was as though the voltage had been turned up: jolts of energy overtook my body and a multitude of uncontrollable images and sequences surfaced. I was attacked by hideous demons, and voracious, destructive monsters ripped me to shreds. I saw visions of disconnected, probing eyes, floating like malevolent planets in a black sky, and I lived through sequences of madness and witchcraft that seemed like memories from other times.

To my horror, I became identified with an agonized crucified Christ as well as with his murderers. I died many deaths, sometimes feeling that they were my own, at other times becoming people throughout history who had died in war, persecution, or torture. I screamed with fear and pain, rolled on the floor in agony. And there was much, much more.

Stan was there throughout most of the episode, gently reassuring me and taking care of my daily needs. He reminded me that throughout history human beings have created rituals as well as forms of meditation, prayer, chanting, dancing, drumming, and other practices designed to bring about such experiences. He said that I was fortunate to have them happening to me so readily.

Even though I had never experienced anything like what I was now going through, I knew intuitively that Stan was right: this event, as frightening and bewildering as it seemed, was a sacred time of sudden expansion. Somehow, through the confusion and the pain, I sensed the positive potential of the experience.

At the end of five days, familiar reality started to reappear, and I began to emerge from what I was describing as the dark night of my soul; I was no longer at the mercy of the visions and experiences of the past days and shakily started to feel interested in familiar daily activities: taking a bath and rummaging in the fridge for a snack. The episode had by no means totally completed itself, but I was at least able to function to some degree in the way I was used to. For months afterward, energetic tremors, extreme physical tensions, intense emotional ups and downs, and visionary sequences punctuated my life. Managing to conduct a "normal" daily life was difficult since I often felt as though I were straddling two worlds: the world of everyday reality and the complex, colorful, and demanding world of my unconscious.

I felt the benefits of the insights I had gained during my crisis. I acknowledged that I was more than my physical body: I also had a vast spiritual self that had been there all the time, waiting for me to discover it. Feeling that my potential was limitless, I recognized that my task in life was to clear away the personal restrictions that kept me from realizing those possibilities. However, I was still deeply troubled by the form this process was taking. I realized that Stan's model explained a lot about the aspects of birth, death, and spirituality, but it did not describe the general trajectory of this process, the strange pattern of physical sensations, or the very specific visions that I was having. That scared me.

What was this process that engaged every aspect of my physical, emotional, and spiritual nature, manifesting itself in strange energy patterns that ran up my legs, bolted up my spine to my head, and then continued over the top of my head and down the front of my body? Why the unrelenting forcefulness of inner activity that engaged my awareness daily and appeared at the most inconvenient times?

Sometime in 1977

Just as these questions were driving me to a point of desperation, I happened upon two books about the Kundalini awakening, an intricate form of spiritual transformation that has been well documented for centuries by Indian yogis. (We have included a description of the Kundalini awakening in chapter 4.) As I read the books, I felt a flood of recognition and reassurance; they contained many, many descriptions that portrayed my experiences exactly. I was elated. Suddenly I had a new map of the inner journey to go by.

I then began another phase of my odyssey; I had passed through a startling initiation, and now that I knew what I was dealing with, I settled into learning to live with this process. I began to discover that certain foods and activities were helpful and that others were best to avoid. And

I tried to keep in mind my new awareness that even the painful times were opportunities for change and sought to cooperate with the experiences and energies when they appeared.

Spring 1980

After I had started to understand and work with my own emergence process, I began to tell my story during the workshops Stan and I led and to talk with others who had had comparable experiences. I was amazed at the number of people who had lived through a journey similar to mine and at the many others who were still struggling, often stuck in their own inner adventures. I began to realize that many individuals who are genuinely engaged in a transformational crisis are routinely misunderstood, misdiagnosed, and mistreated by much of traditional psychiatry and psychology. Profoundly grateful that I had escaped that fate, I felt there should be some kind of alternative understanding and care for those who want it.

With this purpose in mind, I founded the Spiritual Emergence Network, an international resource-and-information network that offers support to those who are in crisis as well as to those around them. A more comprehensive description of SEN appears in appendix I.

August 1989

Three and a half years ago, the most difficult and chaotic manifestations of my spiritual emergence, which had occupied my daily life for twelve years, changed and cleared. The route that took me to this point was complex and painful: I had begun using alcohol to relieve the difficult manifestations of the Kundalini process and, over time, had become an alcoholic (I will discuss my alcoholism and its influence on my transformation process in chapter 5). Without going into detail here, I will say that I have been in recovery for some time. As I write, I have found a state of equanimity, serenity, and connection unlike any I have previously experienced. This does not mean that my life is always simple and easy, but its natural ups and downs no longer overwhelm me. Although I recognize that my inner work is far from complete, I feel a general ease in my existence, and I have developed a deep trust in the wisdom of the spiritual process. After a lifetime of yearning for contact with the force that I perceive to be God, I am finding that, with some effort on my part, it is possible to feel that connection daily. There is a new peace in my life, as well as an appreciation for the beauty of existence.

GOD IN THE LABORATORY: STANISLAV'S STORY

> The most beautiful emotion we can experience is the mystical. It is the sower of all true art and science. He to whom this emotion is a stranger is as good as dead.
>
> ALBERT EINSTEIN

My personal and professional history is somewhat unusual since it was my scientific research and everyday observations in clinical and laboratory work that undermined my initial atheistic worldview and attracted my attention to the spiritual domain. This is not completely unique, since there have been other scientists whose research brought them to a mystical understanding of the universe and to a cosmic type of spirituality. However, it is certainly much more common for the exact opposite to take place: individuals who in childhood had a very strict religious upbringing often find a spiritual worldview untenable when they gain access to the information about the world amassed by Western science.

I was born in 1931 in Prague and spent my childhood partly in that city and partly in a small Czech town. In the early years of my life my interests and hobbies already reflected a great curiosity about the human psyche and culture. My actual involvement with psychiatry and psychology started when I was finishing high school. A close friend of mine lent me, with warm recommendations, Sigmund Freud's *Introductory Lectures to Psychoanalysis*.

Reading this book turned out to be one of the most profound and influential experiences of my life. I was deeply impressed by Freud's penetrating mind, his unrelenting logic, and his ability to bring rational understanding to such obscure areas as the symbolism and language of dreams, the dynamics of neurotic symptoms, the psychopathology of everyday life, and the psychology of art. Since I was close to graduation, I was about to make some serious decisions about my future. Within a

18

few days of finishing Freud's book, I decided to apply to medical school, which was a necessary prerequisite for becoming a psychoanalyst.

In my childhood I was not exposed to religious programming of any kind. My parents had decided not to commit me and my younger brother to a specific church affiliation, wanting us to make our own choice when we came of age. Although I was intellectually interested in religions and Oriental philosophy, I was basically an atheist. Six years of studies at the Charles University School of Medicine in Prague further strengthened my atheistic worldview. A materialistic orientation and mechanistic thinking are characteristic of Western medical training anywhere in the world. Furthermore, in Prague and other Eastern European countries at that time, the education system was dominated by Marxist ideology, which was particularly hostile to any departures from pure materialistic doctrine. Any concepts that would point in the direction of idealism and mysticism were either carefully screened from the curriculum or subjected to ridicule.

I studied a broad spectrum of scientific disciplines under these special circumstances, which only reinforced my conviction that any form of religious belief or spirituality was absurd and incompatible with scientific thinking. I also read mainstream psychiatric literature suggesting that direct spiritual and mystical experiences in the lives of the great prophets, saints, and founders of religions were actually manifestations of mental diseases that had scientific names.

Although the causes of these mental diseases, or psychoses, had so far eluded the determined efforts of countless teams of scientists, the general opinion was that a pathological process of some kind had to underlie such extreme experiences and behaviors. It seemed that it was just a question of time until medicine would explain the exact nature of this problem and discover effective therapeutic measures. Though I had little reason to doubt the beliefs of so many prominent scientific and academic authorities in this regard, I often wondered why millions of people throughout history allowed themselves to be so deeply influenced by visionary experiences if those experiences were nothing but meaningless products of brain pathology. However, this doubt was not strong enough to undermine my trust in traditional psychiatry.

During my medical studies, I joined a small psychoanalytic group in Prague led by three analysts who were members-at-large of the International Psychoanalytic Association. This was all that was left of the Czechoslovakian Freudian movement after the Nazi purges during World War II. We conducted regular seminars in which we discussed various important works from the psychoanalytic literature and selected case histories. Later I underwent a training analysis with the former president of the Czechoslovakian Psychoanalytic Association. I also became a student volunteer at the psychiatric department of the Charles University School of Medicine in Prague to gain early exposure to clinical psychiatry.

As I became better acquainted with psychoanalysis, I started experiencing a deep dilemma and schism in my thinking. The studies I had read by Freud and his followers seemed to offer brilliant and fascinating interpretations of many different aspects of mental life. However, the situation was quite different regarding the practical application of Freudian analysis in clinical work. I realized that it was very exclusive, time-consuming, and ineffective. To be eligible for psychoanalysis, one had to meet special criteria, and many psychiatric patients were automatically excluded as potential candidates. What was even worse was the time factor: those few selected as appropriate subjects had to commit themselves for three to five fifty-minute therapeutic sessions a week for a number of years. The sacrifice of time, energy, and money was enormous in comparison with the results.

I had great difficulty in understanding why a conceptual system that seemed to have all the theoretical answers did not offer more impressive results when applied to real clinical problems. My medical training had taught me that if I really understood a problem, I would be able to do something quite dramatic about it. (In the case of incurable diseases, we at least have some idea of why a problem resists therapeutic efforts and know what would have to change to make it treatable.) But in the case of psychoanalysis, I was asked to believe that although we had a complete understanding of the problems we were working with, we could do relatively little about them over an extremely long period of time.

When I was struggling with this dilemma, the department where I was working received a complimentary parcel from the Sandoz Pharmaceutical Laboratories in Basel, Switzerland. As I opened it, I noticed a mysterious conglomeration of three letters and two numbers: LSD-25. It was a sample of a new experimental substance with remarkable psychoactive properties, discovered in a strange case of serendipity by the leading chemist at Sandoz, Dr. Albert Hofmann. After some preliminary psychiatric work had been done in Switzerland, the company was making samples of this drug available to researchers all over the world, requesting feedback about its effects and potential. Among its possible uses were the exploration of the nature and causes of psychoses, particularly schizophrenia, and the training of psychiatrists and psychologists.

The early experiments conducted in Switzerland showed that minuscule dosages of this amazing substance could profoundly change the consciousness of the subjects for a period of six to ten hours. The researchers found some interesting similarities between these states and

the symptomatology of naturally occurring psychoses. It seemed, therefore, that the study of such "experimental psychoses" could provide interesting insights into the causes of this most enigmatic group of
psychiatric disorders. The possibility of experiencing a reversible "psychotic" state provided a unique opportunity for all professionals working
with psychotic patients to gain intimate acquaintance with their inner
world, understand them better and, as a result, treat them more effectively.

I was extremely excited about the opportunity for such unique training and, in 1956, became one of the early experimental subjects. My first
LSD session was an event that has in its consequences profoundly
changed my professional and personal life. I experienced an extraordinary
encounter and confrontation with my unconscious psyche, which instantly overshadowed my previous interest in Freudian psychoanalysis.
This day marked the beginning of my radical departure from traditional
thinking in psychiatry. I was treated to a fantastic display of colorful
visions, some of them abstract and geometrical, others figurative and full
of symbolic meaning. I also felt an amazing array of emotions with an
intensity I did not know was possible. I could not believe how much I
learned about my psyche in those few hours. One aspect of my first session
deserves special notice, since its significance reached far beyond the level
of psychological insights: my preceptor at the faculty was very interested
in studying the electrical activity of the brain, and his favorite subject
was the exploration of the influence of various frequencies of flashing light
on the brain waves. I agreed to have my brain waves monitored by an
electroencephalograph as part of the experiment.

I was exposed to a strong stroboscopic light between the third and
fourth hour of my experience. At the scheduled time, a research assistant
appeared and took me to a small room. She carefully pasted electrodes
all over my scalp and asked me to lie down and close my eyes. Then she
placed a giant stroboscopic light above my head and turned it on.

At this time, the effects of the drug were culminating, and that immensely enhanced the impact of the strobe. I was hit by a radiance that
seemed comparable to the epicenter of an atomic explosion, or possibly
to the light of supernatural brilliance that according to Oriental scriptures
appears to us at the moment of death. This thunderbolt catapulted me
out of my body. I lost first my awareness of the research assistant and
the laboratory, then the psychiatric clinic, then Prague, and finally the
planet. My consciousness expanded at an inconceivable speed and
reached cosmic dimensions.

As the young assistant gradually shifted the frequency of the strobe
up and down the scale, I found myself in the middle of a cosmic drama

of unimaginable proportions. I experienced the Big Bang, passed through black and white holes in the universe, identified with exploding super-novas, and witnessed many other strange phenomena that seemed to be pulsars, quasars, and other amazing cosmic events.

There was no doubt that the experience I was having was very close to those I knew from reading the great mystical scriptures of the world. Even though my mind was deeply affected by the drug, I was able to see the irony and paradox of the situation. The Divine manifested itself and took me over in a modern laboratory in the middle of a serious scientific experiment conducted in a Communist country with a substance pro-duced in the test tube of a twentieth-century chemist.

I emerged from this experience touched to the core and immensely impressed by its power. Not believing at that time, as I do today, that the potential for a mystical experience is the natural birthright of all human beings, I attributed everything to the effect of the drug. I felt strongly that the study of nonordinary states of mind in general, and those induced by psychedelics in particular, was by far the most interesting area of psychiatry and decided to make it my field of specialization.

I realized that, under the proper circumstances, psychedelic experi-ences—to a much greater degree than dreams, which play such a crucial role in psychoanalysis—are truly, in Freud's words, a "royal road into the unconscious." This powerful catalyst could help to heal the gap be-tween the great explanatory power of psychoanalysis and its lack of ef-ficacy as a therapeutic tool. I felt strongly that LSD-assisted analysis could deepen, intensify, and accelerate the therapeutic process and produce practical results matching the ingenuity of Freudian theoretical specu-lations.

Within weeks of my session, I joined a group of researchers com-paring the effects of different psychedelic substances with naturally oc-curring psychoses. As I was working with experimental subjects, I could not get off my mind the idea of starting a project in which psychoactive drugs could be used as catalysts for psychoanalysis.

My dream came true when I won a position at the newly founded Psychiatric Research Institute in Prague. Its open-minded director ap-pointed me principal investigator of a clinical study exploring the ther-apeutic potential of LSD psychotherapy. I initiated a research project using a series of sessions with medium dosages in patients with various forms of psychiatric disorders. On occasion, we included mental-health professionals, artists, scientists, and philosophers who were interested and had serious motivations for the experience, such as gaining a deeper understanding of the human psyche, enhancement of creativity, or fa-cilitation of problem solving. The repeated use of such sessions became popular among European therapists under the name "psycholytic treatment"; its Greek roots suggest a process of dissolving psychological conflicts and tensions.

I began a fantastic intellectual, philosophical, and spiritual adventure that has now lasted more than three decades. During this time, my worldview has been undermined and destroyed many times by daily exposure to extraordinary observations and experiences. A most remarkable transformation has happened as a result of my systematic study of the psychedelic experiences of others as well as my own: under the unrelenting influx of incontrovertible evidence, my understanding of the world has gradually shifted from an atheistic position to a basically mystical one. What had been foreshadowed in a cataclysmic way by my first experience of cosmic consciousness has been brought to full fruition by careful daily work on the research data.

My initial approach to LSD psychotherapy was deeply influenced by the Freudian model of the psyche, which is limited to postnatal life history and the individual unconscious. Soon after I started working with different categories of psychiatric patients using repeated sessions, it became clear that such a conceptual framework was painfully narrow. While it might be appropriate for some forms of verbal psychotherapy, it was clearly inadequate for situations where the psyche was activated by a powerful catalyst. As long as we used medium dosages, many of the initial experiences of the series contained biographical material from the individual's infancy and childhood, as described by Freud. However, when the sessions were continued, each of the clients moved sooner or later into experiential realms that lay beyond this framework. When the dosages were increased, the same thing happened, but much earlier.

Once the sessions reached this point, I started witnessing experiences that were indistinguishable from those described in the ancient mystical traditions and spiritual philosophies of the East. Some of them were powerful sequences of psychological death and rebirth; others involved feelings of oneness with humanity, nature, and the cosmos. Many clients also reported visions of deities and demons from different cultures and visits to various mythological realms. Among the most astonishing occurrences were dramatic and vivid sequences that were subjectively experienced as past-incarnation memories.

I was not prepared to observe such phenomena in psychotherapeutic sessions. I knew about their existence from my studies of comparative religion, but my psychiatric training had taught me to consider them psychotic, not therapeutic. I was astonished by their emotional power, authenticity, and transformative potential. Initially, I did not welcome this unexpected development in my therapeutic venture. The intensity of the emotional and physiological manifestations of these states was frightening, and many of their aspects threatened to undermine my safe and reliable worldview.

However, as my experience and familiarity with these extraordinary phenomena increased, it became clear that they were normal and natural manifestations of the deeper domains of the human psyche. Their emergence from the unconscious followed upon the appearance of biographical material from childhood and infancy, which traditional psychotherapy considers a legitimate and desirable subject of exploration. Thus it would have been highly artificial and arbitrary to view childhood memories as normal and acceptable and attribute the experiences that followed them to a pathological process.

When the nature and content of these recesses of the psyche were fully revealed, they undoubtedly represented a significant source of difficult emotional and physical feelings. In addition, when these sequences were allowed to run their natural course, the therapeutic results transcended anything I had ever witnessed. Difficult symptoms that had resisted months and even years of conventional treatment often disappeared after experiences such as psychological death and rebirth, feelings of cosmic unity, and sequences that clients described as past-life memories.

My observations of others were in full agreement with those from my own psychedelic sessions: many states that mainstream psychiatry considers bizarre and incomprehensible are natural manifestations of the deep dynamics of the human psyche. And their emergence into consciousness, traditionally seen as a sign of mental illness, may actually be the organism's radical effort to free itself from the effects of various traumas, simplify its functioning, and heal itself. I realized that it was not up to us to dictate what the human psyche should be like in order to fit our scientific beliefs and worldview. Rather, it is important to discover and accept the true nature of the psyche and find out how we can best cooperate with it.

I attempted to map the experiential territories that were made available through the catalyzing action of LSD. For several years, I dedicated all of my time to psychedelic work with patients of various clinical diagnoses, keeping detailed records of my own observations and collecting their own descriptions of their sessions. I believed I was creating a new cartography of the human psyche. However, when I completed a map of consciousness that included the different types and levels of experiences I had observed in psychedelic sessions, it dawned on me that it was new only from the point of view of Western academic psychiatry. It became clear that I had rediscovered what Aldous Huxley called "perennial philosophy," an understanding of the universe and of existence that has emerged with some minor variations again and again in different countries and historical periods. Similar maps have existed in various cultures for centuries or even millenia. The different systems of yoga, Buddhist teachings, the Tibetan Vajrayana, Kashmir Shaivism, Taoism, Sufism, Kabbalah, and Christian mysticism are just a few examples.

The process I was witnessing in others and experiencing myself also had a deep similarity with shamanic initiations, rites of passage of various cultures, and the ancient mysteries of death and rebirth. Western scientists had ridiculed and rejected these sophisticated procedures, believing that they had successfully replaced them with rational and scientifically sound approaches. My observations convinced me that such modern fields as psychoanalysis and behaviorism had only scratched the surface of the human psyche and could bear no comparison to the depth and scope of such ancient knowledge.

In the early years of my research, I became enthusiastic about these exciting new observations and made several attempts to discuss them with my Czech colleagues. I quickly found that my scientific reputation would be at stake if I continued to do so. During the first decade of this work, much of my research was done in isolation, and I had to carefully censor my communications with other professionals. I found only a handful of friends with whom I could openly talk about my findings.

My situation started to change in 1967, when I was awarded a scholarship from a foundation for psychiatric research in New Haven, Connecticut. This made it possible for me to come to the United States and continue my psychedelic research at the Maryland Psychiatric Research Center in Baltimore. During my lectures in various American cities, I connected with many colleagues—consciousness researchers, anthropologists, parapsychologists, thanatologists, and others—whose work resulted in a scientific perspective that resembled or complemented my own.

One important event at this time was my encounter and friendship with Abraham Maslow and Anthony Sutich, the founders of humanistic psychology. Abe had conducted extensive research into spontaneous mystical states, or "peak experiences," and came to conclusions very similar to my own. Out of our joint meetings came the idea of launching a new discipline that would combine science and spirituality and incorporate the perennial wisdom concerning various levels and states of consciousness.

The new movement, which we called "transpersonal psychology," attracted many enthusiastic followers. As their numbers grew, I felt for the first time a sense of professional identity and belonging. However, one problem still remained: transpersonal psychology, although comprehensive and cohesive in its own right, seemed hopelessly separated from mainstream science.

Another decade passed before it became obvious that traditional science was itself undergoing a conceptual revolution of unprecedented proportions. The radical changes that were introduced into the scientific worldview by Einstein's theories of relativity and quantum theory were followed by equally profound revisions occurring in many other disciplines. New connections were being established between transpersonal psychology and the emerging scientific worldview that has become known as the "new paradigm."

At present, we are still lacking a satisfactory synthesis of these developments, which are replacing old ways of thinking about the world. However, the impressive mosaic of new observations and theories that are already available suggests that in the future the old/new discoveries in regard to consciousness and the human psyche might become integral parts of a comprehensive scientific worldview.

Three decades of detailed and systematic studies of the human mind through observations of nonordinary states of consciousness in others and myself have led me to some radical conclusions. I now believe that consciousness and the human psyche are much more than accidental products of the physiological processes in the brain; they are reflections of the cosmic intelligence that permeates all of creation. We are not just biological machines and highly developed animals, but also fields of consciousness without limits, transcending space and time.

In this context, spirituality is an important dimension of existence, and becoming aware of this fact is a desirable development in human life. For some, this process takes the form of unusual experiences that can at times be disturbing and dramatic; these are crises of transformation, for which Christina and I created the term *spiritual emergencies*.

Christina has described her story in the companion prologue with unusual honesty and openness; the years of her spiritual awakening were extremely demanding for both of us. Although I was familiar with nonordinary states of consciousness from my own experiences and from my work with many others, participating in this process around the clock with a person who was emotionally so close to me revealed entirely new aspects and dimensions that remain hidden during work with nonordinary states of consciousness in a professional context. In retrospect, Christina values highly what she has been through, although on occasion she felt stretched to her utmost limits. I can say the same for myself; this extremely difficult period was a time of invaluable learning that only real life can provide.

My beliefs were further reinforced by our observations of the effects of Holotropic Breathwork,™ a powerful method that Christina and I developed. This simple approach—combining accelerated breathing, music, and body work—can induce, in a safe and supportive framework, an entire spectrum of healing experiences comparable to those known from spontaneous transformative episodes; however, unlike the latter, these experiences remain limited to the periods of holotropic sessions.

The concept of spiritual emergency and the guidelines for dealing with the crises of transformation described in this book are results of fourteen years of a stormy personal and professional journey that we shared. From that journey came Christina's idea to found the Spiritual Emergence Network, a worldwide fellowship that supports individuals undergoing crises of transformation in a way that is based on the new principles.

PART ONE

THE STORMY SEARCH FOR THE SELF

CHAPTER 1

WHAT IS SPIRITUAL EMERGENCY?

And like all those who faint away through excess of
pleasure and joy, she remains as it were unconscious
in the divine arms and on the divine breast. She no
longer cares for anything except to abandon herself
to joy, nourished by the divine milk . . . This heavenly
inebriation by which she is delighted and terrified
at the same time . . . this holy madness . . .

SAINT TERESA OF AVILA, *Thoughts on the Love of God*

In modern society, spiritual values have been, in general,
replaced by materialistic considerations and largely ignored. It is now
becoming increasingly evident that a craving for transcendence and a
need for inner development are basic and normal aspects of human nature. Mystical states can be profoundly healing and can have an important
positive impact on the life of the person involved. Moreover, many difficult episodes of nonordinary states of consciousness can be seen as
crises of spiritual transformation and opening. Stormy experiences of
this kind—or "spiritual emergencies," as we call them—have been repeatedly described in sacred literature of all ages as rough passages along
the mystical path.

Spiritual emergencies can be defined as critical and experientially difficult stages of a profound psychological transformation that involves
one's entire being. They take the form of nonordinary states of consciousness and involve intense emotions, visions and other sensory
changes, and unusual thoughts, as well as various physical manifestations. These episodes often revolve around spiritual themes; they include
sequences of psychological death and rebirth, experiences that seem to
be memories from previous lifetimes, feelings of oneness with the universe, encounters with various mythological beings, and other similar
motifs.

31

What Triggers Spiritual Emergency?

In most instances, one can identify the situation that seems to have triggered the transformation crisis. It can be some primarily physical factor, such as a disease, an accident, an operation, extreme physical exertion, or prolonged lack of sleep. Circumstances of this kind can lower psychological resistance by weakening the body and, in addition, function as a powerful reminder of death and the frailty of human life. The most dramatic example in this category is spiritual emergency following a near-death experience associated with a severe biological crisis, which mediates access to very profound transcendental experiences.

In women, a transformation crisis can be triggered by the combination of physical and emotional stress during childbirth. Since delivery is a potentially life-threatening situation, there is an element of death in every birth; this experience thus takes the mother to the very frontiers of individual existence—its beginning and end. This is also the interface between the personal and transpersonal. In some instances, a miscarriage or abortion can play a similar role.

Occasionally, a psychospiritual transformation can begin during intense and emotionally overwhelming lovemaking. Sex also has important transpersonal dimensions: on the one hand, it is a vehicle for transcending the biological mortality of the individual by leading to new birth; on the other it has deep connections with death. The French actually call sexual orgasm "small death" (*petite mort*). Sexual union that occurs in the context of a powerful emotional bond can take the form of a profound mystical experience. All individual boundaries seem to dissolve and the partners feel reconnected to their divine source. Besides being a biological union of two humans, such a situation might be experienced as a spiritual union of the feminine and the masculine principles and appear to have divine dimensions. The deep liaison between sexuality and spirituality is acknowledged and cultivated in the Tantric spiritual traditions.

At other times, the beginning of a spiritual emergency can be traced back to a strong emotional experience, particularly one that involves a serious loss. This can be the end of an important love affair, divorce, or the death of a child, parent, or other close relative. Less frequently, the immediately preceding event is an unexpected financial disaster, a series of failures, or the loss of an important job.

In predisposed individuals, the last straw can be an experience with mind-altering drugs or an intense session of psychotherapy. There have been instances where a transformational crisis started in a dentist's chair with the extraction of a tooth under nitrous oxide. The era of wild unsupervised experimentation with psychedelics catapulted many people into a spiritual opening and some into spiritual emergency. We have also seen situations where a drug prescribed for medical reasons was the precipitating event.

A hypnotic session conducted with the intention of relieving an agonizing migraine headache can unexpectedly lead to the experience of death and rebirth, "past-life memories," and other spiritual domains of the psyche that might be difficult to assimilate. The same is true for experiential-psychotherapy sessions that have not been brought to a successful resolution.

The wide range of seeming triggers of spiritual emergency clearly suggests that the individual's readiness for inner transformation is by far more important than external stimuli. But when we do look for a common denominator or final pathway in the triggering situations, we find that all those situations involve a radical shift in the balance between the unconscious and conscious processes. Something happens that favors the unconscious dynamics to the extent that these override ordinary awareness. Sometimes the ego defenses can be weakened by a biological assault; at other times a psychological trauma interferes with the outward-oriented efforts of the individual, redirecting him or her into the inner world.

The most important catalyst for spiritual emergencies is a deep involvement in various spiritual practices. Many of these have, in fact, been specifically designed to facilitate mystical experiences by isolating the seeker from outer influences and orienting him or her toward the inner world. It is easy to imagine spiritual impulses arising in active forms of worship, such as trance dancing, Sufi whirling, powerful drumming, gospel singing, or continuous chanting. But transformational crises can also be initiated by less dramatic forms, such as sitting or moving meditation, contemplation, and devotional prayer.

As various Oriental and Western spiritual disciplines gain popularity, more and more people seem to experience transformational crises directly related to their practice. We have been repeatedly contacted by persons whose unusual experiences occurred during the practice of Zen, Vipassana Buddhist meditation, Kundalini yoga, Sufi exercises, and Christian prayer or monastic contemplation.

What is Spiritual Emergence?

To understand the problem of spiritual emergency, one has to see it in a larger context of "spiritual emergence," as a complication of an evolutionary process that leads to a more mature and fulfilling way of life.

The mystical teachings of all ages revolve around the idea that the exclusive pursuit of material goals and values by no means expresses the full potential of human beings. According to this point of view, humanity is an integral part of the creative cosmic energy and intelligence and is, in a sense, identical to and commensurate with it. Discovery of one's divine nature can lead to a way of being, on both an individual and a collective scale, that is incomparably superior to what is ordinarily considered the norm.

This was most succinctly expressed by the Neoplatonic philosopher Plotinus, who said: "Mankind is poised midway between the gods and the beasts." Many spiritual systems have described higher levels and states of mind that lead to the realization of one's divine nature and God consciousness. This spectrum of being is characterized by progressively increasing subtlety and refinement, lesser degrees of density, more encompassing awareness, and greater participation in cosmic intelligence.

The best-known system reflecting the far-reaching possibilities of consciousness development is the Indian concept of the seven *chakras*, or psychic energy centers. The chakras are located at different levels of the central axis of the human organism in the so-called energetic or "subtle body." The degree to which the individual chakras are open or obstructed determines the way one experiences the world and relates to it. The three lower chakras govern the forces that drive human behavior prior to spiritual awakening—the survival instinct, sexuality, aggression, competitiveness, and acquisitiveness. The higher chakras represent the potential for experiences and states of being increasingly imbued with cosmic consciousness and spiritual awareness.

In the most general terms, *spiritual emergence* can be defined as the movement of an individual to a more expanded way of being that involves enhanced emotional and psychosomatic health, greater freedom of personal choices, and a sense of deeper connection with other people, nature, and the cosmos. An important part of this development is an increasing awareness of the spiritual dimension in one's life and in the universal scheme of things.

The potential for spiritual emergence is an innate characteristic of human beings. The capacity for spiritual growth is as natural as the disposition of our bodies toward physical development, and spiritual rebirth is as normal a part of human life as biological birth. Like birth, spiritual emergence has been seen for centuries by many cultures as an intrinsic part of life, and, like birth, it has become pathologized in modern society. The experiences that occur during this process cover a wide spectrum of depth and intensity, from the very gentle to the overwhelming and disturbing.

From Spiritual Emergence to Spiritual Emergency

Sometimes the process of spiritual awakening is so subtle and gradual that it is almost imperceptible. After a period of months or years, a person looks back and notices that there has been a profound shift in his or her understanding of the world, values, ethical standards, and life strategies. This change might start by reading a book that contains a message so clear and convincing that it is impossible to ignore. One is left with a longing to know and experience more; then, coincidentally, the author comes to town to give a lecture. This leads to associations with other people who share this excitement, to the discovery of other books, and to attending additional lectures and workshops. The spiritual journey has begun!

At other times, spiritual awareness enters one's life in the form of a deeper and changed perception of certain situations of everyday life. A person might walk into the cathedral in Chartres with a tour group and, completely unexpectedly, feel overwhelmed by the choir and the organ music, by the play of light in the stained-glass windows, and by the grandeur of the Gothic arches. The memory of this rapture and the sense of being connected with something greater than oneself remains. Similar transformations of perception have occurred in people during a raft trip through the majestic beauty of the Grand Canyon or in some other stunning natural setting. For many, the entry into the transcendental domain has been opened by art.

None of these individuals will ever again think of themselves as completely separate. They all have had vivid and convincing experiences that transported them beyond the restrictions of their physical bodies and limited self-concept to a connection with something outside of themselves.

When spiritual emergence is very rapid and dramatic, however, this natural process can become a crisis, and spiritual emergence becomes spiritual emergency. People who are in such a crisis are bombarded with inner experiences that abruptly challenge their old beliefs and ways of existing, and their relationship with reality shifts very rapidly. Suddenly they feel uncomfortable in the formerly familiar world and may find it difficult to meet the demands of everyday life. They can have great problems distinguishing their inner visionary world from the external world of daily reality. Physically, they may experience forceful energies streaming through their bodies and causing uncontrollable tremors.

Fearful and resistant, they might spend much time and effort trying to control what feels like an overwhelming inner event. And they may feel impelled to talk about their experiences and insights to anyone who is within range, sounding out of touch with reality, disjointed, or messianic. However, when offered understanding and guidance, they are usually cooperative and grateful to have someone with whom they can share their journey. The basic criteria for assessing when spiritual emergence has become a crisis are summarized in table 1.

It should be noted that spiritual emergence and spiritual emergency represent a continuum and that it is not always easy to differentiate between them. Throughout this book, we will use the term *spiritual emergency* as a matter of convenience and simplification, even though we will sometimes be talking about situations that might for certain people and under specific conditions better fit the category of spiritual emergence.

The Healing Potential of Spiritual Emergencies

It is important to realize that even the most dramatic and difficult episodes of spiritual emergency are natural stages in the process of spiritual opening and can be beneficial if circumstances are favorable. The activation of the psyche characterizing such a crisis involves a radical clearing of various old traumatic memories and imprints. This process is by its very nature potentially healing and transformative. However, so much psychological material surfaces from various levels of the unconscious that it interferes with the everyday functioning of the person involved. Thus it is not the nature and content of these experiences but their context that makes them seem pathological. Similar states would be not only acceptable but desirable in experiential psychotherapy with expert guidance. But their long duration—unlike therapeutic sessions, these experiences can last days or even weeks—requires special measures.

With these considerations in mind, we created the term *spiritual emergency*. It involves a play on words: the word *emergency*, suggesting a sudden crisis, comes from the Latin *emergere* ("to rise" or "to come forth"). This name thus indicates a precarious situation, but also the potential for rising to a higher state of being. The Chinese pictogram for *crisis* perfectly represents this idea. It is composed of two elementary signs, one of which means "danger" and the other "opportunity."

The recognition of the dual nature of spiritual emergency—danger and opportunity—has important theoretical and practical consequences. If properly understood and treated as difficult stages in a natural developmental process, spiritual emergencies can result in emotional and psychosomatic healing, deep positive changes of the personality, and the solution of many problems in life.

Before we further explore the idea of spiritual emergency and its implications, we need to clarify some of the basic concepts we will be

TABLE 1. DIFFERENCES BETWEEN SPIRITUAL EMERGENCE AND SPIRITUAL EMERGENCY.

Emergence	Emergency
Inner experiences are fluid, mild, easy to integrate.	Inner experiences are dynamic, jarring, difficult to integrate.
New spiritual insights are welcome, desirable, expansive.	New spiritual insights may be philosophically challenging and threatening.
Gradual infusion of ideas and insights into life.	Overwhelming influx of experiences and insights.
Experiences of energy that are contained and are easily manageable.	Experiences of jolting tremors, shaking, energy disruptive to daily life.
Easy differentiation between internal and external experiences and transition from one to other.	Sometimes difficult to distinguish between internal and external experiences, or simultaneous occurrence of both.
Ease in incorporating nonordinary states of consciousness into daily life.	Inner experiences interrupt and disturb daily life.
Slow, gradual change in awareness of self and world.	Abrupt, rapid shift in perception of self and world.
Excitement about inner experiences as they arise, willingness and ability to cooperate with them.	Ambivalence toward inner experiences, but willingness and ability to cooperate with them using guidance.
Accepting attitude toward change.	Resistance to change.
Ease in giving up control.	Need to be in control.
Trust in process.	Dislike, mistrust or process.
Difficult experiences treated as opportunities for change.	Difficult experiences are overwhelming, often unwelcome.
Positive experiences accepted as gifts.	Postive experiences are difficult to accept, seem undeserved, can be painful.
Infrequent need to discuss experiences.	Frequent urgent need to discuss experiences.
Discriminating when communicating about process (when, how, with whom).	Indiscriminate communication about process (when, how, with whom).

using. Foremost among the issues needing clarification are the role of the unconscious in psychotherapy, spirituality and its relation to religion, and, above all, the nature of a group of experiences that modern psychology calls "transpersonal."

The Unconscious, Psychotherapy, and Healing

Human life involves many biological and psychological challenges and traumatic experiences. In infancy and childhood, there are often diseases, injuries, operations, and a variety of emotional assaults. The very process of emerging into this world—human birth—represents a major physical and psychological trauma that lasts many hours or even days. And some of us were exposed to serious crises even during prenatal existence, such as a disease or emotional stress of the mother, various toxic influences, and even impending miscarriage or attempted abortion.

Most of these painful memories are forgotten or repressed, but they do not lose their psychological significance. Indeed, they are recorded deep within us and can exert a powerful influence on our lives. It was the founder of psychoanalysis, the Austrian psychiatrist Sigmund Freud, who first presented convincing evidence that our psyche is not limited to processes that we are aware of but has vast domains that remain below the threshold of consciousness most of the time.

Freud called this dimension of the psyche "the unconscious." He discovered that repressed and forgotten memories from infancy, childhood, and later periods of life can surface in the form of disturbing nightmares. They also constitute important sources of various emotional and psychosomatic disorders, can cause various forms of irrational behavior, and interfere with living our lives in a satisfying way. During the therapeutic process that Freud called psychoanalysis, free associations of the client and the interpretations of the psychiatrist help bring this unconscious material to consciousness and reduce its disturbing influence in everyday life.

Freud's contributions to psychology and psychotherapy were revolutionary and ground breaking. However, his theoretical model remained limited to postnatal biography: he tried to base the explanation of all psychological processes on life history after birth. Similarly, his therapeutic technique of verbal exchange was a relatively weak tool for penetrating into the unconscious and a time-consuming and slow method of healing and transformation.

One of Freud's disciples, the psychoanalytical renegade Otto Rank, extended this model considerably by bringing the attention of professional circles to the psychological importance of the trauma of birth.

Rank's observations, which remained unnoticed for many years, have in the past three decades received powerful confirmation from various experiential psychotherapies. In the last few years, special conferences have been dedicated to problems of prenatal and perinatal psychology, a discipline that studies the influence on the human psyche of experiences occurring before and during birth.

The research of Freud's Swiss disciple Carl Gustav Jung yielded observations that were so astonishing and revolutionary that they have not yet been fully accepted and assimilated in academic circles. Jung came to the conclusion that the human unconscious is not limited to contents derived from individual history. In addition to the Freudian "individual unconscious," there is also the "collective unconscious," which contains the memories and the cultural heritage of all of humanity. According to Jung, the universal and primordial patterns in the collective unconscious, or "archetypes," are mythological in nature. Experiences that involve the archetypal dimensions of the psyche convey a sense of sacredness—or "numinosity," in Jung's terms.

When highly emotionally charged contents from the unconscious are allowed to surface and be fully experienced and assimilated into consciousness, they lose their power to influence us in a negative way. This process is the main objective of depth psychotherapies. Some of the older schools try to achieve this goal by a therapeutic dialogue; more recent innovations involve approaches that facilitate the direct emotional and physical experience of previously unconscious material. Something similar happens in spiritual emergencies—but spontaneously, and often for unknown reasons.

Occasionally, the amount of unconscious material that emerges from deep levels of the psyche can be so enormous that the person involved can have difficulty functioning in everyday reality. However, in spite of its sometimes dramatic manifestations, this stormy event is essentially an attempt of the organism to simplify its functioning, to throw off old negative imprints and programs, and to heal itself. A person who understands this and has a good support system can cooperate with the process and benefit from it.

Spirituality, Religion, and the Experience of the Divine

To prevent miscommunication, we would like to describe our understanding of the term *spirituality* and in what sense we will be using it. The term *spirituality* should be reserved for situations that involve personal experiences of certain dimensions of reality that give one's life and existence in general a numinous quality. C. G. Jung used the word *numinous* to describe an experience that feels sacred, holy, or out of the ordinary. Spirituality is something that characterizes the relationship of an individual to the universe and does not necessarily require a formal structure, collective ritual, or mediation by a priest.

In contrast, religion is a form of organized group activity that may or may not be conducive to true spirituality, depending on the degree to which it provides a context for personal discovery of the numinous dimensions of reality. While at the cradle of all great religions are the direct visionary revelations of their founders, prophets, and saints, in many instances a religion loses its connection with this vital core over time.

The modern term for the direct experience of spiritual realities is *transpersonal*, meaning transcending the usual way of perceiving and interpreting the world from the position of a separate individual or body-ego. There exists an entirely new discipline, transpersonal psychology, that specializes in experiences of this kind and their implications. Insights from the study of transpersonal states of consiousness are of critical importance for the concept of spiritual emergency.

States involving personal encounters with the numinous dimensions of existence can be divided into two large categories. In the first are experiences of the "immanent divine," or perceptions of divine intelligence expressing itself in the world of everyday reality. All of creation—people, animals, plants, and inanimate objects—seems to be permeated by the same cosmic essence and divine light. A person in this state suddenly sees that everything in the universe is a manifestation and expression of the same creative cosmic energy and that separation and boundaries are illusory.

Experiences in the second category do not represent a different perception of what is already known but reveal a rich spectrum of dimensions of reality that are ordinarily hidden from human awareness and are not available in the everyday state of consciousness. These can be referred to as experiences of the "transcendent divine." A typical example would be a vision of God as a radiant source of light of supernatural beauty or a sense of personal fusion and identity with God perceived in this way. Visions of various archetypal beings, such as deities, demons, legendary heroes, and spirit guides, also belong in this category. Other experiences do not involve merely individual suprahuman entities but entire mythological realms, such as heavens, hells, and purgatories, or various sceneries and landscapes unlike anything known on earth.

What interests us at this point are the practical consequences of personal encounters with spiritual realities. For the people who have had them, the existence of the immanent and transcendent divine is not a matter of unfounded belief but a fact based on direct experience—much as our attitude toward the material reality of our everyday life is based on firsthand sensory perceptions. In contrast, a belief is an opinion about the nature of reality based on a specific form of upbringing, indoctrination, or reading of religious literature; it lacks direct experiential validation.

Such transpersonal states can have a very beneficial transformative influence on the recipients and their lives. They can alleviate various forms of emotional and psychosomatic disorders, as well as difficulties in interpersonal relationships. They can also reduce aggressive tendencies, improve self-image, increase tolerance toward others, and enhance the general quality of life. Among the positive aftereffects is often a deep sense of connection with other people and nature. These changes in attitudes and behavior are natural consequences of transpersonal experiences; the individual accepts and embraces them voluntarily, without enforcement by external injunctions, precepts, commandments, or threats of punishment.

Spirituality of this kind, based on direct personal revelation, typically exists in the mystical branches of the great religions and in their monastic orders, which use meditation, repetitive chants and prayers, and other practices to induce such transpersonal states of mind. We have repeatedly seen that spontaneous experiences during spiritual emergencies have a similar potential, if they occur in a supportive and understanding context.

Spiritual Emergencies and Western Psychiatry

From a traditional point of view, it might seem impossible that such dramatic and disorganizing experiences as those that constitute the more extreme forms of spiritual emergency could be part of a natural process, much less a healing and evolutionary one. In the medical model, the psychological and physical manifestations of such states are seen as indicative of a serious disease process. They are referred to as "psychoses," which in mainstream psychiatric thinking implies "diseases of unknown etiology." The assumption is that a biological process, the nature and cause of which have not yet been discovered, is responsible not only for the occurrence of the abnormal experiences, but also for their content.

The fact that the content of transformational states of consciousness is often mystical is seen as further supportive evidence for the disease concept. The worldview created by traditional Western science and dominating our culture is, in its most rigorous form, incompatible with any notion of spirituality. In a universe where only the tangible, material, and measurable are real, all forms of religious and mystical phenomena appear to be products of superstition that suggest a lack of education, irrationality, and a tendency toward primitive magical thinking. When they occur in intelligent, well-educated individuals, they are attributed to emotional immaturity and unresolved infantile conflicts with parental authorities. Personal experiences of spiritual realities are then interpreted as psychotic, as manifestations of mental disease.

Although there are many individual exceptions, mainstream psychiatry and psychology in general make no distinction between mysticism and psychopathology. There is no official recognition that the great spiritual traditions that have been involved in the systematic study of consciousness for centuries have anything to offer to our understanding of the psyche and of human nature. Thus the concepts and practices found in the Buddhist, Hindu, Christian, Islamic, and other mystical traditions, based on centuries of deep psychological exploration and experimentation, are indiscriminately ignored and dismissed, together with various superstitions and naive beliefs of folk religions.

This attitude toward spirituality in general, and spiritual emergencies in particular, has serious practical consequences. Individuals involved in crises of transformation are seen as mentally ill and treated routinely by suppressive medication. However, the belief that we are dealing with a disease in the medical sense is unfounded, since there are at present no clinical or laboratory findings supporting it.

Even if relevant biological changes could be discovered, they would explain only why various elements surface at a particular time from the unconscious—not the contents themselves. And finding a specific trigger for such episodes does not necessarily exclude the possibility that the process itself can be healing. For instance, in the course of deep experiential psychotherapies and various healing rituals, unconscious material surfaces in response to known triggers, such as increased rate of breathing, music, or psychoactive substances.

In addition, there are problems with the clinical diagnosis of psychosis and its different forms. Individual clinicians and researchers disagree considerably about some of the fundamental issues, and the positions of various schools of psychiatry contradict each other. The official classification of psychiatric disorders also varies from country to country, and anthropologists have shown the cultural relativity of what is considered a normal and acceptable form of experience and behavior.

If we approach spiritual emergencies in the spirit of the medical model, the onset of the symptoms would appear to be the beginning of a disease, and their intensity would indicate the seriousness of the situation. According to the alternative approach we are suggesting here, the problems precede the symptoms, but they exist in a latent form. The first appearance of the symptoms is the beginning of the healing process, and their intensity indicates the speed of transformation.

Even in the context of the medical model, a strategy limited to the suppression of symptoms would not be considered satisfactory if a more specific and effective intervention were known and available. The important task of therapy is to lead to a situation where symptoms *need not appear*, not to a situation where they *cannot appear*. We would not appreciate an auto mechanic who solves the problem of a red warning light appearing on our dashboard by pulling out the wire that leads to it.

Thus there are important reasons for recognizing the existence of spiritual emergencies and for extricating them from the framework of the medical model. In individuals undergoing a transformative crisis of this kind, the insensitive use of pathological labels and of various repressive measures, including indiscriminate control of symptoms by medication, can interfere with the positive potential of the process. The ensuing long-term dependence on tranquilizers (with their well-known side effects), loss of vitality, and compromised way of life present a sad contrast to those rare situations where a person's transformative crisis is supported, validated, and allowed to reach completion. It is, therefore, extremely important to clarify the concept of spiritual emergency and to develop comprehensive and effective approaches to its treatment, as well as adequate support systems.

Psychosis Versus Spiritual Emergency

One of the questions most frequently asked during discussions of spiritual emergency is: How does one differentiate between spiritual emergency and psychosis? As we have pointed out, the term *psychosis* is not accurately and objectively defined in contemporary psychiatry. Until that happens, it will be impossible to offer a sharp delineation between the two conditions.

Under the present circumstances, it makes much more sense to ask what characteristics of a nonordinary state of consciousness suggest that one might expect better results with alternative strategies than with treatments based on the medical model. The first important criterion is the absence of any medical condition that can be detected by existing diagnostic tools. This eliminates those states where the primary cause is infection, intoxication, metabolic disorder, tumor, circulatory disturbance, or a degenerative disease. The changes of consciousness in persons who fall into the category of spiritual emergency are qualitatively different from those associated with organic psychoses; they can be relatively easily recognized when one has sufficient experience (for more details, please see table 2 on pages 254–255).

As the term *spiritual emergency* suggests, additional important characteristics of a transformational crisis are an awareness by the person involved that the process is related to critical spiritual issues in life, as well as the transpersonal content of the experiences themselves. Another important hallmark is the ability to differentiate to a *considerable* degree between inner experiences and the world of consensus reality. Persons who are having a spiritual emergency are typically aware of the fact that the changes in their experiential world are due to their own inner processes and are not caused by events in the outside world. Systematic use of the mechanism of projection—disowning one's inner experiences and attributing them to influences coming from other people and from external circumstances—is a severe obstacle to the kind of psychological approach we described here.

People suffering from severe paranoid states, hostile acoustic hallucinations ("voices"), and delusions of persecution consistently engage in projection of such unconscious contents and act under their influence. They cannot be reached with the new strategies, even if some other aspects of their experiences seem to belong to the category of spiritual emergency. Unless it is possible by systematic psychotherapeutic work to create a situation in which they have an adequate insight into the nature of the process and a sufficient degree of trust, such people may require suppressive medication.

The important differences both in the attitude toward the inner process and in experiential style can be illustrated by describing two hypothetical clients who relate their problems to a psychiatrist; they represent opposite poles of a continuum of possibilities. The first comes in for consultation and presents the following account: "In the last three weeks I have been having all kinds of strange experiences. My body is charged with incredible energy. It keeps streaming up my spine and jamming in the small of my back, between my shoulder blades, and at the base of my skull. At times, it is very painful. I have difficulties sleeping and often wake up in the middle of the night sweating and feeling extremely anxious. I have a peculiar sense that I have just come from somewhere far away but do not know where.

"I have visions of situations that seem to be coming from other cultures and other centuries. I do not believe in reincarnation, but sometimes it feels like I am remembering things from previous existences, as if I had lived before. Other times, I see bright lights or images of deities and demons, and other fairy-tale stuff. Have you ever heard about anything like that? What is happening to me? Am I going crazy?"

This person is very bewildered and confused by a variety of strange experiences but is clearly aware that the process is internal and shows a willingness to receive advice and help. This would qualify the process as a possible spiritual emergency and suggest a good outcome.

The second client arrives with a very different attitude, less to ask for advice than to present a clear-cut story, to complain, and to blame: "My neighbor is out to get me. He is pumping toxic gases into my cellar through a pipeline that he secretly constructed. He is poisoning my food and my water supply. I have no privacy in my house; he put a lot of bugging devices all over the place. My health is endangered; my life is threatened. All this is part of a complicated plot that is supported by the Mafia; they have been paying large sums of money to get rid of me. I am inconvenient for them because my high moral principles stand in the way of their plans."

Whatever the causes of this condition are, a client in this category lacks the fundamental insight that this state of affairs has something to do with his own psyche. As a result, he would not be interested in getting any help, other than possible assistance in the fight against his alleged persecutors, such as help in initiating a legal action or debugging the house. In addition, he would likely see the therapist as a potential enemy rather than a helper. For these reasons, he would be a poor candidate for any work based on the principles discussed in this book.

CHAPTER 2

THE DARK NIGHT
OF THE SOUL

The shadow of death and the pains and torments of
hell are most acutely felt, and this comes from the
sense of being abandoned by God . . . a terrible ap-
prehension has come upon [the soul] that thus it will
be forever . . . It sees itself in the midst of the opposite evils, miserable imperfections, dryness and
emptiness of the understanding, and abandonment
of the spirit in darkness.

ST. JOHN OF THE CROSS, *The Dark Night*

These pages will describe some of the most common, crucial, and troublesome areas that surface from the complex and active
inner world of a person in a transformation process, and will draw on
our own experience and on the reports of others. We hope we will not
discourage the reader by delving into these difficult experiences now. The
dark night of the soul is only one aspect of the spiritual journey, and
there are many others that are much more pleasant.

The purpose of dealing with this topic first is to reflect the usual sequence of states during the transformation process. Although there are
many exceptions, most people have to delve into the dark areas and go
through them before they reach a state of freedom, light, and serenity.
For those who take this route, the positive feelings often seem all the
more significant and intense when contrasted with the difficult ones they
encountered previously. Just as a sunrise might look especially bright
and hopeful after a long winter night, so joy can seem particularly powerful after pain.

With this in mind, the following questions arise: What are the dark
internal territories that a person might have to traverse? What do they
feel like? And what kinds of conflicts can be expected to arise?

For someone in a spiritual emergency, whether subtle or more dramatic in form, the task of getting through the day, of functioning in a
familiar way, can become a challenge. The normal, seemingly simple
activities that are part of daily life can suddenly seem troublesome or
overwhelming. Often, individuals in crisis are flooded by internal experi-

ences that are so full of emotion, visual power, and energetic force that they have difficulty separating this vivid inner world from occurrences in the outer world. They may become frustrated as they find it difficult to maintain their attention span. Or the rapid and frequent changes in their state of mind may cause them to panic. Unable to function in their usual way, they can feel powerless, ineffective, and guilty.

One woman describes her frustration: "I could see the things that needed to be done around the house, and it was as though there was a wall between me and the tasks I used to accomplish so effortlessly. I remember going out to do some garden work, feeling that that simple activity would be helpful. Instead, all I could feel was, If I move too fast, I will explode. Artistic and creative projects that used to give me such pleasure were simply too difficult to focus on. Even playing with my children seemed too complex for a while. For that period, it was all that I could do to take care of myself."

Among the most troubling and alarming components commonly confronted by those in spiritual emergency are feelings of fear, a sense of loneliness, experiences of insanity, and a preoccupation with death. While such states of mind are often intrinsic, necessary, and pivotal parts of the healing process, they can become frightening and overpowering, particularly when human support is lacking.

As the gates to the unconscious mind open, a wide variety of repressed emotions and recollections can be released into conscious awareness. Elements of fear, loneliness, insanity, and death can appear, sometimes simultaneously, when one encounters specific memories or experiences from the personal or transpersonal realms. A person may relive serious illnesses or life-threatening accidents as well as other disturbing events from infancy and childhood. Or one might reexperience biological birth, with its complex, chaotic, and dynamic manifestations.

Many memories contain some fear. People from abusive families might find themselves gripped by the terror brought on by the violence of a drunken mother. Others may relive the fear they experienced when they fell from a tree or struggled through whooping cough.

An individual may suddenly feel a childlike sense of loneliness that seems completely inappropriate to his or her present situation; these irrational perceptions may have their origins in an early incident of abandonment by a parent or the lack of bonding with the mother at birth. Similar feelings may result from incidents involving isolation from peers at school or a painful separation during a divorce.

Particularly when remembering a life-threatening event, some individuals may encounter feelings of insanity. They may unexpectedly recall a sequence from their history such as a near-fatal automobile crash, a swimming accident in which they almost drowned, or extreme physical or sexual abuse. As they relive the incident, such people may feel so overpowered and imperiled that they believe they are losing their grip on reality.

These situations can also bring a person into contact with the experience of death. Additional memories related to death stem from the circumstances surrounding birth. One always has some form of essential contact with death within the reliving of birth, with its attendant sense of suffocation and feelings of vital threat. If, during prenatal existence, an individual was in danger of an imminent abortion or miscarriage, he or she might have endured a very convincing fetal survival crisis that can later be relived.

One can also encounter experiences of fear, loneliness, insanity, or death during transpersonal sequences originating from collective or universal domains. The transpersonal realms contain both light and dark elements, and both the "positive" and the "negative" can inspire fear. One may confront a monstrous mythological demon or relive a battle from another time period; to feel some alarm in those situations is inevitable. However, the fact that fear sometimes arises when an individual moves into the realms of light and beauty is somewhat perplexing. In chapter 3, we will address the challenges of the "positive" realms.

An individual may feel loneliness during a convincing identification with a soldier who is separated from a loved one during wartime or with an African mother who grieves the loss of her child through famine. A woman in one of our workshops felt truly insane when, during a session of deep experiential work, she saw herself becoming a madwoman in a medieval asylum. After an hour, when the experience was over, she returned to her usual rational state.

The encounter with death can appear in many forms on the transpersonal level. In what feels like a past-life memory, one can vividly relive being killed as a soldier, slave, martyr, or wartime mother. He or she may confront death in a mythological world, perhaps through identification with the figure of Christ on the cross or with the dismemberment of Osiris.

An individual may identify with an all-human experience of dying, becoming all women who have ever died during childbirth or all men throughout history who have ever been killed in battle. Someone else might become the archetype of Death itself, experiencing it as a universal force in all of its enormity. The following vivid example comes from a woman whose spiritual emergency involved many realistic experiences of death:

"All around me I could see swirling images of death: gravestones, crosses, a grinning skull and crossbones. I saw hundreds of bloody bat-tlefields, concentration camps, and hospital wards; there were scenes of dying everywhere. I felt as though I was both reviewing and participating in all of death throughout history. And then my experience shifted and I suddenly felt as though I, whoever that was, was responsible for it all; I had become Death itself, the Grim Reaper, the Pale Horseman, and it was I who was calling humanity away from life."

It is easy to mistakenly associate the emotions and sensations involved in suddenly available memories with one's immediate life situation. For example, a man who is reexperiencing the imminent threat of dying during birth may develop a deep concern about his health or an unusually strong reaction to films or television shows that portray death. He may feel constantly menaced by potential dangers in his surroundings and may even fear for his physical safety. Without realizing it, he can panic in enclosed places, fearing elevators and crowded subways.

Someone like this may develop thanatophobia, or excessive fear of death, in which he or she is driven by an obsessive concern that a heart attack or stroke is imminent. When the full experience of birth emerges into conscious awareness, with its wide range of emotions and physical sensations, the person develops the insight that this is the source of his or her fears, and they dissipate.

Facing Fear

The element of fear is a natural piece of the mosaic of change. Fear in some form usually accompanies a spiritual emergency, whether it is a mild sense of concern in anticipation of daily events or an enormous, free-floating terror that does not seem to be attached to any familiar aspects of one's life. Some anxiety is appropriate to such an individual's situation: not only are many of his or her familiar belief systems breaking down, but he or she has become exceedingly emotional. The body feels as though it is falling apart, with new physical stresses and bothersome pains. Much of the fear feels completely illogical, however, as though it has very little to do with the person involved. Sometimes the individual in crisis can deal with various fears relatively easily, and on other occasions the feel-ings of fear seem to expand into utterly uncontrollable panic.

In most human lives, there are many kinds of fear, from the gross, obvious forms, such as terror of physical harm or death, to the more subtle ones, such as anxiety about asking directions from a stranger. In spite of their various fears, most people are able to function well in everyday life without being overwhelmed by them. During many spiritual emergencies, however, daily fears are intensified and concentrated, often becoming unmanageable. They might take the form of free-floating anxiety or crystallize into several general kinds of fear.

Fear of the unknown. To some extent, this is common to many human beings. When our lives take us in an unfamiliar direction, we often automatically respond by becoming apprehensive and then resistant. Some individuals can plunge into the unknown relatively undaunted, with what appears to be enviable courage. But many people, if they move into unexplored territories at all, do so against their will or at best very prudently.

For those in spiritual emergencies, fear of the unknown can become tremendously magnified. Their inner states often change so quickly that they become very fearful of what might come next. They are constantly being introduced to unfathomed realms within, new awarenesses, and undiscovered possibilities. A woman who is very materialistic may have a spontaneous out-of-body state and learn that she is more than her physical identity. A man will suddenly live through a complex visual and emotional sequence that seems to come from another time and place. His experience propels him toward thoughts about reincarnation, a concept totally foreign to him.

These kinds of abrupt events can be very frightening for those who are unprepared. Such people feel uncertain about where they are going or how they will feel, and so much rapid change leads to the fear that they are losing control of their lives. They may even long for the familiarity of the safe, old way of being, for the quieter and less demanding, if somewhat unhappy, existence from which they came.

Fear of losing control. A man who has spent many years working toward a successful family life may have his future well mapped out and may feel very much in charge of his existence. When his wife develops a terminal illness, his life goes in a very different direction than he had planned. His dream is shattered, and the emotional stress that ensues may initiate a transformation process in him. Very painfully, he realizes that he does not have power over the forces of life and death, that he is subject to forces beyond his command.

Many people spend years feeling that their world is orderly and that they have complete authority over their lives. When they discover that they are not entirely in control of their own life trajectory, they are sometimes enormously relieved. At other times, they become very frightened, especially if they are heavily identified with being in charge. They will likely ask themselves, If I am not the authority, who is? And is he, she, or it trustworthy? Can I abandon myself to some unknown force and know that I will be taken care of?

Confronted with the fear of losing control, the mind and the ego become very ingenious in their efforts to hang on; people in this situation may create a complex system of denial, telling themselves that they are just fine the way they are and do not need to submit to change, or that the changes that they feel are just illusory. They may intellectualize the states of mind that they are having, creating elaborate theories to explain them away. Or they may simply try to avoid having them altogether. Sometimes the anxiety itself becomes a defense; hanging on to one's feelings of fear may successfully keep one from growing too rapidly.

There is another form of losing control that is much less gradual and more dramatic. At times during a spiritual emergency, someone might become overwhelmed by powerful episodes during which he or she completely loses control of his or her behavior. Such an individual may explode with anger and tears, shake violently, and scream in a way that he or she has never done before. This uninhibited release of emotion can be immensely liberating, but before it happens, one might be stricken with a tremendous fear of and resistance to the power of the feelings involved. After this kind of outburst, the person may also feel frightened and ashamed as he or she realizes the power of the expression.

Other fears. In some forms of spiritual emergency, physical sensations or reactions can be interpreted as fear. People can feel consumed by strange and at times overpowering bursts of energy. They might feel pulsing electrical charges, uncontrollable tremors, or sensations of some unknown force streaming throughout their systems. Their heart rate may increase and their body temperature rise. Why does this happen? These manifestations are often a natural physiological accompaniment to abrupt changes in consciousness; they may also be specific characteristics of a certain form of spiritual emergency, such as the awakening of Kundalini.

People who are not prepared for or are unfamiliar with these phenomena can be very dismayed to have them suddenly become part of everyday life. Since they are used to a certain norm of bodily sensations, they usually feel some anxiety during the onset of such strange new feelings and can easily mistake the sensations for fear itself. A woman involved in intense meditation practice remembers her reaction:

"I went to my spiritual teacher and told him about the strange feelings of anxiety that were now part of my life. I especially felt them at night or when I tried to meditate: my heart would race, my body would shake, and I found myself perspiring a lot. When he heard these things, he laughed and explained that these were the workings of the Kundalini Shakti. He said, 'Remember, when you feel these things, it is not fear attacking you. It is God moving through you.' I have thought of that many times since then, and it has given me great comfort."

One can also encounter fear of insanity, fear of death, and fear of universal annihilation, which we will explore later in this chapter.

Feelings of Loneliness

Mirabai, a fifteenth-century Indian poet, wrote:

> *My eyes fill with tears.*
> *What shall I do? Where shall I go?*
> *Who can quench my pain?*
> *My body has been bitten*
> *By the snake of "absence,"*
> *And my life is ebbing away*
> *With every beat of the heart.*

Loneliness is another intrinsic component of spiritual emergency. It can range from a vague perception of separateness from other people and the world to a deep and encompassing engulfment by existential alienation. Some of the feelings of inner isolation have to do with the fact that people in spiritual emergencies have to face unusual states of consciousness that they may not have heard anyone describe and that are different from the daily experiences of their friends and family. However, existential loneliness seems to have very little to do with personal or outside influences.

Many people in a transformation process feel isolated from others by the nature of the experiences they are having. As the inner world becomes more active, one may feel the need to temporarily withdraw from daily activities, becoming preoccupied with intense thoughts, feelings, and internal processes. Relationships with other people may fade in importance, and the person may even feel disconnected from the familiar sense of who he or she is. As this is happening, one may feel an encompassing sense of separation from oneself, from other people, and from the surrounding world. For those in this state, even familiar human warmth and reassurance are unavailable.

A young teacher tells of the loneliness he experienced during a spiritual emergency: "I used to lie in bed next to my wife at night and feel completely, undeniably alone. She had been a great help and comfort to me during my crisis. But during this period, nothing she could do would help—no amount of cuddling, no degree of encouragement."

We have often heard individuals in spiritual emergency say, "No one has ever gone through this before. I am the only one who has ever felt this way!" Not only do such people feel that the process is unique to them, but they might also be convinced that no one in history has ever experienced what they are feeling. Perhaps because they feel so special, they may also believe that a certain trusted therapist or teacher is the only one who can sympathize and help. Their strong emotions and unfamiliar perceptions are taking them so far from their previous existence that they easily assume they are abnormal. They feel that something is very wrong with them and that no one will be able to understand them. If they have therapists who are mystified as well, their feelings of intense isolation increase.

Even if people in this stage are aware of the variety of theoretical maps and spiritual systems that describe similar states, they will find a difference between studying them and being in the middle of them. This is illustrated by the example of Sarah, a graduate student in anthropology:

Sarah's class notes were full of descriptions of Indian shamanic life and ritual in central Mexico. When she later encountered vivid and realistic shamanic elements as part of her spiritual emergency, she could not make the connection between her studies and her experiences until some time later. In the classroom, her relationship to the subject matter had been strictly intellectual; her assumption was that the behavior and perceptions of the Indians had no relevance to her. Her transformative states had been so immediate and encompassing that she was unable to recognize them from her exclusively scholarly approach.

During the existential crisis, one feels cut off from the deeper self, higher power, or God—whatever one depends on beyond personal resources to provide strength and inspiration. The result is a most devastating kind of loneliness, a total and complete existential alienation that penetrates one's entire being. This was expressed by a woman after her spiritual emergency: "I was enveloped by an abiding, enormous loneliness. I felt as though every cell of me was in a state of extreme solitude. I had dreams of standing on a windy cliff, looking into a dark sky, yearning to connect with God; I was only met with more darkness. It was more than human abandonment; it was total."

This deep sense of isolation appears to be available to many human beings, regardless of their history, and is often a central ingredient of spiritual transformation. Irina Tweedy, a Russian woman who studied with a Sufi master in India, wrote in *The Chasm of Fire*:

> The Great Separation was here . . . a peculiar, special feeling of utter loneliness . . . it cannot be compared to any feeling of loneliness we all experience sometimes in our lives. All seems dark and lifeless. There is no purpose anywhere or in anything. No God to pray to. No hope. Nothing at all.

This sense of extreme isolation is reflected in the desolate prayer of Jesus on the cross: "My God, my God. Why hast Thou forsaken me?" People who are lost in this place frequently cite the example of Christ's darkest hour in an attempt to explain the extent of this monumental feeling. They cannot find any connection to the Divine; instead, they have an enduring, wrenching sense of abandonment by God. Even when one is surrounded by love and support, one can become imbued with profound and bitter loneliness. When a person descends into the abyss of existential alienation, no amount of human warmth can change it.

Not only do those facing such an existential crisis feel isolated, but they also feel insignificant, like useless specks in a vast cosmos. The universe itself appears to be absurd and pointless, and any human activities seem trivial. Such people may see humankind as being involved in a rat-race existence that has no useful purpose. From this vantage point, they cannot see any kind of cosmic order and have no contact with a spiritual force. They may become extremely depressed, despairing, and even suicidal. Frequently, they have the insight that even suicide is no solution; it seems that there is no way out of their misery.

ISOLATING BEHAVIOR

An individual in a spiritual emergency may appear to be "different" for a while. In a culture of established norms and often rigid expectations, one who begins to change internally may not seem to fit. He or she may show up at the job or the dinner table one day wanting to talk about new ideas or insights: for example, feelings about death, questions about birth, remembrances of long-obscured family history, unusual perspectives on the problems of the world or the basic nature of the universe.

The foreign quality of these concepts and the intensity with which a person presents them may prompt colleagues, friends, and family members to withdraw, and his or her already-present sense of loneliness becomes magnified. One's interests and values may change, and one may no longer be willing to participate in certain activities. An evening of drinking with the boys no longer holds the appeal that it used to; it may even seem repugnant.

People in this position can feel very different because of the nature of the experiences they are having. They may feel that they are growing and changing while the rest of the world is sitting still, that no one can follow them. They may be drawn to activities that people close to them do not understand or support. Their sudden interest in prayer, in chanting, in meditation, or in some esoteric system such as astrology or alchemy may seem "weird" to family and friends and may increase their need to withdraw.

If an individual in this stage becomes classified as a psychiatric patient, the labels and treatment he or she is given will often compound his or her sense of isolation. Feelings of separateness are reinforced each time he or she is given the verbal or nonverbal message "You are sick. You are different."

People in a transformation process may also change their appearance. They might cut or grow their hair or be attracted to clothes that reflect a departure from the norm. Examples can be found in the psychedelic culture of the sixties and seventies, when many people had spiritual insights and, instead of expressing them in ways acceptable to the established society, felt moved to convey them by forming a separate or "counter" culture characterized by expressive clothing, jewelry, hairstyles, and even brightly painted cars.

Other examples can be found in various spiritual groups. Initiates into Zen Buddhism may be expected to shave their heads and live a life of outward simplicity. Followers of the guru Rajneesh not only wore clothes of a certain color but also donned a *mala*, or rosary, containing the teacher's picture and changed their given names to Indian ones. As part of Orthodox Judaism, men often wear yarmulkes and beards and follow a strict religious lifestyle at home. An accepting community of fellow spiritual practitioners will tolerate or even encourage this kind of behavior. However, someone who decides to suddenly adopt such obvious expressions while living outside a supportive situation may experience further isolation.

For many people in spiritual emergency, transformation happens without these kinds of alienating external manifestations. In others, however, more apparent changes in conduct occur. For some, these new ways of behaving are temporary stages in spiritual development, while for others they may become a permanent part of a new lifestyle.

Experiencing "Insanity"

During a spiritual emergency, the logical mind is often bypassed and the colorful, rich world of intuition, inspiration, and imagination takes over. Reason becomes restrictive, and true insight takes one beyond the intellect. For some individuals, this excursion into the visionary realms can be exciting, spontaneous, and creative. But more frequently, since it does not involve states of mind that they consider normal, many people assume that they are going crazy.

When the dissolution of rationality occurs as part of spiritual development, it frequently brings about the death of old mental restrictions or narrow-mindedness, which is sometimes mandatory before a new, expanded understanding and increased inspiration can take its place. What is actually disappearing is not one's reasoning ability, although it may seem that way for a while, but the cognitive limitations that keep one constricted and unchanging.

While this is happening, linear thinking is at times impossible, and the person feels mentally agitated as the conscious mind is bombarded with unblocked material from the unconscious. Strange and disturbing emotions are suddenly available, and once-familiar rationality is useless in explaining such occurrences. This can be a very frightening juncture in spiritual development. However, if an individual is truly engaged in the emergence process, it is only temporary and can be a very important stage of transformation.

In *The Chasm of Fire*, Irina Tweedy relates her feelings of insanity:

> Half unconscious, I suddenly noticed in the dark room around me some kind of whirling, dark, grey mist . . . and soon I could distinguish most hideous things, or beings; leering, obscene, all coupled in sexual intercourse, elemental creatures, animal-like, performing wild sexual orgies. I was sure that I was going mad. Cold terror gripped me; hallucinations, madness; no hope for me—insanity—this was the end . . . The creatures were nearer now, all round my bed . . . All those evils must have been in me! Merciful God help me! There's no escape for me but an Indian mental asylum; a padded cell!

Sometimes, unfamiliar patterns of unusual meaningful coincidences may seem to govern the workings of the world, replacing the more predictable, seemingly manageable known order. At other times, people might experience total internal chaos; their logical ways of structuring their reality break down, and they are left with a confused and disorganized lack of continuity. Completely at the mercy of a dynamic inner world filled with vivid drama and gripping emotions, they cannot function in an objective, rational mode. They may feel as though this is the final destruction of any shred of sanity, and they are fearful that they are headed toward total, irreversible madness.

This experience of insanity is recalled by a woman after her spiritual emergency: "I felt as though my mind was being shattered into millions of pieces. I couldn't hang on to thoughts as I knew them; there were just fragments. My husband tried to talk to me, but I couldn't absorb his words. Nothing made any sense. Everything was completely jumbled and confused. I had visions of myself as a chronic patient on the back ward of some state hospital for the rest of my life. I was sure that this was the way I would be forever."

Certain spiritual traditions offer an alternative view of this kind of "madness." "Holy madness" or "divine madness" is known and acknowledged by various spiritual traditions and is distinguished from ordinary insanity; it is seen as a form of intoxication by the Divine that brings extraordinary abilities and spiritual instruction. In traditions such as Sufism and the Native American culture, sacred figures recognized as fools or buffoons are known to embody this state. Revered seers, mystics, and prophets are often described as inspired by madness.

Divine madness is described by the Greek philosopher Plato as a gift from the gods:

> The greatest blessings come by way of madness, indeed of madness that is heaven-sent. It is when they were mad that the prophetess at Delphi and the priestesses at Dodona achieved so much for which the states and individuals in Greece are thankful; when sane, they did little or nothing . . . madness [is] a divine gift, when due to divine dispensation.

In the Okinawan culture such a state is called *kamidari*. It is a period when a person's spirit suffers, a time of trial during which he or she cannot operate rationally. The community supports such an individual, recognizing the distraught condition as a sign that he or she is close to God. Afterward, such a person is regarded as one who has a divine mission, perhaps that of healer or teacher.

Confronting Symbolic Death

Confrontation with the issue of death is a pivotal part of the transformation process and an integral component of most spiritual emergencies. It is often part of a powerful death-rebirth cycle in which what is actually dying is old ways of being that are inhibiting an individual's growth. From this point of view, everyone dies in some form many times during the course of a lifetime. In many traditions, the notion of "dying before dying" is essential to spiritual advancement. Coming to terms with the fact of death as part of the continuity of life is seen as tremendously liberating, releasing one from the fear of death and opening one to the experience of immortality. As the seventeenth-century Christian monk, Abraham a Santa Clara wrote: "A man who dies before he dies does not die when he dies."

Swami Muktananda's description of his own encounter with death in *Play of Consciousness* vividly describes not only the experience of dying, but also his movement into rebirth:

> I was terrified of death. My prana [breath, life force] ceased. My mind functioned no longer. I felt that my prana was passing out of my body . . . I lost all power over my body. Like a dying man, whose mouth is agape and arms outstretched, I emitted a strange noise and collapsed on the floor . . . I lost consciousness completely.
>
> I got up after about an hour and a half and felt amused, saying to myself, "I died a short while ago, but I am alive again!" I stood up feeling deep calm, love, and joy. I realized that I had experienced death . . . Now that I knew what it meant to die, death ceased to have any more terror. I became completely fearless.

Many people have largely negative associations with the subject of death; they believe that it is the end of everything, the ultimate dispossession, the final retribution. They regard death as a fearsome unknown, and when it comes up as part of their inner experience, they become terrified.

The encounter with death can manifest itself in several forms. One is the confrontation with one's own mortality. Someone who has avoided the subject of dying will likely have difficulty with a deep experience that shows him or her that this life is transitory and that death is certain. Many people subconsciously retain the childhood notion that they are immortal and, when faced with the tragedies life has to offer, discard them with the general statement, "That happens to other people. It will not happen to me."

When a spiritual emergency brings such individuals to the essential understanding of their mortality, they become extremely resistant. They will do anything to avoid the subject, perhaps actively trying to stop the process through frantic work, excessive talking, or brief relationships, or by taking depressive drugs or alcohol. In conversation, they might try to avoid the subject of death or laugh it away, returning instead to relatively safe topics. Others may suddenly become sharply aware of the aging process, their own and that of the people close to them.

Some arrive at an unexpected awareness, such as this one described by a teacher: "I had been playing with the concept of my own mortality for some time. I knew about some of the Christian and Buddhist ideas about impermanence, but I hadn't really accepted them as anything pertaining to me. Then came the day that the *Challenger* space shuttle blew up. As I watched on television, I saw those seven astronauts waving happily as they climbed aboard the vehicle that turned out to be their death trap. They had no way of knowing that these were the last minutes of their lives. All they really could be sure of was that moment of vitality and soon, that would be gone. Watching that horrible drama, I got it! It is true what the philosophers had been describing: our lives are ephemeral, and all we truly have is the present moment. No past, no future. Just now."

This kind of insight can be devastating to people who are unwilling or unable to confront their fear of death; but it can be liberating for those who are ready to accept the fact of their mortality, since full acceptance of death can free them to enjoy each moment as it arises.

Another common experience is the death of restricted ways of thinking or being. As a person begins to change, he or she finds it necessary to drop some of the limitations that have been preventing growth. Sometimes, this happens slowly and almost at will, through a very regulated form of therapy or spiritual practice that requires one to consciously release old restrictions. Or it may occur automatically as part of one's development.

However, for many people experiencing a spiritual emergency, this process is rapid and unexpected. Suddenly, they feel as though comfort and security are being ripped away as they are thrust in an unknown direction. Familiar modes of being are no longer appropriate but have yet to be replaced by new ones. An individual caught in this shift feels unable to hang on to any recognizable reference points in life and fears that he or she will find it impossible to return to old behaviors and interests. One may feel as though all that he or she has ever been or has ever cared about is dying and that the process itself is irreversible. Such a person may be consumed by tremendous grief over the death of the old self.

The state of detachment from roles, relationships, the world, and oneself is another form of symbolic death. It is well known in many spiritual systems as a primary goal of inner development. Detachment is a necessary occurrence in life that naturally takes place at the moment of death, the time when each human being fully understands that we cannot take our material possessions, earthly roles, and relationships with us into the world beyond. Meditation practice and other forms of self-exploration allow seekers to confront this experience before physical death in order to free themselves to fully enjoy what they have in life.

The poet T. S. Eliot wrote:

> *In order to possess what you do not possess*
> *You must go by the way of dispossession.*
> *In order to arrive at what you are not*
> *You must go through the way in which you are not.*

In Buddhism, attachment, or clinging to the material world, is seen as the root of suffering, and releasing it as a key to spiritual liberation. This idea is familiar in other traditions and is echoed by Patanjali in the Yoga Sutras: "By absence of all self-indulgence at this point, when the seeds of bondage to sorrow are destroyed, pure being is attained."

More or less radical detachment occurs regularly during the emergence process and can be rather confusing and distressing when it appears. As a person begins to transform, his or her relationship to loved ones, activities, and roles in life will start to shift. A man who has assumed that his family belongs to him will discover that his attachment to his wife and children serves only to bring him great pain. He may even gain the insight that the only constant thing in life is change and that he will eventually lose whatever he thinks he has.

A woman who is very identified with her role as an aerobics instructor will recognize that she will not be able to maintain her physical excellence forever and will realize that none of the months of intensive training will change that; in fact, her investment of time and energy make the reality more difficult to accept. An industrialist who has spent a lifetime making money and accumulating possessions will reluctantly acknowledge that he cannot take it with him and that he will eventually lose it all.

These kinds of insights can lead to the realization that death is the ultimate equalizer and that even if one denies its reality in life, it will eventually take its toll. During the transition toward this experience, individuals must undergo a painful procedure of letting go of worldly concerns that keep them attached, thereby perpetuating suffering. The process of detachment is itself a form of death, the death of attachment. In some people, the impulse toward detachment is so strong that they become fearful that they are literally preparing for imminent physical death.

Individuals in this stage of spiritual emergence often develop the misconception that completing this inner shift means moving away from meaningful associations in daily life, and they confuse their newly introduced need for internal detachment with outer aloofness. They may feel an insistent inner urging to free themselves from restricting conditions, and if they do not have the insight that the process of detachment can be completed internally, they mistakenly act it out in their daily lives. During the sixties and early seventies, many people who reached this place during experimentation with mind-altering techniques and drugs acted it out externally, literally letting go of family and social roles and creating a counterculture that attempted to represent their newfound understanding.

A lawyer attending one of our workshops had arrived at this juncture during his spiritual journey and came to us, desperately concerned: "Does this mean I am going to have to leave everything that I have worked for all this time? I love my family and my work. I've been married for twenty years and I am very devoted to my wife. My law practice is thriving, and I am good at what I do. But everything inside is telling me that I am going to have to leave it all behind. Am I about to die? What do I do?"

After some discussion, he realized that it was not necessary to renounce a good and productive lifestyle and that his emergence process was not taking him toward physical death. Instead, he had arrived at a very common and natural stage of detachment in which he needed to give up his emotional attachments to important elements in his life. He was able to see that what would die at that point would be only his restrictive, clutching relationship to his familiar roles and that this inner letting go would ultimately liberate him to function more effectively.

An important way of experiencing symbolic death during transformation is the ego death. During the process of spiritual emergence, a person moves from a relatively limited way of being to a new, expanded condition. Often, in order to complete this shift, it is necessary for an old mode of existence to "die" in order to make way for a new self; the ego must be destroyed before a larger self-definition becomes available. This is known as ego death. This is not the death of the ego that is necessary to handle daily reality; it is the death of old personality structures and unsuccessful ways of being in the world, which is necessary for the advent of a happier and freer existence. Ananda K. Coomaraswamy writes, "No creature can attain a higher level of nature without ceasing to exist."

Ego death can happen gradually, over a long period of time, or it may occur suddenly and with great force. Although it is one of the most beneficial, most healing events in spiritual evolution, it can seem disastrous. During this stage, the dying process can sometimes feel very real, as though it were no longer a symbolic experience but instead a true biological disaster. Usually, one cannot yet see that waiting on the other side of what feels like total destruction of the ego is a broader, more encompassing sense of self.

These lines from D. H. Lawrence's *Phoenix* reflect this devastating but transformative process:

Are you willing to be sponged out, erased, cancelled,
made nothing?
Are you willing to be made nothing?
dipped into oblivion?
If not, you will never really change.

When people are immersed in the ego-death process, they often feel overwhelmed and ravaged, as though all that they are or were is collapsing without any hope for renewal. Since the identities of such individuals appear to be disintegrating, they are no longer sure of their place in the world or of their validity as parents, employees, or effective human beings. Outwardly, old interests are no longer relevant, ethical systems and friends change, and they lose confidence that they are functioning reliably in daily life. Inwardly, they may experience a gradual loss of identity. They sense that their physical, emotional, and spiritual selves are being unexpectedly and forcefully shattered. They may feel that they are literally dying, suddenly having to face their deepest fears.

After going through an ego-death experience, a middle-aged woman remembers her feelings of total destruction: "Afterwards, someone congratulated me on my courage at putting the pieces of myself back together. But there were no pieces left, not even a shred. Everything I thought I was had been demolished."

A very tragic misunderstanding that can occur at this juncture is the confusion of the desire for the ego death with the impulse to actually kill oneself. One can easily confuse the wish for what we can call "egocide" with the drive toward suicide. People in this stage are often driven by a forceful inner insistence that something in them has to die. If the internal pressure is strong enough and if there is no understanding of the dynamics of the ego death, they may misread these feelings and act them out through self-destructive behavior. Or they may talk incessantly about killing themselves, causing grave concern to those around them.

With therapy, spiritual practice, and other forms of self-exploration, it is possible to complete the symbolic experience of dying internally, without taking the body along. One can die inwardly and still remain alive and healthy.

One of the most encompassing encounters with death is the experience of the destruction of the world or the universe. The confrontation with the fact of one's own mortality and the ego death take place within individual, personal realms. However, sometimes that same sense of imminent annihilation extends to a transpersonal level; one can live through vivid sequences of the destruction of all of life on earth or of the planet itself. He or she may confuse this inner event with outer reality and come to fear that the world's existence is being threatened.

Further, this same experience can expand to include the destruction of the solar system or of the entire cosmos. One can see visions of exploding stars and physically identify with all of matter being dissolved into a black hole. One feels completely powerless, and efforts to arrest this enormous disaster are futile.

Swami Muktananda describes his own dramatic meditation experience in *Play of Consciousness*:

> As I sat down, my legs locked themselves in the lotus posture. I looked around. The flames of a vast conflagration were raging in all directions. The entire cosmos was on fire. A burning ocean had burst and swallowed the entire globe . . . I was very frightened . . . I could still see the earth submerged in the waters of dissolution. The whole world . . . had been destroyed.

In recent times, we live with the reality that our entire planet is threatened by nuclear destruction, and a great deal of fearfulness about the situation is appropriate. However, someone in a spiritual emergency may encounter a very vivid internal experience of a nuclear catastrophe, and the fear that arises at this stage can seem beyond personal anxiety. If a person faces such an apocalyptic inner event, it is frequently followed by a sequence of planetary or universal restructuring. He or she enters a new world, reintegrated and radiant, and the cosmos has been restored to a loving and benevolent order.

CHAPTER 3

ENCOUNTERING THE DIVINE

Suddenly a great light from heaven shone around me . . . Those who were with me indeed saw the light and were afraid . . . So I said, "What shall I do, Lord?" And the Lord said to me, "Arise and go into Damascus, and there you will be told all things which are appointed for you to do." And since I could not see for the glory of that light, being led by the hand of those who were with me, I came into Damascus.

SAUL OF TARSUS on the road to Damascus, Acts 22:6–11

So far, we have focused on the troublesome or negative inner territories that one can traverse during the dark night. However, individuals in a spiritual emergency also frequently encounter light, ecstatic, or divine domains within themselves. As could be expected, these states generally present fewer difficulties than the others. Some people simply feel blessed by such experiences and are quietly able to learn from them and consciously apply their lessons in everyday life. However, these "positive" mystical states are not necessarily without problems; there are those who struggle with them, and they can even become part of the crisis of transformation.

Both the dark and light realms are common and important aspects of spiritual emergence, and although we use the terms *negative* and *positive*, we do not mean to imply that one is more or less worthwhile than the other. Both areas are necessary and complementary components of the healing process.

Some people are able to contact the positive or mystical areas relatively easily as part of the course of existence. One may encounter them in simple activities or in natural settings. In an inspired passage in Eugene O'Neill's play *Long Day's Journey into Night*, Edmund tells of an experience he had as he sailed on a ship:

I lay on the bowsprit, facing astern, with the water foaming into spume under me, the masts with every sail white in the moonlight, towering high above me. I became drunk with the beauty and singing rhythm of it, and for a moment I lost myself—actually lost my life. I was set free! I dissolved into the sea, became white sails and flying spray, became beauty and rhythm, became moonlight and the ship and the high dim-starred sky! I belonged without past or future, within peace and unity and wild joy, within something greater than my own life, or the life of Man, to Life itself! To God, if you want to put it that way . . . Like the veil of things as they seem drawn back by an unseen hand. For a second, there is meaning.

One may also discover the transcendental realms unexpectedly during physical exercise, such as dance or sport. This is perhaps due to focused concentration on the activity, bodily exertion, or increased breathing rate; the same elements are involved in techniques developed by many meditative practices, which allow one to go beyond the ordinary, logical world. The basketball player Patsy Neal writes in *Sport and Identity*:

> There are moments of glory that go beyond the human expectation, beyond the physical and emotional ability of the individual. Something unexplainable takes over and breathes life into the known life . . . Call it a state of grace, or an act of faith . . . or an act of God. It is there, and the impossible becomes possible . . . The athlete goes beyond herself; she transcends the natural. She touches a piece of heaven and becomes the recipient of power from an unknown source.

Some have mystical experiences during meditation, and others as part of the dramatic, overwhelming transformative process of spiritual emergency. These states are sudden, all-consuming, and radical, completely altering a person's perception of himself or herself and the world. Whatever way the divine realms come into a person's life, they share certain general characteristics.

The Nature of Transcendental or Mystical Experience

The emotions and sensations associated with the heavenly inner realms are usually the opposite of those that a person may encounter in the dark regions. Instead of painful alienation, one can discover an all-encompassing sense of unity and interconnectedness with all of creation. Instead of fear, one may be infused with ecstasy, peace, and a deep feeling of support by the cosmic process. In the place of experiencing "madness" and confusion, one often finds a sense of mental clarity and serenity. And instead of an abiding preoccupation with death, one can connect with a state that feels eternal, understanding that one is at once the body and also all that exists.

Due in part to their ineffable and boundless nature, the divine domains are more difficult to describe than the dark regions, although poets and mystics of all ages have created beautiful metaphors to approximate them. During some spiritual states, one sees the ordinary environment as a glorious creation of divine energy, filled with mystery; everything within it appears to be part of an exquisite interconnected web. The poet William Blake captures this knowledge of the imminent divine:

> To see a World in a Grain of Sand
> And a Heaven in a Wild Flower,
> Hold Infinity in the palm of your hand
> And Eternity in an hour.

Other experiences involve a revelation of dimensions that one is not aware of in everyday life: they transcend time and space and are inhabited by celestial and mythological beings. These experiences are often accompanied by intense sensations of a potent spiritual force that floods the body. People perceive the mystical realms to be pervaded by a sacred or numinous essence and an unfathomable beauty, and they frequently see visions of precious gold, sparkling jewels, unearthly radiance, luminescence, and brilliant light. In *Leaves of Grass*, the mystical poet Walt Whitman writes:

> As in a swoon, one instant,
> Another sun, ineffable full-dazzles me,
> And all the orbs I knew, and brighter, unknown orbs;
> One instant of the future land, Heaven's land.

As well as being filled with resplendent divine light, the transcendental domains are often described as existing beyond the ordinary senses. The American poet Henry David Thoreau writes:

> I hear beyond the range of sound,
> I see beyond the range of sight,
> New earths, and skies and seas around,
> And in my day the sun doth pale his light.

One often experiences the Divine as eternal, unchanging, and timeless, as characterized by the Chinese philosopher Lao Tsu in the *Tao te Ching*:

There is a thing inherent and natural,
Which existed before heaven and earth.
Motionless and fathomless.
It stands alone and never changes;
It pervades everywhere and never becomes exhausted.
It may be regarded as the Mother of the Universe.
I do not know its name.
If I am forced to give it a name,
I call it Tao, and I name it as supreme.

Many people who experience these inner dimensions recognize them as part of the boundless, expansive essence of each human being, which is usually obscured by the problems and concerns of daily life. Because of their clarity and vividness, transcendent states frequently feel more real than "ordinary" reality; people often compare the discovery of these realms to awakening from a dream, removing opaque veils, or opening the doors of perception. Sometimes they acquire new insights and intricate knowledge about the life process from sources within them that are not ordinarily available.

Just as one may encounter the desolating area of ego death during the dark night of the soul, one can also encounter a kind of positive ego death in the transcendental realms. Here, personal boundaries temporarily dissolve and one can feel oneself merging into the external world or into the cosmos. One of the most common kinds of positive disintegration is that in which people feel as though they are losing themselves in the immanent divine, which is displayed in the surrounding environment. They may feel their individual definition fading as they melt into the familiar world of people, trees, animals, or inorganic nature. During another form of this experience they often feel themselves merge with divine realms that transcend daily reality.

Alfred Lord Tennyson writes of this state:

More than once when I
Sat all alone, revolving in myself
The word that is the symbol of myself,
The mortal limit of the Self was loosed,
And passed into the nameless, as a cloud
Melts into heaven.

This experience often takes the form of a gentle ego loss, a dissolution of ego structures that is necessary in order to reach a larger definition of self. The Indian philosopher and saint Sri Ramana Maharishi likened this process to that of a sugar doll that goes for a swim and melts into the ocean of consciousness. A more dramatic form of positive ego death is a sudden confrontation with the light, compared by the mystics to the moth that flies into the divine flame and is instantly consumed.

Encounters with the divine regions during the process of spiritual emergence are extremely healing. Reaching them, one often feels positive emotions such as ecstasy, rapture, joy, gratitude, love, and bliss, which can quickly relieve or dissolve negative states such as depression and anger. Feeling oneself to be part of an all-encompassing cosmic network often gives a person who has problems with self-esteem a fresh, expanded self-image.

Those who have such experiences early in their process usually feel lucky; they develop a philosophical overview that accompanies them through future challenges. They feel that even though things can become tough, at least they have an idea of where they are going. It is like getting a glimpse of the mountain top, and then, even if one has to return to its base to climb it, having the perspective that there is a reward waiting at the end of the journey. This is by far preferable to the situation of the person who spends months tunneling through difficult emotions and sensations without any idea of what the goal is.

These positive experiences do not necessarily occur as a logical stage in a linear progression, as a prize at the end of a difficult search. Many people find that they have to clear away personal problems or emotional blockages before these areas can open up; when they become available, one may feel as though their appearance is due to the hard work beforehand. However, other individuals spontaneously connect with transcendent places within themselves, even though they have not done any work on difficult issues. In many spiritual emergencies, people are treated to brief tastes of these realms periodically, and find that they become more and more available as time goes by.

Problems Created by Mystical or Transcendental Experiences

In spite of the generally benevolent qualities of positive states, there are two areas of difficulty that can arise when people have mystical experiences: conflicts within oneself in accepting or dealing with the transcendental realms, and problems when the experience interfaces with the environment. Further, there are many times when these areas overlap.

PROBLEMS WITHIN THE PERSON

Many people feel unprepared for the scope of the sacred realms. These are unknown realities and states of mind, and allowing them into one's consciousness usually means giving up familiar concepts of what is real. Such people may also feel that they are not strong enough for the profound impact of the sensory and physical manifestations of mystical experiences or that they are not sufficiently open to handle their power. The American spiritual teacher Ram Dass compares such a person to a toaster, and his or her reaction to "sticking your plug into 220 volts instead of 110 volts and everything fries." Receiving this enormous physical, mental, emotional, and spiritual input can feel overpowering, and a natural reaction can be to recoil.

A similar response may occur during a powerful experience of luminosity. Sometimes, people feel that their eyes are too weak or too clouded to handle the intensity of dazzling light, literally fearing that if they allow the experience in, they will be permanently blinded. As this is happening, they may feel a great deal of physical pain in and around their eyes.

A meditator recalls the terror she felt during a "positive" transpersonal state: "It was so strange . . . I had read about the experience of light in books on spirituality and had only heard it described as blissful. I had wished for that kind of state for a long time, and had tried many forms of inner work to get there. But when it actually happened, I was terrified. It was awesome; it was painful and terrible and wonderful all at once. I felt as though it was too much, that I couldn't contain it all. I thought of Moses and the burning bush, how it was so bright that he had to turn away. I felt unprepared, that I wasn't expanded or clear enough to take it in."

Although the suffering that occurs during a mystical encounter may feel destructive and violent at first, with time people often recognize it as the pain of spiritual opening and growth. They may even come to welcome it as a sign of their connection with the Divine, as described by Saint Teresa of Avila:

> The pain was so sharp that I moaned but the delight of this tremendous pain is so overwhelming that one cannot wish it to leave one, nor is the soul any longer satisfied with anything less than God. It is a spiritual, not bodily pain, although the body has some part, even a considerable part, in it. It is an exchange of courtesies between the soul and God.

The experience of positive ego disintegration, described earlier, can also present problems. While some may welcome the opportunity as liberating and expansive, for those who are very attached to their individual identities this juncture can be very frightening, and they may try to resist or fight it. Although this state of ego loss is transitory, people who are in it feel that it is very permanent. In the limbo between who they knew themselves to be and who they are becoming, they may ask, "Who am I? Where is this taking me? And how can I have confidence in what is happening?"

Some people may not trust the reality of their newfound possibilities or may be afraid that the states they experience are signs of mental illness. They may feel that they are straying too far from the ordinary. They may even fear that after touching the Divine, they will have changed so much that others around them will immediately see that they are "different" and think they are either special or crazy.

Others may struggle with the transcendental realms, no matter how beautiful and serene they are, because they do not feel worthy of the experience. We have known several individuals with lifelong self-image problems who feel undeserving of any experience that is too pleasurable or auspicious. Often, the more benevolent their spiritual state is, the more actively they try to resist it.

Some individuals become depressed after having visited the transcendent domains because their daily life looks bleak and uninteresting in comparison to the radiance and liberation they have tasted. A therapist writes about returning to the limitations of the physical body after a mystical experience:

"In that illuminated state, I felt completely boundless and free, surrounded and filled with brilliant light, and washed by an enormous sense of peace. As I began to return to the everyday world, I felt that my new, expanded Self was being funnelled back into a constricted unit: my physical, everyday self. My body felt like a steel trap, ensnaring and holding all of my possibilities. I felt the pain and drama of daily life beginning to press in on me, and I cried as I yearned to return to the freedom that I had discovered."

Some people in this situation may indeed yearn to stay in an expanded, pleasant state, to the exclusion of their daily responsibilities. Or they may want so badly to repeat the experience that they are closed to the possibility that other stages on their spiritual journey, while not as beautiful or extraordinary, are just as important. As a result, they may prevent themselves from cooperating with their further development by resisting and even judging anything less than a positive mystical state.

PROBLEMS WITH THE INTERFACE IN DAILY LIFE

Often, individuals benefit from their encounter with the divine but have problems with the environment. In some instances, people talk to those close to them about a powerful mystical state. If their family, friends, or therapists do not understand the healing potential of these dimensions, they may not treat them as valid or may automatically become concerned about the sanity of the loved one or client. If the person who has had the experience is at all hesitant about its validity or concerned about his or her state of mind, the concern of others may exaggerate these doubts, compromising, clouding, or obscuring the richness of the original feelings and sensations.

Difficulties also arise when transcendent encounters occur in situations where they may be misunderstood. People generally find it less problematic to be overwhelmed by a rapturous mystical state within the safe confines of a meditation room or their bedroom than in the middle of a shopping mall or an airport terminal. If an individual is not in a supportive situation during the dissolution of personal boundaries, he or she is likely to have temporary difficulty operating in the external world. For example, such a person may feel unsure of physical coordination or movement and may appear to be clumsy and disoriented. If, at the same time, he or she is having to interact with a restaurant waiter or an airport security guard, the behavior might be easily misunderstood.

Others may be afraid that if they allow such expanded experiences to enter their lives, their new awareness will bring with them additional, unwanted duties or responsibilities to the people around them or to the world in general. One may ask, "Does this revelation mean that I have to do something with it? Am I supposed to help other people to see what I have seen? Does this give me a special role in the world?"

Or they may have the opposite reaction: they may feel that they have been blessed with divine Providence, and that therefore they deserve special recognition and an elevated status that places them above ordinary concerns. They may have had a very real insight that their existence is part of an intricate, interconnected cosmic order; as a result, they might feel that God will take care of everything and that they are therefore exempt from much responsibility in life.

Closely related to this can be the way in which people act out such insights. If they have connected with what they feel to be God or a Higher Power, or with a celestial being such as Jesus or Buddha, they may allow this state to distort their ego or their sense of personal identity. Rather than understanding that they have tapped a universal reality that is potentially available to everyone, they feel that it is exclusively their own. Instead of emerging from the experience with the understanding that they are divine and so is everyone and everything else, they feel that they are God and have a message for the world. Such people may develop messianic tendencies, which, when expressed, may alienate them from others.

CHAPTER 4

VARIETIES OF SPIRITUAL EMERGENCY

From the unreal lead me to the real.
From the darkness lead me to light.
From death lead me to immortality.
Brihad-Aranyaka Upanishad

The common denominator of all crises of transformation is the manifestation of various aspects of the psyche that were previously unconscious. However, each spiritual emergency represents a unique selection and combination of unconscious elements—some of them biographical, others perinatal, and still others transpersonal. These three categories of experiences were briefly described earlier and will be discussed in chapter 7. Within the psyche there are no boundaries; all its contents form one continuum with many levels and many dimensions. One should not, therefore, expect spiritual emergencies to come in types or forms with sharp boundaries such that they can be easily distinguished.

However, it is possible and useful to define certain types of spiritual emergencies that have enough specific and characteristic features to differentiate them. The following list of forms is based on our many years of experience with people undergoing such crises, on information from colleagues who do similar work, and on the study of related literature. As we define, describe, and discuss each of them, it is important to keep in mind that their boundaries are somewhat blurred and in many cases overlap.

- Episodes of unitive consciousness (peak experiences)
- The awakening of Kundalini
- Near-death experiences
- Emergence of "past-life memories"
- Psychological renewal through return to the center
- The shamanic crisis
- Awakening of extrasensory perception (psychic opening)

73

- Communication with spirit guides and channeling
- Experiences of close encounters with UFOs
- Possession states

Episodes of Unitive Consciousness (Peak Experiences)

> In this light my spirit suddenly saw through all, and in and by all the creatures, even in herbs and grass, it knew God, who he is, and how he is, and what his will is; and suddenly in that light my will was set on, by a mighty impulse, to describe the being of God. But because I could not presently apprehend the deepest births of God in their being and comprehend them in my reason, there passed almost twelve years before the exact understanding thereof was given me.
>
> Jacob Boehme,
> *Aurora: Dawning of the Day in the East*

The American psychologist Abraham Maslow described a category of mystical experiences characterized by dissolution of personal boundaries and a sense of becoming one with other people, with nature, the entire universe, and God; he coined for them the term *peak experiences*. In his writings, he expressed sharp criticism of the traditional position of Western psychiatry that such experiences are indications of mental disease. Maslow demonstrated beyond any doubt that peak experiences often occur in normal, well-adjusted people. He also observed that if they are allowed to reach natural completion, they typically result in better functioning in the world and are conducive to what he called "self-actualization" or "self-realization"—a fuller capacity to express one's creative potential.

The psychiatrist and consciousness researcher Walter Pahnke developed a list of basic characteristics of a typical peak experience, based on the work of Abraham Maslow and W. T. Stace. He used the following criteria to describe this state of mind:

- Unity (inner and outer)
- Strong positive emotion
- Transcendence of time and space
- Sense of sacredness (numinosity)

- Paradoxical nature
- Objectivity and reality of the insights
- Ineffability
- Positive aftereffects

As this list indicates, an individual having a peak experience feels a sense of overcoming the usual divisions and fragmentations of the body and mind and reaching a state of complete inner unity and wholeness; this usually feels very healing and beneficial. One also transcends the ordinary distinction between subject and object and experiences a state of ecstatic union with humanity, nature, the cosmos, and God. This is associated with strong feelings of joy, bliss, serenity, and peace.

Individuals experiencing mystical consciousness of this type have a sense of leaving ordinary reality, where space has three dimensions and time is linear, and entering a timeless, mythical realm where these categories no longer apply. In this state, eternity and infinity can be experienced within seconds of clock time. Another important experiential quality of unitive consciousness is a sense of numinosity, a term C. G. Jung used to describe a profound feeling of sacredness or holiness that is associated with certain deep processes in the psyche. The experience of numinosity has nothing to do with previous religious beliefs or programs; it is a direct and immediate awareness that we are dealing with something that has a divine nature and is radically different from our ordinary perception of the everyday world.

Descriptions of such experiences are usually full of paradoxical statements that violate the basic laws of logic. The mystical state might be referred to as being without any specific content yet all-containing. While it does not present anything concrete, nothing seems to be missing since it contains all of existence in a potential form. A person describing it can talk about a complete loss of the ego and simultaneously claim that his or her sense of identity was infinitely expanded so that it encompassed the entire universe. Others can say that they feel utterly insignificant, awed, and humbled through the experience and yet have a sense of accomplishment of cosmic proportions. While they feel themselves to be, in a sense, nothing, they also feel that in another sense they are commensurate with God.

During mystical experiences, one can feel that one has access to ultimate knowledge and wisdom in matters of cosmic relevance. This does not usually involve specific information about the material world, although mystical states have occasionally been sources of valid information that could be practically utilized. More typically, it is a certain comprehensive insight into the essence of existence described in the Upanishads as "knowing That, the knowledge of which gives the knowledge of everything." This knowledge of the true nature of existence is usually perceived as being ultimately more real and relevant than all scientific theories or perceptions and concepts of our everyday life.

Ineffability is a very characteristic feature of mystical states. It is virtually impossible to describe to others the nature of these experiences, their profound meaning, and their significance, particularly to those who have never had them. Almost all accounts of mystical states contain laments about the total inadequacy of words for such a task. Individuals who have had experiences of this kind often hold to the fact that the language of poetry, although imperfect, is the best vehicle for describing these states. The immortal verses of great transcendental poets of the East, such as Omar Khayyam, Rumi, Kabir, Mirabai, and Kahlil Gibran, as well as Hildegard von Bingen, William Blake, Rainer Maria Rilke, and others from our own tradition, attest to this fact.

If experiences of this kind are allowed to run their course, they can have a profound and lasting influence on one's general well-being, life values, and overall strategy for existence. They often result in better emotional and physical health, an increased appreciation for life, and a more loving, accepting, and honest attitude toward fellow human beings. They can drastically reduce intolerance, aggression, irrational drives, and unrealistic ambitions.

There are certain situations in life that are particularly conducive to peak experiences. In many instances, ego dissolution occurs when one is overwhelmed by the perception of something that is exquisitely beautiful. This often happens in extraordinary natural settings—while scuba diving in coral-reef gardens, sailing on the ocean or white-water rafting on wild rivers, camping in the desert, hiking in the high mountains, hot-air ballooning, or hang-gliding. Experiences of this kind happened to several astronauts during the flights to the moon and while orbiting the earth.

Another important source of peak experiences is inspired art; here the ecstatic rapture can be felt by the creative or performing artist, as well as the sensitive admirer. Many experiences of unitive consciousness have been evoked by the splendor of the Egyptian pyramids, Hindu temples, Gothic cathedrals, Moslem mosques, and the Taj Mahal, or by inspired music, paintings, or sculptures. Love, romance, and erotic rapture also frequently trigger powerful unitive experiences. It might come as somewhat of a surprise that peak experiences also occur frequently during rigorous training and competitive encounters in various sports. Michael Murphy and Rhea White have offered many amazing examples of such states in their book *The Psychic Side of Sports*.

Considering the positive nature and potential of peak experiences, it might seem puzzling that they can become a source of spiritual crisis. The main reason for such complications is a lack of real understanding about nonordinary states of consciousness in Western culture. As a result, we are unable to recognize the value of such experiences, accept them, and support them. The prevailing attitude in traditional psychiatry and among the general public is that any deviations from the ordinary perception and understanding of reality are pathological. Under these circumstances, an average Westerner undergoing a mystical state will tend to question his or her sanity and resist the experience. Relatives and friends will very likely support such an attitude and suggest psychiatric help. Many people in the midst of a peak experience have been sent to psychiatrists who gave them pathological labels, interrupted their experience with tranquilizing medication, and assigned them the role of lifelong psychiatric patients.

The Awakening of Kundalini

Sometimes the Spiritual Current rises through the spine, crawling like an ant. Sometimes, in samadhi, the soul swims joyfully in the ocean of divine ecstasy, like a fish. Sometimes, when I lie down on my side, I feel the Spiritual Current pushing me like a monkey and playing with me joyfully. I remain still. That Current, like a monkey, suddenly with one jump reaches the Sahasrara (crown center). That is why you see me jump up with a start. Sometimes, again, the Spiritual Current rises like a bird hopping from one branch to another. The place where it rests feels like fire . . . Sometimes the Spiritual Current moves up like a snake. Going in a zigzag way, at last it reaches the head and I go into samadhi. A man's spiritual consciousness is not awakened unless his Kundalini is aroused.

The Indian saint Ramakrishna

Descriptions of this form of spiritual emergency can be found in ancient Indian literature; its manifestations are attributed to the activation or awakening of a form of subtle energy called the Serpent Power or Kundalini. According to the yogis, Kundalini (literally, "the coiled one") is the energy that creates and sustains the cosmos. In the human body, it resides in its latent form at the base of the spine. It has the potential to purify and heal the mind and body, mediate spiritual opening, and raise one to a higher level of consciousness.

Dormant Kundalini is traditionally represented as a serpent coiled three and a half times around the lingam, the phallic symbol of male generative power. Among the situations that can lead to Kundalini awakening are intense meditation, the intervention of an advanced spiritual teacher or guru, and certain specific maneuvers and exercises of Kundalini yoga. On occasion, childbirth and passionate lovemaking can play a critical role. In some instances, people experience spontaneous arousal of Kundalini: it can happen unexpectedly, in the middle of everyday life, without an obvious trigger.

Activated Kundalini changes into its fiery form, or Shakti, and rises up the spine, flowing through the conduits of the subtle body, a non-physical field of energy that the yogis say infuses and surrounds the physical body. Clearing away the effects of old traumas, it opens the seven spiritual centers, called *chakras*, that are located in the subtle body along an axis corresponding to the spine. Beside various difficult experiences associated with this purging process, individuals undergoing Kundalini awakening often describe ecstatic states associated with reaching higher levels of consciousness. Among these, the *samadhi*, or union with the Divine that occurs when the process reaches the seventh or "crown" chakra (Sahasrara), deserves special notice. This process, although regarded by the yogis as highly desirable and beneficial, is not without dangers. Ideally, people undergoing intense Kundalini awakening should have the guidance of an experienced spiritual teacher.

The Shakti energy moving through the body brings into consciousness a broad spectrum of previously unconscious elements: memories of psychological and physical traumas, perinatal sequences, and various archetypal images. As this is happening, people in this form of spiritual crisis experience a rich spectrum of emotional and bodily manifestations called *kriyas*. They have intense sensations of energy and heat streaming up their spines, and their bodies are often overcome by violent shaking, spasms, and twisting movements. Their psyche can be unexpectedly flooded by powerful waves of emotions, such as anxiety, anger, sadness, or joy and ecstatic rapture. An overwhelming fear of death, loss of control, and impending insanity are also frequently concomitants of extreme forms of Kundalini awakening.

Individuals involved in this process might find it difficult to control their behavior; during powerful rushes of Kundalini energy, they often emit various involuntary sounds and their bodies move in strange and unexpected patterns. Among the most common manifestations of this kind are unmotivated and unnatural laughter or crying, talking in tongues, singing previously unknown songs and spiritual chants, assuming yogic postures and gestures, and imitating a variety of animal sounds and movements.

The sensory manifestations of Kundalini awakening can be very rich and varied. People involved in this process often describe colorful visions of beautiful geometrical patterns, brilliant lights of supernatural beauty, and complex scenes of deities, demons, and saints. They experience inner sounds that range from simple humming, buzzing, and the chirping of crickets to celestial music and choirs of human voices. At times they might smell exquisite perfumes and balms: some refer to an indescribably sweet fragrance of a divine nectar. Particularly common are intense sexual arousal and orgastic feelings that may be either ecstatic or painful. This deep connection between Kundalini and sexual energy is the basis of a yogic practice called Tantra, where ritual sexual union is used as a vehicle for inducing spiritual experiences.

Careful study of the manifestations of Kundalini awakening confirms that this process, although sometimes very intense and shattering, is essentially healing. In connection with experiences of this kind, we have repeatedly observed over the years the dramatic alleviation or complete clearing of a broad spectrum of emotional as well as physical problems including depression, various forms of phobias, migraine headaches, and asthma. However, in the course of Kundalini awakening, various old symptoms can also be temporarily intensified and previously latent ones become manifest. On occasion, they can simulate different psychiatric and medical problems, and may even be misdiagnosed as such.

Although the concept of Kundalini found its most sophisticated and elaborate expression in the Indian scriptures, important parallels exist in many cultures and religions around the world. One of the most interesting examples is the trance dance of the African !Kung bushmen of the Kalahari Desert. They regularly conduct all-night rituals during which the women sit on the ground drumming and the men move in a circle in rhythmic monotonous movements. One after another, the participants enter a profound altered state of consciousness associated with the release of powerful emotions such as anger, anxiety, and fear. They are often unable to maintain an upright position and are overcome by violent shaking. Following these dramatic experiences, they typically enter a state of ecstatic rapture. According to the bushman tradition, the dance releases from the base of the spine a cosmic healing force called *ntum*, or "medicine." This is then passed by direct physical contact from one person to another.

Concepts similar to Kundalini and the system of the chakras also exist among North American Indian tribes. The Hopis envision centers of psychic energy that closely resemble the chakras. Joseph Campbell often pointed out parallel elements in Navajo sand paintings. Ideas related to Kundalini and the chakras can also be found in Tibetan Buddhism, Taoist yoga, Korean Zen, and Sufism.

However, the activation of Kundalini is not a phenomenon limited to non-Western cultures. In the Christian tradition, manifestations resembling Kundalini have been described during the practice of the so-called Jesus prayer or hesychasm. And unmistakable signs of Kundalini awakening have recently been observed in thousands of modern Westerners. Gopi Krishna, a world-renowned spiritual teacher from Kashmir who personally experienced a profound and dramatic Kundalini crisis, spent many years trying to alert the Western world to the existence and importance of this phenomenon.

The credit for bringing the Kundalini concept to the attention of Western professional circles goes to the California psychiatrist and eye doctor Lee Sannella. In his pioneering book, *The Kundalini Experience: Psychosis or Transcendence*, he described the form the awakening of Kundalini takes in our culture, approaching it from the point of view of Western medicine. Sannella put special emphasis on the medical significance of the Kundalini syndrome. He pointed out that it can simulate many psychiatric and even medical problems, such as psychoses, hysteria, eye disorders, heart attacks, gastrointestinal diseases, pelvic infections, epilepsy, and even multiple sclerosis. For these reasons, Sannella considers a medical examination by an informed clinician to be particularly important in this type of spiritual emergency.

Near-Death Experiences

Then I saw my whole past life take place in many images, as though on a stage at some distance from me. I saw myself as the chief character in the performance. Everything was transfigured as though by a heavenly light and everything was beautiful without grief, without anxiety, and without pain. The memory of very tragic experiences I had was clear but not saddening. I felt no conflict or strife; conflict had been transmuted into love. Elevated and harmonious thoughts dominated and united the individual images, and like magnificent music a divine calm swept through my soul. I became ever more surrounded by a splendid blue heaven with delicate roseate and violet cloudlets. I swept into it painlessly and softly and I saw that now I was falling freely and under me a snowfield lay waiting . . . Then I heard a dull thud and my fall was over.

Albert Heim describing his near-fatal fall in the Swiss Alps

Death is one of the few universal experiences of human existence. It is the most predictable event in our life, yet the most mysterious one. Since immemorial times, the fact of our mortality has been an inexhaustible source of inspiration for artists and mystics. The idea of survival of consciousness after death and of the posthumous journey of the soul appears in folklore, mythology, and spiritual literature of all times and cultures. Special sacred scriptures have been dedicated to the description and discussion of the experiences associated with death and dying.

In the past, Western scientists ignored what they called "funeral mythology," considering it to be a product of the fantasy and imagination of primitive peoples unable to face and accept the fact of their mortality. This situation started to change dramatically after Elisabeth Kübler-Ross attracted the attention of professional circles to the area of death and dying and Raymond Moody published his best-selling book *Life after Life*. Moody's work was based on the accounts of 150 people who had had near-death experiences; it essentially validated the descriptions found in the Tibetan and Egyptian books of the dead, in the European *Ars Moriendi*, and other similar guides for the dying from other times and cultures. It became clear that the process of dying can be associated with an extraordinary inner journey into the transpersonal domains of the psyche.

Although there are individual variations, the experiences of the people who come close to death seem to follow a general pattern. One's entire life up to that point can be reviewed in the form of a colorful, incredibly condensed replay within seconds of clock time. Consciousness can detach from the body and move around with great independence and freedom. Sometimes it floats above the scene of the accident and observes it with curiosity and detached amusement; at other times it travels to distant locations.

Many people experience passage through a dark tunnel or funnel to a source of light whose radiance and brilliance are beyond human imagination. This light has an exquisite, supernatural beauty and is endowed with definite personal characteristics. It radiates infinite all-embracing love, forgiveness, and acceptance. Moody uses the term *Being of Light* to describe the nature of this experience; many people refer to it quite explicitly as God. This encounter often has the form of an intimate personal exchange that involves profound lessons about life and the universal laws; this provides a context for looking at one's own past and evaluating it by these cosmic standards. In the light of this new information, one makes the decision of whether to return to ordinary reality. People who have had this experience and have come back to life usually return with a deep determination to live in a way that is congruent with the principles they have learned.

Near-death experiences can thus be powerful catalysts of spiritual awakening and consciousness evolution. An encounter with the transpersonal source in the form of the Being of Light leads to profound changes of personality that are very similar to the aftereffects of spontaneous peak experiences described by Maslow: an increase in self-esteem and self-confidence, and a decreased interest in status, power, and material pursuits. These are associated with a heightened appreciation for nature and life, deep ecological concerns, and a love for one's fellow human beings. However, the most striking consequence is the awakening of a spirituality that has a universal quality. It transcends the divisive interests of religious sectarianism and resembles the best of mystical traditions and the great spiritual philosophies of the East in its all-embracing quality and transcendence of ordinary boundaries.

Near-death experiences of this kind occur in over one-third of the people who come close to losing their lives. They are independent of sex, age, intelligence, level of education, religious beliefs, church affiliation, and other similar characteristics. It also does not seem to make a difference whether one actually suffers serious biological damage; often the mere exposure to a situation where one might lose one's life is sufficient.

The reason near-death experiences frequently lead to a spiritual emergency is that they involve an unusually abrupt and profound shift in the experience of reality in people who are entirely unprepared for this event. A car accident in the middle of rush-hour traffic or a heart attack while jogging can catapult one into a fantastic visionary adventure within seconds. Unfortunately, the people who provide assistance often are not aware that such emergencies have an important psychological and spiritual dimension. Moody reported, for example, that in only one of the 150 cases he studied was the attending physician at all familiar with near-death experiences. This is astonishing considering that medicine is a discipline that professionally deals with death and dying on a daily basis.

Since the time of the publication of Moody's book, the situation has changed. Many additional scientific studies have confirmed and refined his original findings. Their results have been published in popular books and have appeared repeatedly in the mass media. Professionals now have an intellectual knowledge of the phenomena surrounding near-death situations, and so do most of their clients. Unfortunately, this information has yet to find sufficient application in day-to-day clinical work with people in emergency.

Emergence of "Past-Life Memories"

The patient was getting deeply involved in the process and described that she was engaged in a vicious battle in ancient Persia. Suddenly, she experienced a sharp pain in her chest which was penetrated by an arrow. She was lying on the ground dying in the dust on a hot day.

In the blue sky above her, she noticed vultures, approaching her in large circles. They all landed and surrounded her, waiting for her to die. While she was still alive, some of them approached her and started tearing pieces of her flesh.

Screaming and beating around herself, she fought a desperate, but losing battle with the scavanger birds. Finally, she surrendered and died. When she emerged from the experience, she was free from the phobia of birds and feathers that had tormented her for many years.

A hypnotic regression described in Stanislav Grof's
The Adventure of Self-Discovery

One category of transpersonal phenomena occurring in spiritual crises deserves special attention, because of its great practical importance and the key role it has played in the religions of many cultures: so-called past-life memories, or karmic experiences. They belong to the most colorful and dramatic manifestations of nonordinary states of consciousness. These are experiential sequences taking place in other historical periods and/or other countries. They usually depict emotionally charged events and portray the protagonists, physical settings, and historical circumstances with astonishing detail. An important characteristic of karmic experiences is a conviction that these events are personal memories from a previous lifetime.

Whether or not we see these experiences as supporting evidence for a belief in reincarnation, they are important psychological phenomena with great healing and transformative potential. Experiences of this kind clearly provided inspiration for the Indian concepts of rebirth and the law of karma. According to these teachings, our existence is not limited to one lifetime but consists of a long chain of successive incarnations. We do not generally remember the events from previous incarnations except on special occasions, when isolated memories of important events from past lives emerge into our consciousness. Yet we are responsible for our actions in all of them. Because of the inexorable effects of the law of karma, our present life is shaped by the merits and debits of the preceding ones, and our current actions, in turn, influence our future destiny.

To appreciate the psychological importance of past-life experiences, we have to realize that the concept of reincarnation, which is based on them, was nearly universal in ancient and preindustrial cultures. It is the cornerstone of the great Indian spiritual systems—Hinduism, Buddhism, Jainism, and Sikhism—and of the Tibetan Vajrayana. The broad spectrum of other cultures and groups that have shared the belief in past lives is very rich; it includes the ancient Egyptians, American Indians, the Parsees, the Polynesian cultures, and the Orphic cult of ancient Greece. It is not commonly known that similar concepts also existed in Christianity before A.D. 553, when they were banned by a special council in Constantinople under the Emperor Justinian in connection with the teachings of Father Origen.

Another important aspect of past-life memories is their extraordinary therapeutic and transformative potential, which has been repeatedly confirmed by psychotherapists and consciousness researchers who study nonordinary states. When the content of a karmic experience fully emerges into consciousness, it can suddenly explain many otherwise incomprehensible aspects of one's daily life. Strange difficulties in relationships with certain people, unsubstantiated fears, peculiar dislikes and attractions, as well as obscure emotional and psychosomatic problems now seem to make sense as karmic carryovers from a previous lifetime. These very often disappear when the experiences are completed. We have repeatedly observed, after someone has had a powerful past-life experience, the alleviation or complete elimination of severe psychosomatic pains, depression, phobias, psychogenic asthma, migraine headaches, and other problems that had previously resisted a variety of conventional treatments.

Past-life memories can also be a source of considerable problems. When they are close to consciousness, but not close enough to become fully manifest, they can have a profound impact on the psyche and cause serious emotional and physical distress. The person involved can experience strange feelings and sensations in different parts of the body that do not have a basis in everyday reality. He or she can notice various unsubstantiated fears of certain people, situations, and places or, conversely, irresistible attractions. One can feel sharp pains in the body or feelings of suffocation for which there is no medical cause. The picture of an unknown face, scenery, or object might recurrently emerge into consciousness.

All these elements are meaningful parts of a karmic pattern that has not yet fully surfaced. Experienced out of context, they are incomprehensible and seem completely irrational. In our experiential workshops, many people were able during sessions of Holotropic Breathwork™ to identify, fully relive, and resolve various past-life memories that had for months or years been sources of serious emotional difficulties.

Other problems can occur when a strong karmic experience begins emerging into consciousness in the midst of everyday life and profoundly disturbs normal functioning. The person involved might feel compelled to act out certain elements of the underlying karmic theme before it is made fully conscious and understood or "completed." We have seen situations where individuals who were under the influence of an emerging past-life memory identified certain people from their current life as their karmic partners—either enemies or soul mates. As a result they harassed them, seeking confrontation or connection. Such situations can cause much confusion and embarrassment.

Experiential completion of a past-life memory does not necessarily mean the end of problems. Even if the inner process comes to an end and its implications have been accepted, some people might encounter an additional challenge. They have now had a profound and meaningful experience of certain realities that are alien to our culture and have the task of reconciling this fact with the traditional worldview of Western civilization. This might be easy for people who do not have a strong commitment to a well-articulated philosophical or scientific worldview. They might simply find the experience interesting, revealing, and beneficial; they accept the new information and do not feel much need to analyze it.

However, those with a strong intellectual orientation and with much investment in rational understanding might feel that a rug has been pulled out from under their feet and that they are losing solid ground. They may enter a period of unpleasant confusion as a result of having had a convincing and meaningful experience that threatens to undermine and invalidate their belief system.

Psychological Renewal Through Return to the Center

The religious imagery described the patient as another Christ, leading the fight against the Devil; like Christ, he was to be sacrificed and rise again. The Garden of Eden figured prominently: it was once occupied by Father, Son, and Holy Ghost, but then taken over by the Devil. Interwoven with this were stories of four kings of the four directions, and a major conflict between the King of the North and the South.

As a mythical hero the patient found himself performing great wonders. As King Richard the Lion-Hearted, he killed a tiger and strangled a serpent just after he was born. As a Japanese hero he took on the form of a serpent and acquired a "vicious power to strike back"; he killed a tarantula who was a Japanese mother dressed for battle, and he overcame several monsters.

John Perry, *The Far Side of Madness*

This important type of transformational crisis has been described by the California psychiatrist and Jungian analyst John Perry, who gave it the name *renewal process*. Perry's experiences with this type of crisis came from many years of psychotherapy with young people in acute episodes of nonordinary states of consciousness. These people were allowed and encouraged to go through the process without suppressive medication. Perry also founded a specially designed facility that made this approach possible; it was based in San Francisco and was called Diabasis.

People involved in the renewal process experience dramatic sequences that involve enormous energies and occur on a scale that makes these individuals feel they are at the center of events that have global or even cosmic relevance. Their psyche becomes a fantastic battlefield where the forces of Good and Evil are engaged in a universal combat that seems critical to the future of the world.

These visionary states seem to replay history in reverse, taking these individuals further and further back—to their own roots, to the origins of humanity, to the creation of the world, and to the ideal pristine state of paradise. This is often associated with a conviction that this process offers an opportunity for correcting some serious errors and accidents that happened in the past, both individual and universal, and for creating a better world.

Another important aspect of the renewal process is a great preoccupation with death in many different forms. Individuals engaged in this type of crisis might feel that it is essential for them to understand the nature of dying and death and what functions these have in the universal order. They might experience a connection with the afterlife and communication with their ancestors. The idea of ritual killing, sacrifice, and martyrdom seems particularly significant and appealing.

For those undergoing this radical psychological renewal, the problem of opposites is also an issue of special interest. They are fascinated by the differences between sexes, sexual change, homosexuality, and transcendence of sexual polarity.

When the episode is allowed to proceed beyond the initial turmoil and confusion, the experiences become increasingly pleasant and gradually move toward a resolution. The process often culminates in the experience of "sacred marriage," a blissful union with an ideal partner. This can be either an imaginary archetypal figure or an idealized person from one's life on whom this role is projected. The sacred marriage can have as protagonists such archetypal figures as Adam and Eve, the King and the Queen, the Sun and the Moon, Shiva and Shakti, and similar pairs; it usually means that the masculine and feminine aspects of the personality are reaching a new psychological balance. In women, it can take the form of a sacred marriage to Christ.

At this time, the process seems to be reaching the center or organizing principle of the psyche that C. G. Jung referred to as the Self. This transpersonal center represents our deepest and true nature and is probably closely related to the Hindu concept of Atman-Brahman, the Divine Within. In visionary states, the Self appears in the form of a radiant source of light of supernatural beauty, precious stones and metals, shining pearls, exquisite jewels, and other symbolic variations.

Individuals who connect with this glorious inner domain usually interpret this achievement as a personal apotheosis, a cosmic happening that elevates them to an exalted human role or raises them above the human condition altogether—a great leader, world savior, or even the Lord of the Universe. They may feel that they have conquered death and may have a profound sense of spiritual rebirth. In this context, women frequently experience giving birth to a divine child with some extraordinary mission, while men more often experience themselves as reborn into this new role.

As the process of renewal reaches its completion and integration, the visions bring images of an ideal new world—usually some form of a harmonious society governed by love and justice, which has successfully overcome all ills and evils. In this final arrangement, the number four often plays an important role; in Jungian psychology, this number is seen as an archetypal symbol of the Self and of wholeness.

The final drama can involve four kings, four countries, or four political parties. This is often reflected in spontaneous drawings with motifs of four axes, four quadrants, four cardinal points, or four rivers. The appearance of quadrated circles seems to be a particularly important indication that the process is approaching successful resolution. As the intensity of the experiences subsides, the individual realizes that the entire drama was a psychological transformation that was by and large limited to the inner world and becomes ready for reentry into everyday reality.

To an uninformed observer, the experiences of people involved in a renewal process seem so strange and extraordinary that it might seem logical to attribute them to some exotic process or a serious disease affecting the functioning of the brain. However, Perry did not let himself be deceived by the unusual nature of the experiences. He came to this work equipped with a solid knowledge of Jungian psychology and an encyclopedic cultural background. Allowing the experiences to take their spontaneous course, he was soon able to recognize that this process was by its very nature healing and restorative.

Among Perry's most important contributions was the insight that the renewal process has a profound meaning and order and is linked to important aspects of human history. He realized that the sequences his clients experienced during their acute episodes were identical to the themes of the ritual dramas that were enacted during New Year festivals in all major cultures of the world at the time when the kings were seen as incarnations of gods. The mythological roots of these experiences and their connection to human history will be explored in chapter 6.

The healing and transformative potential of the renewal process, as well as its connection with an important stage of human cultural history, makes it highly unlikely that we are dealing here with erratic products of mental disease. Perry offers an explanation that is radically different from the position of mainstream psychiatry; according to him, this process signifies a major step in the direction of what Jung called "individuation"—a fuller expression of one's deeper potential.

The Shamanic Crisis

There is a power we call Sila, which is not to be explained in simple words. A great spirit, supporting the world and the weather and all life on earth, a spirit so mighty that what he says to mankind is not through common words, but by storm and snow and rain and the fury of the sea; all the forces of nature that men fear. But he has also another way of communication: by sunlight and calm of the sea, and little children innocently at play, themselves understanding nothing . . . No one has seen Sila; his place of being is a mystery, in that he is at once among us and unspeakably far away.

Eskimo shaman, as recorded by explorer Knut Rasmussen

This form of psychospiritual transformation bears a deep resemblance to the initiatory crises of shamans—healers and spiritual leaders of many aboriginal peoples. Anthropologists refer to the dramatic episodes of nonordinary states of consciousness that mark the beginning of the healing career of many shamans as the "shamanic illness." It is the most ancient form of transformational crisis, but it would be a mistake to consider it a phenomenon that is limited to the remote past or to exotic and so-called primitive cultures.

We have repeatedly seen very similar experiences in modern-day Americans, Europeans, Australians, and Asians, in the form both of spontaneously occurring episodes lasting many days, and of brief transient sequences during psychedelic sessions and Holotropic Breathwork. In this context, we will describe the nature of shamanic crisis as an important form of spiritual emergency. In chapter 6, we will explore shamanism as a historical and cultural phenomenon.

Visionary adventures of this kind typically involve a journey into the underworld—the realm of the dead. There one is attacked by vicious demonic entities and exposed to unimaginable ordeals culminating in experiences of death, dismemberment, and annihilation. As in shamanic crises, the final annihilation can be experienced as being killed, torn to pieces, or swallowed by specific animals who function as initiators. The same animals may appear later in the roles of spirit guides, protectors, and teachers. This experience of total annihilation is typically followed by resurrection, rebirth, and ascent to celestial regions. This process of psychological death and rebirth seems to be closely related to reliving the trauma of biological birth, although this connection by no means provides a full explanation of the shamanic crisis.

Also characteristic is a rich spectrum of transpersonal experiences that provide profound insights into realms and dimensions of reality that are ordinarily hidden to human perception and intellect. Some of them mediate profound connection with and attunement to the creative energies of the universe, the forces of nature, and the world of animals and plants. Others involve various deities, spirit guides, and particularly power animals—helpers and protectors in animal form.

People experiencing sequences of this kind often feel a special connection with nature—with the ocean, rivers, mountains, celestial bodies, and various life forms. Many are seized by sudden artistic inspiration through which they receive poems, songs, or ideas for rituals to be performed. Some of these rituals can be identical with those actually practiced by shamans of various cultures. And, like shamans, some develop unusual insights into the nature of various emotional and psychosomatic disorders and ways of detecting and healing them.

Awakening of Extrasensory Perception (Psychic Opening)

> Then I looked again. Something was wrong. This wall had no windows, no furniture against it, no doors. It was not a wall in my bedroom. Yet somehow it was familiar. Identification came instantly. It was not a wall, it was the ceiling. I was floating against the ceiling, bouncing gently with any movement I made. I rolled in the air, startled, and looked down.
>
> There, in the dim light below me, was the bed. There were two figures lying in the bed. To the right was my wife. Beside her was someone else. Both seemed asleep. This was a strange dream, I thought. I was curious. Whom would I dream to be in bed with my wife? I looked more closely and the shock was intense. I was the someone in the bed!
>
> Robert Monroe, *Journeys Out of the Body*

Many spiritual traditions and mystical schools describe the emergence of various paranormal abilities as a natural but potentially dangerous stage in consciousness development. Fascination and obsession with psychic phenomena are usually seen as a dangerous trap for the seeker's ego and an unfortunate distraction from genuine spiritual pursuits. In the more advanced stages that follow the overcoming of this critical obstacle, heightened intuition and psychic abilities can become integral parts of one's life. At that time, they are integrated into the new mystical worldview and do not present problems.

It is thus not surprising that a considerable increase in intuitive abilities and the occurrence of psychic or paranormal phenomena are extremely frequent concomitants of various forms of spiritual emergency. Practically any type of transpersonal experience can under certain circumstances provide astonishing information that the individual could not have acquired in conventional ways and that appears to come from paranormal sources. In addition, many individuals in transformational crisis report specific instances of extrasensory perception, such as remote viewing, precognition, telepathy, and other psychic phenomena. However, occasionally the influx of information from nonordinary sources becomes so overwhelming and confusing that it dominates the picture and becomes a major problem.

The most extreme and dramatic manifestations of a psychic opening are out-of-body experiences. Here consciousness seems to separate from the body, assumes various degrees of independence and freedom, and acquires the ability to perceive the environment without the mediation of the senses. People experiencing such disembodied states are able to observe themselves from the ceiling, witness events in other parts of the building, or "travel" to various distant locations and perceive accurately what is happening there. As we will see later, such states are particularly frequent in near-death situations, where their authenticity has been confirmed by systematic clinical studies.

Another extrasensory phenomenon that often occurs in persons experiencing a dramatic psychic opening is the capacity to tune so deeply into the inner processes of others that it results in telepathy. Their insights can be remarkably accurate and may be aimed at various areas that people ordinarily like to hide. Many people in crisis tend to indiscriminately verbalize their telepathic insights, which offends and irritates those whom the insights concern and aggravates further an already tense situation. On occasion, this can be one of the factors that lead to unnecessary hospitalization.

In some instances, individuals undergoing spiritual emergency can have various forms and degrees of awareness concerning the future. Sometimes this is related to events that are about to happen, at other times to those that will occur in the remote future. They can also exhibit perceptions of situations in other parts of the world, particularly if these involve people to whom they are emotionally close. The frequent occurrence and accumulation of such psychic events can be very frightening and disturbing, since they seriously undermine the notion of reality prevalent in industrial societies.

Another experience that often presents serious problems for people undergoing dramatic psychic opening is the occasional loss of their own identity and mediumistic identification with other persons. They can assume the other person's body image, posture, gestures, facial expression, emotions, and even thought processes. Accomplished shamans, psychics, and spiritual healers are often able to enter such states at will and use them for acquiring insights into other people's problems, and diagnosing and healing various disorders. However, inexperienced people in crises of psychic opening are often surprised by the sudden and unsolicited occurrence of such phenomena and find the loss of control and personal identity that they entail very frightening.

Individuals in spiritual crises often report that their lives abound in various extraordinary coincidences that connect the elements of their inner reality, such as dreams and visionary states, with events in the everyday world. This phenomenon was first recognized and described by C. G. Jung, who called it synchronicity. He defined *synchronicity* as an acausal connecting principle that accounts for meaningful coincidences linking individuals and situations in separate locations or across time. Extraordinary synchronicities accompany many forms of spiritual emergency, but they seem to be particularly common in crises of psychic opening.

Traditional psychiatry insists on strictly causal explanations and has not yet accepted the phenomenon of synchronicity. Psychiatrists usually dismiss any allusions to meaningful coincidences as distorted perception and misinterpretation of facts due to a pathological process. The technical term used in this context is *delusion of reference*, which means that the person sees connections where there really are none. In the Newtonian-Cartesian image of the universe, there is no place for meaningful coincidences; every improbable coincidence either is a chance happening or exists only in the imagination of the perceiver.

Transpersonal research has shown that in the process of spiritual opening people often experience genuine synchronicities in Jung's sense. All those who have access to the facts—about both the inner experiences and the corresponding events in the external world—recognize the extraordinary nature of these situations. The connections are very specific, deeply meaningful, and often even contain an element of cosmic humor. Everything considered, it is highly implausible that such coincidences can be understood in causal terms or that they are due to chance alone. At present, the concept of synchronicity is not limited to psychology. Many avant-garde scientists, including quantum-relativistic physicists, have embraced the principle of synchronicity as an important alternative to strictly causal explanations.

The accumulation of psychic happenings of various kinds can be very disturbing. When such episodes are so overwhelming and convincing that it is difficult to dismiss them, the situation becomes very frightening, since the old foundations of security have been shattered and one feels like an entirely naive and uninformed newcomer in an unknown and mysterious world.

When one becomes familiar and comfortable with psychic events and abilities, one might encounter problems of a different kind. It is easy to become fascinated by the opening realm of psychic phenomena and interpret their occurrence as an indication of one's own superiority and special calling. Since the goal of the spiritual path is transcending the ego, such an attitude represents a great danger of ego aggrandizement and inflation.

Communication with Spirit Guides and Channeling

> I do not believe that I could get the equivalent of Seth's book on my own. This book is Seth's way of demonstrating that human personality is multidimensional, that we exist in many realities at once, that the soul or inner self is not something apart from us, but the very medium in which we exist . . . Seth may be as much a creation as this book is. If so, this is an excellent instance of multidimensional art, done at such a rich level of unconsciousness that the "artist" is unaware of her own work and as much intrigued by it as anyone else.
>
> Jane Roberts, *Seth Speaks*

In nonordinary states of consciousness, one can assume different roles in relation to the various entities and situations encountered in the inner world. It is possible to be an uninvolved observer, to actively participate in the sequences, or to actually identify with various elements of the scenario. However, occasionally one can come into contact with an entity that appears to be entirely separate from and independent of one's own inner process. He or she offers a personal relationship and continues to play the role of guide, protector, teacher, or superior source of information. In the literature on psychic phenomena, such figures are usually referred to as spirit guides.

In some instances, the subject is able to recognize the nature of these beings; at other times the spirit guides introduce themselves and explain where they come from and what their mission is. They usually appear to be discarnate humans, suprahuman entities, or deities, inhabiting higher planes of consciousness and endowed with extraordinary wisdom. Sometimes they resemble human beings; at other times they look like a radiant source of light. There are also instances where they do not appear in any detectable form but their presence can be sensed. They communicate with their protégés through direct thought transfer or through other extrasensory means. Occasionally, they have human voices and send verbal messages.

A special example of experiences in this category is channeling, a phenomenon that in recent years has become very popular among the

American public and has received extensive coverage in the media: an individual becomes a mediator, or channel, for messages that come from a source allegedly outside of his or her individual consciousness. These messages are transmitted through speaking in trance, automatic writing, or telepathic transfer. The quality of the channeled material varies, and the question of the ultimate source of the information has been the subject of many speculations and conjectures. However, channeling can be a healing and transformative experience for the recipient, and channeled information has often been of value to others as a guide for personal growth and consciousness evolution.

Channeling has played an important role in the history of humanity. Among the channeled spiritual teachings are many scriptures of enormous cultural influence, such as the ancient Indian Vedas, the Koran, and the Book of Mormon. Many passages in the Zoroastrian sacred text Zend-Avesta and in the Bible also have their origin in experiences of this kind.

Among the important sources for channeling in the twentieth century is an entity who called himself "the Tibetan"; both Alice Bailey and Madame Blavatsky acknowledged him as the source of their spiritual writings. The Italian psychiatrist Roberto Assagioli credited the same entity as the real author of his psychological system called psychosynthesis.

During his lifetime, C. G. Jung had many transpersonal experiences. Prominent among these was a dramatic episode during which he channeled his famous text *Seven Sermons for the Dead*; the entity that inspired it introduced himself as the Gnostic Basilides. Jung also had powerful experiences with the spirit guide Philemon and left a painting portraying him. His experiences with this entity convinced him that various aspects of the psyche can assume a completely autonomous function.

One of the most popular contemporary channeled texts is the best-selling book *A Course in Miracles*; it is very highly acclaimed by lay people, as well as by many professionals who use it as a basis for lectures, seminars, and courses. It was channeled by Helen Schucman and dictated by an entity who called himself Christ. Schucman was a traditionally trained psychologist, atheist, and disbeliever in the paranormal, with a solid university position and good professional credentials. When she started hearing an inner voice mediating information that was entirely new to her, she went into a state of profound conceptual confusion, with doubts about her sanity.

The main reason such experiences trigger a serious crisis is that Western society traditionally has only ridicule and pathological labels for phenomena of this kind. However, it is not easy for channelers to completely ignore and discard their experiences in view of the extraordinary nature and quality of the information that can be received. For instance, on occasion channeling can bring absolutely accurate data from areas of knowledge that the recipient has never been exposed to. This seeming proof of the existence of spiritual realities can lead to serious philosophical confusion for those who had previously held a very different belief system.

In some instances, the experience of channeling can be intense and intrusive and may seriously interfere with everyday life. Another problem is the danger of ego inflation in the channeler. The spirit guides are usually perceived as very advanced and evolved beings; they appear to be on a high level of consciousness and have superior intelligence and extraordinary moral integrity. The channelers might interpret their having been chosen as proof of their own superiority.

Experiences of Close Encounters with UFOs

And I'm coming before a bright light—crystals, bright, bright light, and clear crystals that have rainbows all in it. It is all crystal all around—all forms of crystal. I don't know what it is. I'm afraid! I want to go back! And the bright light up ahead! I want to go back. They are taking me through these crystals. That bright light is up ahead . . . Oh, that bright light. We are stopping and the two are getting off the thing. And I'm just there, before the light.

Betty Andreasson describing her encounter in *The Andreasson Affair*

Since 1947, when the American civilian pilot Keneth Arnold saw in the mountains near Mount Rainier unidentified flying objects and gave them the name flying saucers, the subject of UFOs and extraterrestrial visits and encounters has caused considerable controversy. Some reports describe daytime visions of unusual objects and nighttime visions of strange lights; others tell of landed spacecrafts and crews and even of interactions with them. The extreme forms of such experiences involve abductions or visits to the interiors of the spacecrafts and participation in flights to more or less distant extraterrestrial locations. According to an anonymous Gallup poll, about 5 million Americans have observed things in the sky that they could not explain and that belong in this category.

Discussions about UFOs are usually understood as attempts to determine whether or not the earth has been visited by extraterrestrial beings and spacecrafts. However, the experiences of such encounters have an important psychological and spiritual dimension. They can often precipitate serious emotional and intellectual crises that have much in common with spiritual emergencies. C. G. Jung considered this phenomenon to be so important that he made it the subject of a special essay, entitled *Flying Saucers: A Modern Myth of Things Seen in the Skies*. It was based on careful historical analysis of legends about flying discs and actual apparitions that had occasionally caused mass hysteria. Jung came to the conclusion that UFO phenomena might be archetypal visions originating in the collective unconscious rather than extraterrestrial spacecraft. Other researchers have pointed out the similarity of these experiences with other transpersonal states and emphasized their transformative potential.

Whether these experiences originate in actual extraterrestrial contacts or within the psyche, they share many characteristics with various transpersonal states in general, and with certain forms of spiritual emergency in particular. Individuals reporting UFO sightings usually talk about lights that have an extraordinary supernatural quality and do not resemble anything known on earth—descriptions that are strongly reminiscent of visions of light occurring in mystical states and other nonordinary states of consciousness.

UFO researcher Alwin Lawson has also pointed out that the "extraterrestrial visitors" fall into several major categories, the same that one finds in world mythology and religion, suggesting that they might have their origins in the collective unconscious. Abduction reports often contain references to physical procedures, such as scientific examinations and experiments, that are extremely painful. In this they resemble experiences in shamanic crises or various ordeals of initiates in rites of passage conducted by aboriginal cultures.

Accounts of the people who were allegedly abducted or invited for a ride describe the alien spacecrafts and their cosmic flights in a way that is reminiscent of Ezekiel's biblical vision of the flaming machine or the legendary chariot of the Vedic god Indra. The cities of advanced civilizations visited during these journeys and the fabulous landscapes of alien planets bear a strong resemblance to the visionary experiences of paradises, celestial realms, and cities of light known from spiritual literature of various cultures.

The experiences of encounters with and abduction by what appear to be extraterrestrial spacecrafts and beings can often precipitate serious emotional, intellectual, and spiritual crises. Keith Thompson, a psychologist and ardent researcher of UFO phenomena, has quite explicitly compared the experiences of people involved in these situations with those of initiates undergoing rites of passage. Thompson pointed out that, like such initiates, those experiencing UFO phenomena have been exposed to levels and dimensions of reality that are ordinarily hidden to human perception and have been profoundly transformed by their experiences. They lost connection with their society and are in a state of liminality, betwixt and between. They cannot return to the culturally shared illusion of reality, which has been shattered by their experience, and have not succeeded in creating a new, more encompassing one.

Unlike the initiates, however, who receive a warm welcome by a society that honors their new belief system and actually enacts rituals with the explicit intention of revealing certain hidden realities, those involved with UFO experiences continue to live in a culture whose worldview they no longer share. This lack of acceptance by society can create a crisis much like that precipitated by near-death experiences and other forms of spiritual emergency.

There are additional reasons that the experience of a UFO encounter can precipitate a psychospiritual crisis; the issues here are similar to those we discussed in relation to spirit guides and channeling. The extraterrestrial civilizations involved are usually perceived as being much more advanced than the population of our planet, not only in terms of science and technology, but also morally and spiritually. Communication and contact with them typically has a very strong mystical quality and involves a sense of higher teaching that leads to universal insights.

Under these circumstances, the recipients of such special attention might themselves start feeling exceptional. They might conclude that they were chosen for an unusual task by beings from an advanced civilization because of some extraordinary personal qualities.

Possession States

Suddenly, Flora started complaining that the pain of the facial cramps was becoming unbearable. In front of my eyes, the spasms were grotesquely accentuated and her face froze into what can best be described as a "mask of evil." She began to talk in a deep male voice and everything about her was so different that I could not see much connection between her present appearance and her former self. Her eyes had an expression of indescribable evil and her hands were spastic and claw-like.

The alien energy that had taken over her body and voice introduced itself as the Devil. "He" turned directly to me, ordering me to stay away from Flora and to give up any attempts to help her. She belonged to him and he would punish anybody who would try to invade his territory. What followed was quite explicit blackmail, a series of dismal intimations of what would happen to me, my colleagues, and the research program, if I decided not to obey.

Stanislav Grof, *The Adventure of Self-Discovery*

This form of psychospiritual crisis is characterized by an uncanny sense that one's psyche and body have been invaded and are being controlled by an alien entity or energy that has personal characteristics. This feeling can be occasional and intermittent or may persist for long periods of time. People suffering from such a condition perceive this entity as malevolent, hostile, and disturbing; it is "ego alien"—coming from outside and not belonging to one's personality. When it becomes identified, it appears to be a discarnate entity, a demonic presence, or consciousness of an evil person trying to take over by means of hexing rituals and black magic.

This condition can manifest itself in different forms, with varying degrees of intensity. In many instances, the alien energy remains latent and can cause a broad spectrum of problems, while its real nature remains hidden. It can be the driving force behind serious psychopathology, such as various forms of antisocial or even criminal behavior, suicidal depression, murderous aggression or self-destructive tendencies, promiscuous and deviant sexual impulses, or excessive consumption of alcohol and drugs. Sometimes the "possession state" underlying these problems is not identified until the individual enters experiential psychotherapy and is exposed to methods that activate the unconscious mind.

In experiential therapy, the problem can suddenly become manifest. In the middle of the session, the "possessed" person suddenly develops severe cramps and spasms; the eyes and face assume a wild and terrifying expression, the body and the extremities become contorted, and the voice becomes deep and has an otherwordly quality. When the facilitators allow and encourage full manifestation and expression of this condition, the behavior of the person can become quite extreme. He or she can flail around, scream, vomit, choke, and even experience a temporary loss of control and consciousness. Sessions of this kind can resemble exorcisms in the Christian church or the exorcist rituals of various aboriginal cultures.

In other cases, the alien energy is so close to the surface that the "possessed" individual is aware of it most of the time and has to spend an enormous amount of effort to prevent it from becoming manifest. In the extreme and most dangerous form, the defense mechanisms fail and the problem manifests itself uncontrollably in the midst of everyday life. Its manifestations, which in the right therapeutic context could be healing and transformative, can under these circumstances lead to highly destructive and self-destructive forms of acting out.

Such demonic possession clearly belongs to the group of spiritual emergencies, even if it looks on the surface to be very different and is often associated with the most objectionable forms of psychopathology.

Individuals in this kind of predicament experience a true dark night of the soul. They often feel bad, abominable, and cut off from the stream of life and from the Divine. Relatives, friends, and often even therapists tend to ostracize the "possessed" person, partly because of moral judgment, and partly because of profound metaphysical fear. This contributes even further to feelings of desperate loneliness and anxiety associated with the condition itself.

However, there are more important reasons that the possession state should be considered a spiritual emergency. The demonic archetype that causes it is by its very nature transpersonal and represents a necessary counterpoint to the Divine, being its polar opposite or negative mirror image. It also often functions as a screen hiding access to the Divine, like the terrifying guardian figures at the gateways of Oriental temples. When the person is given an opportunity to confront and express the disturbing energy in a supportive and understanding setting, a profound positive spiritual experience often results, one that has an extraordinary healing and transformative potential.

CHAPTER 5

ADDICTION AS SPIRITUAL EMERGENCY

As the hart panteth after the water brooks, so panteth
my soul after thee, O God.
Psalm 42.1

As we felt the new power flow in, as we enjoyed peace
of mind, as we discovered we could face life successfully, as we became conscious of His presence,
we began to lose our fear of today, tomorrow, or the
hereafter. We were reborn.
Alcoholics Anonymous

It is possible that for many people, behind the craving for
drugs or alcohol is the craving for transcendence or wholeness. If this
is so, then drug and alcohol dependency, as well as the multitude of
other kinds of addiction, may be in many cases forms of spiritual emergency. Addiction differs from other forms of transformative crisis in that
the spiritual dimension is often obscured by the apparent destructive
and self-destructive nature of the disease. In other varieties of spiritual
emergencies, people encounter problems because of spiritual or mystical
states of mind. In contrast, during addiction many difficulties occur
because the quest for the deeper dimensions within is not being carried
out.

Alcoholics and other addicts describe their decline into the depths of
addiction as "spiritual bankruptcy" or "soul sickness," and the healing of
their impoverished soul as "rebirth." Since many spiritual emergencies
follow this same trajectory, many lessons in assistance during transformation crises can be learned from successful alcohol and drug-abuse
treatment programs.

Because of the rampant problem of drug and alcohol addiction in
the world, and since it is an area of great interest, we feel that it deserves
a special chapter. In these pages, we will explore the idea of addiction
as a form of spiritual emergency and offer some thoughts about the

lessons that each field can learn from the other. But first we would like to discuss the roots of our interest in the subject.

Christina has personally experienced the depths and drama of both spiritual emergency and chemical dependency, and it was initially through her intimate involvement with each that she began to consider the possibility that the two are related. In the following pages, Christina will continue her story, as begun in her prologue.

Christina's Story, continued

My spiritual emergence preceded my addiction to alcohol, and yet the process of "hitting bottom" with this disease and going into recovery was for some reason the key to resolving many of the dramatic problems that had occurred during the years of the Kundalini awakening. It has become very clear to me that both my spiritual crises and my alcoholism have been essential elements in my transformation process, although beforehand I would never have imagined that addiction could have the profound positive impact on my life that it has had.

In telling this story, I in no way intend to glamorize the horribly degrading, self-destructive, and potentially lethal life of an alcoholic. Although many people move through their addictions into a freer, more enlightened, more productive life of quality recovery, thousands do not. I would never recommend this extremely dangerous form of spiritual emergency as a route to transformation.

Before I discovered alcohol as a tranquilizer, I had not used it to any great extent. Although I drank socially during my days in Honolulu, I controlled it successfully and drank very little after being introduced to yoga. However, that changed with the onset of the chaotic Kundalini activity.

Stan and I were traveling all over the globe, keeping arduous schedules of seminars and lectures. In our workshops, I was dealing with large numbers of people involved in intense emotional exploration, and although our work was exciting, I constantly felt depleted from the continuous attention I was giving to others.

In addition, I was having to cope daily with my own demanding inner states, never knowing when they would hit me or what they would entail. I found myself in a desperate struggle to balance my complex internal world of seemingly interminable experiences, visions, and strange physical energies with an equally complex external world. I discovered that when the airline cocktail cart rolled around, a couple of drinks would take the edge off, and I increasingly turned to alcohol for relief.

What I did not know is that certain families have a predisposition toward alcoholism and that this disease had affected a number of my family members; for this reason, as well as others, I was a prime candidate. I was hooked very quickly. As the alcoholism progressed rapidly, it became difficult to distinguish the manifestations of the Kundalini process (the tremors, mood swings, and gastrointestinal problems) from those of the disease. The resulting confusion, combined with my unshakable denial of the fact that I had a problem, made for a deadly combination.

I also found myself in a horrible dilemma: I had had a spiritual awakening and was "on the path," assisted by a loving teacher, and yet I could not stop using alcohol. I would visit Swami Muktananda, feel loved, accepted, and connected, and then go home to drink. Many times I asked myself, "How can a seeker continue to do something this bad?" and I began to believe that I was not really involved in a true spiritual journey.

Like a flash fire, my addiction swept rapidly through my life, becoming particularly destructive after Muktananda's death in 1982; I had grown very close to him, and I was devastated when my support and teacher was no longer available. In January 1986, after having been hospitalized twice for severe dehydration and liver problems, I entered a treatment center for alcoholism and chemical dependency.

Even then, I clung tenaciously to my familiar way of being, even though it was extremely destructive, unhealthy, and dishonest. I knew that my life was not working, that I was physically extremely sick and suicidal. But I hung on to the illusion that I was different from the other alcoholics and addicts around me because of the "important" people I knew, the exotic places I had been, the "consequential work" that I had done, the "high" spiritual experiences that I had had. The elaborate story that I was telling myself and others kept me from looking at the reality of the glaring truth: I was undeniably an alcoholic, with all of the problems faced by any other drunk.

Finally, on the tenth day, with loving but firm guidance from the treatment-center staff, I gave up every shred of my defenses and admitted defeat. The combination of the work we did in treatment, the natural progression of my disease, and the news of a young friend's death from an overdose of alcohol and drugs took me to the bottom with a crash.

That experience is difficult to describe exactly. It was like being hit by an enormous truck that demolished every aspect of who I had been. I felt as though every aspect of my life were slipping away, including myself. There was nothing left to hold on to, and even if there had been, I no longer had the strength to grasp it. I had no choice but to give up. Some larger force was obviously in charge.

Somehow, that state of total physical, emotional, and spiritual bank-ruptcy was the internal death experience that I had been looking for. I had had two episodes of spiritual emergency. In spite of the depths that I had reached during those periods, I had never fully completed the process of "ego death," a necessary prelude in many transformative crises to healing and rebirth.

During the second episode, the content of my experiences centered almost exclusively around the issue of death. Even though the states during that crisis were powerful and unrelenting, I was never able to finish them. Intellectually, I knew that after resolving a powerful con-frontation with death, the process almost always moves into a period of spiritual rebirth. Instead, I was left physically and psychically weak from days of activity. I now realize that I had kept myself stuck through my use of alcohol as a tranquilizer. Instead of completing the ego-death experience internally, I had been acting it out externally through the horrifying self-destructive drama of alcoholism.

Immediately following the final downfall, a profound and awesome period of healing began automatically. I did not have to search for the grace that came into my life at that point. It simply appeared. Among the many miracles it brought with it was the complete clearing of the dramatic manifestations of the Kundalini. The almost-daily involvement with strange and sudden experiences ceased, freeing me to pursue fresh creative projects. I felt a new connection with myself and with the world around me, and became deeply aware of a higher source that offers me guidance. And I came to implicitly trust the emergence process as it continues, the same process that I fought and resented for many years.

The inner work is far from completed, and I know that I will die inwardly many more times, but that holds wondrous excitement for me rather than dread. To my great delight, I now find that many of Muk-tananda's teachings are reflected in my spiritual recovery program. I am daily grateful that I lived through my excursion into alcoholism, and have developed a strong urge to try to use that experience to benefit others.

A Closer Look at Addiction

With this story as background, let us now look, in greater detail, at the three statements made at the beginning of this chapter:

For many people, behind the craving for drugs, alcohol, or other addictions is the craving for the Higher Self or God. Many recovering people will talk about their restless search for some unknown missing piece in their lives and will describe their vain pursuit of a multitude of substances, foods, relationships, possessions, or powerful positions in an effort to fulfill their unrewarded craving. In retrospect, they acknowledge that there was a tragic confusion, a misperception that told them that the answers lay outside themselves.

Some even describe the first drink or drug as their first spiritual experience, a state in which individual boundaries are melted and everyday pain disappears, taking them into a state of pseudo-unity, as acknowledged by William James in the following passage from *The Varieties of Religious Experience*.

> The sway of alcohol over mankind is unquestionably due to its power to stimulate the mystical faculties of human nature, usually crushed to earth by the cold facts and dry criticisms of the sober hour. Sobriety diminishes, discriminates, and says no; drunkenness expands, unites, and says yes.

After hitting bottom with their disease and becoming part of a spiritual recovery program, recovering addicts will exclaim, "This is what I was looking for!" Their newfound clarity and connection with a Higher Power and with other human beings offers them the unitive state that they had been seeking, and the insatiable yearning diminishes.

William James acknowledged the role of spirituality in recovery: "The only cure for dipsomania [an archaic name for alcoholism] is religiomania." The great Swiss psychiatrist Carl Gustav Jung believed the same thing. In January 1961, Jung wrote to Bill Wilson, the cofounder of Alcoholics Anonymous:

> Craving for alcohol [is] the equivalent on a low level of the spiritual thirst of our being for wholeness, expressed in medieval language: the union with God . . . Alcohol in Latin is "spiritus," and you use the same word for the highest religious experience as well as for the most depraving poison. The helpful formula therefore is: "spiritus contra spiritum."

This idea of "spiritus contra spiritum," the employment of the Divine Spirit against the ravages of "spirits," or liquor, has become the basis of many treatment programs. To understand why this is so, it may be helpful to look at the recent history of addiction. We will specifically address chemical dependency, since this is the area toward which most attention and professional experience has been directed; however, many of the other forms of addiction (for example, food, sex, relationships, gambling) may be substituted in some places. We also focus on alcohol since it is the drug that we know the best, but most of the ideas that we are discussing apply to addiction to other drugs such as cocaine, crack, heroin, and marijuana.

A great number of people were raised with the belief that alcoholism and drug addiction represent ethical shortcomings and that people with such a disorder are bad. The prevailing image of an addict or alcoholic was that of a male skid-row bum with days of unattended stubble on his chin, wallowing unconsciously through his remaining days in an intoxicated stupor and intolerable poverty. He was an unethical human being who had fallen on hard times without the proper moral integrity to exert self-control over his situation or willpower over his drug. Audiences gasped in horror as they watched Frank Sinatra shoot heroin in *The Man with the Golden Arm* and Jack Lemmon sink into moral disintegration in *The Days of Wine and Roses*.

Relatively recently, this perspective has changed. In the 1950s, the American Medical Association recognized alchoholism as a disease. It also became known as a combination of a physical allergy to alcohol plus a compulsion to drink, which has an unknown origin. This disease affects the physical, emotional, and spiritual makeup of the victim. It was now known to be a predictable illness that is progressive and ultimately fatal if left untreated. Researchers attempted to try to isolate the genetic and chemical variables. Hope was offered to those suffering from addiction that this deadly disease could be successfully treated through abstinence. The self-help fellowship of Alcoholics Anonymous grew, recovery programs sprang up, and literature proliferated. A popular phrase among recovering groups became, "We are not bad people trying to be good; we are sick people trying to get well."

Soon people from all walks of life, relieved to know that they were ill rather than evil, began to come forth with their stories in an effort to offer reassurance to others. Movie stars, dress designers, society matrons, physicians, politicians, lawyers, and even the wife of a president of the United States all admitted to their bouts with chemical dependency. It became increasingly clear to the general public that this problem touches every facet of society, not simply the forgotten derelicts.

The twelve-step fellowships such as Alcoholics Anonymous, Narcotics Anonymous, and others exhibited a higher success rate than most forms of therapy in helping addicts and alcoholics stay off drugs and alcohol. Not only did such systems work toward daily abstinence, but they also actively focused on a sophisticated, detailed scheme to help people to create better lives, lives of quality sobriety and spiritual maturity. They emphasized the necessity of abandoning a sense of control over one's life, entrusting it instead to a Higher Power or God "as we understand God."

These programs encouraged people to become honest with themselves and others, doing what they could to correct the "wreckage of [their] past," but also focusing on the opportunities and blessings of the present moment with the dedication not to personally create more difficulties. They motivated people to practice prayer and meditation, offering the possibility of a "spiritual awakening," and to transform their intimate exposure to the pain and problems of addiction into service to others. Soon, professionals began to recognize the tremendous effectiveness of such programs and to build them into recovery plans that include the concept of a Higher Power.

In many cases the intense and sometimes overpowering craving for drugs, alcohol, food, sex, or other objects of addiction is really a misplaced yearning for wholeness, a larger sense of self, or God—one that cannot be satisfied in the external world. When the true object of this craving, an experience of the Higher Power, becomes available and even partially fulfills this consuming desire, the desire diminishes. How is this related to spiritual emergency?

For many people, drug and alcohol dependency and other addictions are forms of spiritual emergency. As with many other forms of spiritual emergency, the journey of the addict or alcoholic to the bottom and into recovery is often an ego-death and rebirth process. The death-rebirth cycle has been recognized as a natural and lawful pattern throughout history by many cultures. Just as spring reliably follows winter year after year, so the development of a new life automatically follows a full experience of the destruction of the old. This principle applies to the dynamics of many forms of spiritual emergence, including addiction.

The important role of the ego death during a transformational crisis has been previously discussed; this experience has a direct parallel with the alcoholic's or addict's experience of "hitting bottom." In both cases, a person comes to the point at which his or her life is not working successfully and he or she is rendered completely powerless to control its trajectory. During the ego death, whether it occurs in an episode of spontaneous spiritual awakening or at the bottom of an individual's drinking career, everything that one is or was—all relationships and reference points, all rationalizations and protections—collapse, and the person is left naked, with nothing but the core of his or her being.

From this state of absolute, terrifying surrender, there is nowhere to go but up. As part of the rebirth that follows this devastating death, one easily opens to a spiritually oriented existence during which the practice of service becomes an essential impulse. Life becomes manageable, with help from a higher power, and one develops a new attitude toward handling life's ups and downs as they appear. Many people are surprised to find a constant, unending benevolent source within that offers them strength and guidance. They develop the insight that life without spirituality is trivial and unfulfilling.

In the process of hitting bottom with drugs or alcohol, some people lose everything; their health, family, home, job, and money slide away as a direct result of their disease, and they are left externally destitute. Others manage to keep their outer world relatively intact. However, all alcoholics and other addicts experience an internal loss, a "spiritual bankruptcy" or "soul sickness," that cuts them off from their inner resources and from the world around them. They enter the soul's dark night and wrestle with the demons of fear, loneliness, insanity, and death that are so common in other forms of spiritual emergency.

Whatever their circumstances, each addict or alcoholic moves progressively toward a total emotional, physical, and spiritual annihilation. As that experience approaches, suicide often seems to be the only way out of such a desperate dilemma; someone helplessly caught in the spiral toward desctruction does not understand that this process of inner dying, of complete surrender, is the turning point, the gateway into a new way of being: it is the opportunity for "egocide," so often mistaken for suicide, the dark night that comes before the dawn of healing.

Unfortunately, many literally enact the death phase of this elemental death-rebirth process and become part of the already grim statistics concerning drug- and alcohol-related deaths. But those who make it into recovery regularly discover a new, spiritual life that includes a newfound honesty, openness, flexibility, love, and trust in God and in themselves, elements that are common in the new life after a spiritual emergency. The key to this redemption has been the complete surrender of the illusion that one is in control of one's life and the acceptance of help from a Higher Power, as outlined in the first three steps of the Alcoholics Anonymous program:

1. We admitted we were powerless over alcohol—that our lives had become unmanageable.

2. Came to believe that a Power greater than ourselves could restore us to sanity.

3. Made a decision to turn our will and our lives over to the care of God *as we understood God*.

According to Buddhist teachings, the root of all suffering is attachment. With this in mind, it is easy to see that chemical dependency is an extreme form of attachment, a kind of forced suffering. Becoming physically and psychologically addicted to a substance harnesses one to it, as well as to the destructive and self-destructive behavior implicit in its use. Breaking out of the resultant misery is an immense and total letting go of a manipulative, ruinous way of existing; as with other kinds of spiritual emergency, one then naturally progresses toward a new freedom. This does not imply that one automatically becomes exempt from problems; however, instead of trying desperately to control and exploit one's life, one develops an attitude of collaboration with its dynamics. It is the difference between a boxing match, in which a person clashes with existing forces, and the flowing practice of martial arts, when one waits to see the direction in which the movement and energy are proceeding and cooperates with it.

For many people, a sudden, profound spiritual awakening triggers their movement into a life of sobriety; these elevating life-changing events often happen in most unlikely places: jail cells, gutters, hospitals, the floor of one's home, the toilet stall of a bar. For others, such transformative movement happens gradually during recovery, over a period of time; William James calls this the "educational variety" of religious experience, one that grows gradually over time.

Whatever the route, many people who have known the depths of alcoholism or drug addiction, have hit bottom, and have emerged into a new life develop some kind of relationship with a Higher Power of their own definition: a community of people, the inner self, the creative force, or God. It becomes dramatically clear that when left to their own devices, such individuals could not effectively manage their own lives. For many, the fact that they lived through the total emotional, physical, and spiritual devastation is a miracle, made possible only with help from a greater source and the natural tendency of the organism to seek wholeness.

Bill Wilson, the cofounder of Alcoholics Anonymous, spoke and wrote eloquently about alcoholism and the need for the spiritual dimension in recovery. Wilson's transformation began in a hospital room, where, desperately sick, he received medical treatment after one of his many binges. His biographer writes:

Now, there was nothing ahead but death or madness. This was the finish, the jumping-off place. "The terrifying darkness had become complete," Bill said . . . In his helplessness and desperation, Bill cried out, "I'll do anything, anything at all!" He had reached . . . a state of complete, absolute surrender. . . . He cried, "If there be a God, let Him show Himself!"

[Wilson's words follow:] "Suddenly, my room blazed with an indescribably white light. I was seized with an ecstasy beyond description . . . I stood upon [the summit of a mountain], where a great wind blew. A wind, not of air, but of spirit. In great, clean strength, it blew right through me. Then came the blazing thought, 'You are a free man.' . . . a great peace stole over me and . . . I became acutely conscious of a Presence which seemed like a veritable sea of living spirit. I lay on the shores of a new world . . . For the first time, I felt that I really belonged. I knew that I was loved and could love in return."

Bill Wilson never drank again, and went on to cofound Alcoholics Anonymous. However, even after such a true revelatory event, Wilson had his doubts as to the validity of his experience. Soon afterward, when his mind had had time to start doubting his awakening, he hesitatingly described it to his physician, asking, "Doctor, is this real? Am I still perfectly sane?" Fortunately, Dr. William Duncan Silkworth had read about such experiences and, although he had never encountered anyone who had actually had one, was able to reassure Wilson as to his sanity, encouraging him to develop his newfound awareness and identity.

This automatic inclination to question or negate a transformative experience is a familiar theme in work with spiritual emergency. Because such a mystical state is so far from ordinary perception, one easily misinterprets it as crazy. Some may find that it seriously violates a strong atheistic belief, as Wilson did, and so try to discard it. Others may feel that they do not deserve such grace.

Many lessons can be learned from successful treatment programs. Since the field of spiritual emergency is relatively new in our culture, there have not been much data collected or many treatment modalities explored. However, many chemical-dependency treatment programs include a spiritual dimension. The alcoholism and drug-abuse world can offer models that could be adapted by those in a spiritual emergence process, as well as by those assisting them. Self-help fellowships such as Alcoholics Anonymous, along with good treatment centers and chemical-dependency programs, provide some of the few sanctuaries in this culture where people can move through a life-changing rite of passage with support, understanding, and love. We would like to see the same opportunities made available for those going through a spontaneous spiritual emergency. Halfway houses that offer protection and assistance to alcoholics and addicts making their way back into society can also provide inspiration for those working with people in a transformational crisis.

Addiction and Spiritual Emergency

There are two connections between spiritual emergence and chemical dependency that are based on our informal observations; we hope they will assist in the further understanding of both addiction problems and spiritual emergency.

Some people develop alcoholism, drug dependency, or other addictions during a spiritual emergency. We are increasingly meeting people in a transformation process who have turned to addictive substances in an attempt to ease the stress of that intense period. Alcohol or drugs can provide a temporary escape from the pressures, pain, and chaos of the inner world and from the alienation that one may feel from the external world. This can be complicated if, in a state of unrest, a person seeks the help of a sympathetic but uninformed psychiatrist who prescribes addictive tranquilizers. Although the moderate use of tranquilizers might be indicated in certain situations, their frequent use to suppress the process is contrary to the full expression required during a spiritual emergency. And for many people—especially those with addictive tendencies—such medications can be easily abused.

Also, one of the primary manifestations of experiences such as the Kundalini awakening is tremendous energy. Especially during highly aroused states, a great deal of this energy is expressed through physical movement and emotional outpourings, often depleting one's physical resources. The individual subsequently finds himself or herself craving sweets, needing to replace the carbohydrates that have been expended. It is only a small step from candy to alcoholic beverages such as port, which has a high sugar content.

Many addicts and alcoholics have a highly developed sensitivity, intuition, or mystical nature, which, while sought after in other cultures, causes them trouble in the modern world and contributes to their addictive behavior. This became apparent when we realized that one of the most frequent statements made by recovering people is, "I always felt different, like an outcast. But when I took my first drink or my first drug, the pain of separation suddenly faded and I felt as though I belonged." As we mentioned previously, for many people this sense of connection may be a sad caricature of the state of mystical union, a pseudosatisfaction of an intense craving for a larger sense of self. But there might be another reason for this behavior, which is also linked to the innate human impulse toward spiritual emergence.

A large number of people who become addicts or alcoholics have grown up in dysfunctional families, frequently in situations of emotional, physical, and sexual abuse, and often with parents who are chemically dependent. The psychic Anne Armstrong has described in her lectures the emotional violence in her family that caused her to develop and depend upon her acutely intuitive nature as a way of surviving. Where ordinary coping mechanisms failed, she became able through her increasingly strong intuition to outguess and outmaneuver those who threatened her.

This appears to be the case with many people who are raised in such an atmosphere: unable to get along successfully by directly approaching family members, they refine their sensitivities and natural psychic inclinations. Children of drunken, angry parents quickly learn instinctive ways to take care of themselves; perhaps they teach themselves to read their parent's moods and gestures or to predict their actions through precognitive impressions.

These children often retreat to their inner worlds for protection, comfort, and a sense of connection; they might escape into daydreams, create imaginary friends and adventures, or read for hours. They can spend a great deal of time in nature or participating in sports, or may find their way to the local church. They might develop a strong relationship with their creative or mystical nature, and may have true spiritual experiences along the way. For such people, spiritual emergence can begin in childhood—initiated, as are many other transformative processes, by extreme physical or emotional stress.

Then, after years of refining their intuition and creativity, they enter our culture—going to school, forming relationships, and, later, finding a job. Here they are forced to live daily within a society in which rationality is the accepted mode of operation and intuition is seen as weak or flaky. They experience terrible pain and constant rejection as they try to fit themselves into a world that is constructed around logic and reason.

They may also feel an unidentified longing to return to the inner realms that gave them consolation, security, and a relationship to something beyond their individual suffering. When the first drink or drug comes along, their problems seem to be solved. Their distress diminishes, and their differences become diffused as their individual boundaries seem to melt and they move toward a state of pseudo-unity. They become more relaxed socially as they take part in a highly acceptable activity. If they are predisposed to alcoholism or drug dependency, as their parents may have been, they can become addicted within a short time.

These observations regarding the complex relationship of alcoholism, drug addiction, and other dependencies with spiritual emergency are only a beginning; with time, many others will likely arise that could also be the subject of serious research. We feel that it is essential in the treatment of either chemical dependency or spiritual emergency for the person in crisis, as well as those surrounding him or her, to be aware of the connection between the two. If a person is in a spiritual emergency, it is necessary to look for abuse of drugs or alcohol; if one has problems with chemical dependency, it can be helpful to look for other indications of a spiritual emergence. It is important for professionals who work in the area of addiction to recognize and encourage the intuitive, creative, and spiritual dimensions of their clients and to offer them recovery programs in which these aspects can be developed.

The fact that alcoholism and drug dependence, as well as other addictions, are in many cases a form of spiritual emergency has far-reaching implications. For example, there are millions of people in the United States, the Soviet Union, Japan, Europe, and Australia, as well as other regions of the world, who are suffering from the ravages of alcoholism and drug addiction. One of our dreams is that, with loving guidance and understanding, each of the countless addicts and alcoholics who are teetering on the brink of rebirth will make the step into a spiritual way of living; perhaps if these individuals find some degree of serenity within, they will have a positive impact on the global community as it struggles toward peace.

PART TWO

CHARTS FOR THE INNER JOURNEY

CHAPTER 6

SPIRITUAL LESSONS FROM OTHER TIMES AND CULTURES

Now the real treasure, to end our misery and trials,
is never far away, it is not to be sought in any distant
region; it lies buried in the innermost recess of our
own home, that is to say, our own being ... But
there is the odd and persistent fact that it is only
after a faithful journey to a distant region, a foreign
country, a strange land, that the meaning of the inner
voice that is to guide our quest can be revealed to us.
HEINRICH ZIMMER

If we look to other cultures and historical periods, we find
convincing supportive evidence for the basic assumptions underlying the
concept of spiritual emergency. Throughout history, most cultures had
a great appreciation for nonordinary states of consciousness. They often
possessed extraordinary knowledge of the cartography of the inner journey and developed a variety of technologies of the sacred—methods for
inducing spiritual experiences—because they highly valued the positive
potential of such states. These mind-altering techniques combined various forms of drumming, chanting, dancing, breathing, fasting, physical
pain, social isolation, and even ingestion of plants with psychedelic properties.

This chapter explores several areas of human culture that are particularly relevant to spiritual emergency. The first is shamanism, humanity's
most ancient religion and healing art. Closely related to shamanism are
the so-called rites of passage, powerful rituals conducted in many cultures
at the time of important biological and social transitions.

Another fascinating phenomenon is the initiation into the ancient
mysteries of death and rebirth, such as those conducted in Greece, Egypt,
Rome, Mesoamerica, and other parts of the world. The most important

sources of information about spiritual emergencies are the scriptures of the great religions of the world and their mystical branches.

Among them, books of the dead had a very special position; they were used as guidebooks for the dying, as well as manuals for meditation practices and initiatory procedures.

The Shaman's Way

> I felt a great, inexplicable joy so powerful that I could not restrain it but had to break into song, a mighty song with room for only one word: joy, joy! . . . and then in the midst of such a fit of mysterious and overwhelming delight I became a shaman, not knowing myself how it came about. I have gained my enlightenment, the shaman's light of brain and body.
>
> Eskimo shaman quoted in *Ecstatic Religions*

Shaman is a term that anthropologists use for a special kind of medicine man or woman, witch doctor, or healer who employs nonordinary states of consciousness to heal himself or herself or others, foresee the future, open channels of extrasensory perception, and communicate with animals, elements of nature, and beings in the worlds beyond.

At the very core of shamanism is the notion that during unusual states of consciousness one can make beneficial visionary journeys to other realms and dimensions of reality. The early shamans were the first explorers and cartographers of such inner landscapes.

Shamanism is a universal phenomenon. It is also extremely ancient; its beginnings can be traced back to the Cro-Magnon man of the Paleolithic era. Many rock paintings and carvings on the walls of the great caves of Altamira, Font de Gaume, Les Trois Frères, and others depict shamanic motifs.

Archeological, historical, and anthropological research indicates that the basic features of shamanism and its technologies of the sacred have remained relatively unchanged through tens of thousands of years. They have survived migrations over half of the globe, while many other aspects of the cultures involved underwent dramatic changes. These facts suggest that shamanism engages levels of the human psyche that are primordial, timeless, and universal.

Throughout the ages, enormous amounts of knowledge have been amassed by shamans around the world, passed on to apprentices, and confirmed again and again by the profound personal experiences of these healers and those they helped. The very term *shaman* is very likely derived from the Tunguso-Manchurian verb *sa*—meaning "to know." A literal translation of the Tungus word *saman* is, then, "the person who knows." As guardians of the ancient knowledge of nonordinary states of consciousness, shamans represent extremely valuable sources of information about the processes involved in crises of transformation.

Several important aspects of shamanism are of great relevance to the concept of spiritual emergency. Many shamans are launched into their careers as healers by a dramatic episode of emotional and psychosomatic turmoil that often reaches proportions that Western psychiatry would consider psychotic. Yet a future shaman emerges from this crisis in an improved state of health and as a fully functioning individual.

Second, an accomplished practicing shaman has the capacity and the means to enter nonordinary states of consciousness at will, states that would again be considered psychotic. However, he or she can function during these experiences, utilize them for a variety of purposes, and return from them without any negative aftereffects. And third, among the capacities of a shaman is the ability to induce nonordinary states in others and guide them in a way that results in healing or is beneficial in some other way.

THE SHAMANIC CRISIS

Let us now take a closer look at the aspect of shamanism that is the most significant for the concept of spiritual emergency—the stormy beginning of the career of many shamans all over the world. This is a profound emotional and psychosomatic crisis that many Western anthropologists and psychiatrists refer to as *shamanic illness*. This term reflects the bias of our culture against nonordinary states of consciousness, as well as the strong disease orientation of contemporary psychiatry.

In some instances, the "shamanic disease" can be triggered by a physiological crisis; there are stories about Siberian or Eskimo shamans whose initiation occurred when they were afflicted with smallpox or some other infectious disease or were recovering from a severe injury. At other times, no obvious precipitating factors are present and the entire episode seems to be of a purely psychological and spiritual nature.

Within hours or days, the future shaman develops a deep alteration of consciousness during which he or she loses contact with the everyday reality and may appear to external observers to be dying or going crazy. These changes can take many different forms. Sometimes, these people appear to be agitated, move around at a hectic pace, and make strange grimaces and gestures. At other times they may behave in an opposite fashion, withdrawing and spending hours in a reclining position, completely self-absorbed, or even in a condition approaching loss of consciousness and stupor. The speech of the novice shaman can become incoherent and incomprehensible. He or she might appear to be possessed by evil spirits or may seem to communicate with deceased people, whom he or she may believe to be former shamans who want to instruct and guide the shaman-to-be during this initiation.

The spectrum of visionary experiences during a shamanic crisis is very rich. In the course of this inner journey, the novice shaman experiences visits to other realms of reality, many of which are fantastic and mythological in nature. He or she has to brave icy winds, burning forests, stormy rivers, and bloody streams. During these visits, the involuntary traveler experiences encounters with ancestors, spirit guides, deities, demons, and other beings. Among these, "power animals" play a particularly significant role; they are spirits or nonordinary aspects of various animal species who can become guides and helpers of the shaman. During these adventures, the initiate learns the rules and taboos of the inner life and the laws of the higher natural order. Guardian spirits in animal and human form appear at different times to offer guidance through funerary landscapes—dangerous and terrifying regions of the underworld.

The experiences of the shamanic crisis vary in detail from culture to culture but seem to have a basic core with three characteristic phases. The visionary adventure begins with a gruesome journey into the underworld, the realm of the dead. This is followed by an ecstatic experience of an ascent into the celestial regions and the acquisition of supernormal knowledge. The final stage is a return and the integration of the extraordinary adventure into everyday life.

During the visionary journey into the underworld, the future shamans experience attacks by vicious demons and evil spirits who expose them to incredible tortures and cruel ordeals. The malevolent entities scrape the flesh from the bones of their victims, tear out their eyeballs, suck out their blood, or boil them in heated cauldrons. The tortures culminate in the experience of dismemberment and total annihilation. In some cultures this final destruction is mediated by an initiatory animal who tears the novice apart or devours him. Depending on the ethnic group, this can be a bear, wolf, jaguar, giant snake, or any of a variety of others.

This experience is followed by a sequence of rebirth or resurrection. The novice shaman has a sense of receiving new flesh, new blood, and new eyes, being charged with supernatural energy and connected with the elements of nature. Feeling reborn and rejuvenated, he or she experiences an ascent to the Upper Worlds. The symbolism of this phase again varies from culture to culture and from one historical period to another. One can have an experience of being abducted by an eagle or another bird traditionally associated with the sun, or of being actually transformed into such a creature. The ascent can also take the form of climbing the World Tree—an archetypal structure that connects the lower, middle, and upper worlds of the visionary realm. In some cultures, a mountain, rainbow, or ladder plays a similar role. This phase often culminates with a sense of reaching the realm of the sun and fusing and uniting with its energy.

The essential aspects of the shamanic crisis can be illustrated by the following classical description of an extreme form of initiation of an Avam-Samoyed Siberian shaman, as recorded by the Russian anthropologist A. A. Popov:

> Stricken with smallpox, the future shaman remained unconscious for three days, so nearly dead that on the third day he was almost buried. He saw himself go down to Hell and, after many adventures, was carried to an island, in the middle of which stood a young birch tree which reached up to heaven. It was the Tree of the Lord of the Earth, and the Lord gave him a branch of it to make himself a drum.
>
> Next he came to a mountain. Passing through an opening, he met a naked man plying the bellows at an immense fire on which there was a kettle. The man caught him with a hook, cut off his head, chopped his body to bits and put them all into the kettle. There he boiled the body for three years, and then forged him a head on the anvil. Finally, he fished out the bones, which were floating in a river, put them together, and covered them with flesh.
>
> During his adventures in the Other World, the future shaman met several semidivine personages, in human or animal form, and each of them revealed doctrines to him or taught him secrets of the healing art. When he awoke in his yurt among his relatives, he was initiated and could begin to shamanize.

Whatever specific symbolic form the shamanic journey takes, the common denominator is always the destruction of the old sense of identity and an experience of ecstatic connection with nature, with the cosmic order, and with the creative energy of the universe. In this process of death and rebirth, shamans experience their own divinity and attain profound insights into the nature of reality. They typically gain an understanding of the origin of many disorders and learn how to diagnose and heal them.

If this process is successfully completed and the extraordinary experiences are well integrated into everyday consciousness, the result is dramatic emotional and psychosomatic healing and a profound personality transformation. The individual can emerge from this crisis in an incomparably better condition than when he or she entered it. This includes not only an increased sense of well-being, but also a highly improved social adaptation that makes it possible to function as a venerated leader of the community.

DIFFERING VIEWS OF THE SHAMANIC CRISIS

With few exceptions, Western experts agree that the shamanic crisis represents a severe form of pathology, although opinions differ as to the appropriate clinical label. The most frequent diagnoses given to such states are schizophrenia or some other form of psychosis, hysteria, and epilepsy. Yet anthropologists and psychiatrists who have intimate knowledge of shamanism, including firsthand experiences of the shamanic state of consciousness, refuse to see the shamanic crisis as a mental disease. They assert that this clinical approach reflects Western culture's preference for consensus reality, lack of a genuine understanding of altered states of consciousness, and strong tendency to pathologize all such states without discrimination. Michael Harner, who is both an anthropologist and an initiated shaman, calls this attitude ethnocentric, because it expresses a strong cultural bias. He also refers to it as "cognicentric," meaning that it uses as its exclusive source of knowledge information originating in the ordinary state of consciousness.

In view of the often dramatic positive results of the shamanic crisis, it is certainly more appropriate to consider this condition to be—at least potentially—an amazing process of healing and profound restructuring of personality that facilitates resolution of a variety of life problems. Its therapeutic potential compares very favorably with the best treatment procedures available to Western psychiatry. As we mentioned earlier, we have observed sequences indistinguishable from the shamanic crisis in a variety of settings: in psychedelic sessions, in our experiential work with breathing and music, and during the course of spiritual emergencies of modern Westerners.

Traditional scientists often attribute the appreciation that non-Western societies show for shamans to the fact that these societies are unable to discriminate the abnormal from the supernormal because of their lack of education and scientific knowledge. This explanation is in sharp conflict with the experiences of those who have had intimate contact with shamans and shamanic cultures. Such people have a clear understanding that bizarre experiences and behaviors are not enough to qualify one as a shaman. While some individuals are seen as great shamans, others are considered sick or crazy. In order for someone to be considered a shaman, following the initiatory crisis he or she has to show at least adequate functioning in everyday reality. In many instances, the social adjustment of shamans is clearly superior to other members of the group.

Shamans are typically active participants in social, economic, and even political affairs of the tribe. They are hunters, farmers, gardeners, craftsmen, artists, and often responsible family members. The tribe sees them as important guardians of the psychological, spiritual, and ecological equilibrium and as intermediaries between the seen and the unseen worlds. The master shaman has to be at home in nonordinary as well as ordinary reality and operate successfully in both; this is seen as evidence of genuine shamanic power.

All these facts are difficult to reconcile with the idea that shamans are ambulant psychotics or otherwise severely disturbed individuals, although their entry into the shamanic career might have been marked by extreme emotional and psychosomatic turmoil. The observations from the world of shamanism thus bring into sharp relief the need to discriminate between pathological states that have to be medically treated and transformative states that have a positive potential and should be supported.

Rites of Passage

Another important source of information about culturally sanctioned crises of transformation is the ritual events anthropologists call rites of passage. Here the cultural understanding and appreciation of the positive value of nonordinary states of consciousness goes one step further: while in the case of shamanic crises, social groups accept and value spontaneously occurring episodes of altered states of consciousness, with rites of passage they actually use various techniques that have been specifically developed to induce such episodes.

Ceremonies of this kind existed in many cultures of antiquity and are being performed to this day in preindustrial societies. Their main purpose is to redefine, transform, and consecrate individuals, groups, and even entire cultures. Rites of passage are conducted at times of critical change in the life of an individual or a culture. Their timing frequently coincides with major physiological and social transitions, such as childbirth, circumcision, puberty, marriage, menopause, and death.

Similar rituals are associated with initiation into warrior status, acceptance into a secret society, calendrical festivals of renewal, healing ceremonies, and geographical moves. In all these situations, the individual or social group leaves behind one mode of being and moves into totally new life circumstances. This transition is typically dramatic and is associated with unusual experiences that often are terrifying and psychologically disorganizing.

The term *rite of passage* was coined by Arnold van Gennep, the author of the first scientific treatise on the subject. Van Gennep recognized that in all the cultures he had studied, rituals of this kind followed a standard pattern with three distinct stages: separation, transition, and incorporation. In the first stage, separation, the individual is removed from his or her social fabric—family, clan, and the rest of the tribe. At this time, the neophyte can be completely alone or can share this unsettling situation with peers or age-mates.

Loss of the familiar network and absence of a new one to replace it leads him or her to a state of liminality, a condition of being betwixt and between. During this period of separation, one can feel intense grief over the loss of the old way of being. One can also become fearful and anxious—afraid of uprootedness, of the unexpected, and of the unknown. This situation bears a deep similarity to spiritual emergency, where familiar reality is forcefully replaced by the challenges of the inner world. However, in group initiations that occur in tribal rites of passage, this frightening period of separation has its positive side; as a result of it, the neophytes develop a deep sense of bonding and community with each other.

During this time, the initiators teach the novices the culture's cosmology and mythology and prepare them for the next stage of transition. This happens indirectly through mythical stories, songs, and dances, or directly by descriptions of the experiential territories they will traverse. Such a preparation is very important for the outcome of the transformative process. The neophytes learn that the journey, strange and ominous as it might seem, has a universal and timeless dimension. It has been and will be traveled by many others—sacred ancestors, as well as past and future initiates. The knowledge of this broader context has the potential to reassure the novices and help them face the difficult aspects of the transformation process.

In the next stage—transition—initiates move from intellectual learning to powerful direct experiences of nonordinary states of consciousness. The practices used by different cultures to induce such states cover a wide range: some are relatively gentle, such as suggestion, group pressure, monotonous chanting and dancing, fasting, and sleep deprivation; others are more drastic, involving agonizing pain and mutilation of the body, strangling and choking, or extreme physical exertion and exposure to vital danger. Also among the common mind-altering techniques are social or even sensory isolation and, conversely, sensory overload by strong acoustic and optical stimuli. Some of the most powerful tools of ritual transformation over the centuries have been various plants with psychedelic properties.

In the course of a typical rite of passage, the experiences and behaviors of the neophytes—and often those of the initiators as well—can be most unusual and extravagant. As in the case of the shamanic crisis, a Western observer with traditional psychiatric training would very likely label them as psychotic.

We take for our example a complex rite of passage—the Okipa festival of the Mandans, a tribe of Plains Indians who lived on the Missouri River. We have deliberately chosen a ritual that involves extreme physical pain and mutilation; it shows how highly some cultures value transformative experiences and how much they are willing to sacrifice in their pursuit. Naturally, many other rites of a similar kind are not nearly as radical.

Although its core was initiation of young men into adulthood and warrior status, it also included ceremonial dances for the purpose of securing successful buffalo hunts and appeasing evil spirits, and a celebration of the subsiding of the mythological flood.

At the beginning of the ritual, a ceremonial figure painted with white clay and wearing a splendid robe led the group of young male initiates covered with clay of different colors to the ceremonial site; he represented the First Man, the Original Ancestor. They entered a large round lodge and sat down around its sides. After smoking his sacred medicine pipe, the First Man gave the initiates an encouraging talk and appointed an old medicine man to be the Master of the Ceremonies.

Among the roles of the appointed Master of the Ceremonies was to make sure that none of the young men escaped from the lodge, ate, drank, or slept during the four days of preparation for the ordeal. Through prayers, he also maintained connection with the Great Spirit, asking for the success of the procedure. During this preparation time, participants enacted a number of rituals and provided various forms of entertainment outside the lodge around the Great Canoe, a reminder of the flood. They chanted many prayers to the Great Spirit, asking for continuous supplies of buffaloes and encouragement for the young initiates.

Much of their energy was focused on invocations of the Evil Spirit, O-Kee-hee-dee. (The effort to come to terms with the dark aspects of existence is characteristic of the rites of passage and healing ceremonies in many cultures.) On the fourth day, a masked figure representing O-kee-hee-dee finally appeared, almost naked and painted mostly black, with occasional white. He stormed the village adorned with a colossal wooden penis that had a black shaft and a large vermillion head; he ran around in a frenzy, chasing women and wreaking havoc.

The general panic and chaos kept building until it reached a sudden turning point. The Master of the Ceremonies confronted the Evil Spirit and immobilized him by the charm of his sacred pipe. O-kee-hee-dee, bereft of his magic power, was tantalized, ridiculed, and humiliated, particularly by the women, and chased out of the village. The women's triumphant return with his gigantic penis as a trophy was the signal for the beginning of the ordeal in the lodge.

There the young initiates were raised above the ground on cords attached to skewers piercing their flesh. Weights consisting of heavy objects, such as shields, bows, quivers, and buffalo skulls, were suspended from the skewers, and the initiates were rotated with a pole until they lost consciousness. They were then lowered to the ground, and when they regained consciousness, their little fingers were chopped off by a hatchet and offered to the Great Spirit. With the weights still attached to their bodies, they were taken outside to the ceremonial area.

The final stage of the Okipa ceremony was the Last Race. The young men had to run in large circles, dragging the weights behind them, each striving to endure longer than his peers, without collapsing—or "dying," as it was called. Even after they fainted, totally exhausted by physical exertion and excruciating pain, they were dragged around until all of the weights were torn out. Their mangled bodies lay on the ground until the initiates regained consciousness and staggered through the crowds to their lodges. There they were welcomed by their relatives, who congratulated them on their great achievement. The immature youngsters who they had been were considered to have died in this ordeal and been reborn as adults and brave warriors.

Whatever most Westerners might think of such extreme experiences and behaviors, the typical result of ceremonies of this kind is often a considerable increase in emotional and physical well-being, an enhanced sense of personal strength and independence, feelings of deep connection with nature and the cosmos, and a sense of social belonging and cohesion. The inner experiences and external events of the rite of passage communicate a profound message to the neophytes, the core insight of all human transformative processes, including spiritual emergencies: one can suffer through the chaos of liminality and dying, undergo an experience of total annihilation, and yet emerge feeling healed, reborn, rejuvenated, and stronger than before. This awareness reduces greatly the fear of death and enhances one's ability to enjoy life.

Although in the Okipa rite of passage a significant part of the transformative ordeal was enacted in a realistic and concrete way, this is not the only alternative. Various mind-altering techniques of a much gentler kind can trigger similar sequences of suffering, death, and rebirth, by activating the psyche's own inner repositories. A purely symbolic experience of this kind will have an identical impact on the person involved. In spiritual emergencies, episodes of this kind often occur spontaneously.

The third stage in van Gennep's triad is that of incorporation. It involves the reintegration of the individual into his or her community in a new social role defined by the type of ceremony: an adult, a parent, a warrior, etc. However, the person who returns is not the same as the one who entered the initiation process. As a result of a deep psychological transformation, he or she has a new and much expanded worldview, a better self-image, and a different system of values. All this is the result of a deliberately induced crisis that reaches the very core of the initiate's being and is at times frightening, chaotic, and disorganizing. The rites of passage are thus another example of a situation in which a period of temporary disintegration and turmoil leads to greater sanity.

The two examples of "positive disintegration" we have discussed so far—the shamanic crisis and the experience of the rite of passage—have many features in common, but they also differ in some important ways. The shamanic crisis invades the psyche of the future shaman unexpectedly and without warning; it is spontaneous and autonomous in nature. In comparison, rites of passage are a product of the culture and follow a predictable time schedule; the experiences of the initiates are the result of specific mind-altering technologies developed and perfected by previous generations. In cultures that venerate shamans and also conduct rites of passage, the shamanic crisis is considered to be a form of initiation much superior to the rite of passage. It occurs in individuals as a result of a higher power and is thus seen as an indication of divine choice and special calling.

Mythology, the Hero's Journey, and Ritual Madness

> Nothing is higher than these mysteries. They have sweetened our character and softened our customs; they have made us pass from the condition of savages to true humanity. They have not only shown us the way to live joyfully, but they have taught us to die with hope.
>
> Cicero, *De Legibus*

The ancient mysteries of death and rebirth provided another important social context for transformative experiences. In them, initiates identified with various mythological figures who had died and had been brought back to life.

THE FUNCTION OF MYTHOLOGY IN
THE PSYCHE AND SOCIETY

It is usually assumed that myths are products of human intellect and imagination. Our own concepts are radically different; besides our personal experiences in this area, we have been strongly influenced by the work of Carl Gustav Jung and, more specifically, by many years of close friendship with the mythologist Joseph Campbell. The work of these two seminal thinkers brought a conceptual revolution into the understanding of mythology. According to Jung and Campbell, myths are not fictitious stories about adventures of imaginary characters in nonexistent countries and thus arbitrary products of individual human fantasy. They originate in the collective unconscious of humanity and are manifestations of the primordial organizing principles of the psyche and the cosmos that Jung called archetypes.

Archetypes express themselves through the individual psyche and its deeper processes, but they do not originate in the human mind and are not its products. They are in a sense supraordinated to it and function as its governing principles. According to Jung, certain powerful archetypes can even influence historical events and the behavior of a particular culture. The "collective unconscious," Jung's name for the place where they reside, represents a shared cultural heritage of all humanity throughout ages.

In mythology, the basic archetypal themes in their most general and abstract form show universal distribution. In different cultures and at various periods in history, one can find specific variations of these basic mythological motifs. A powerful universal archetype is, for example, the Great Mother Goddess; in various cultures, this figure takes the forms of a specific local mother goddess, such as Isis, the Virgin Mary, Kybele, or Kali. Similarly, the concept of heaven, paradise, and hell can be found in many cultures of the world, but the specific form of these archetypal domains varies from one instance to another.

THE HERO WITH A THOUSAND FACES

In 1948, after many years of systematic study of the mythologies of various cultures of the world, Joseph Campbell published his ground-breaking book *The Hero with a Thousand Faces*, a masterpiece that in the following decades had a profound influence on a large number of thinkers from different fields. Analyzing a broad spectrum of myths from various parts of the world, Campbell realized that they all seemed to contain variations of one universal archetypal formula, which he called the monomyth. This was the story of the hero, either male or female, who leaves his or her home ground and, after fantastic adventures, returns as a deified being. Campbell found that the archetype of the hero's journey typically has three stages, which are similar to those we described earlier as characteristic sequences in traditional rites of passage: separation, initiation, and return. The hero leaves the familiar ground or is forcefully separated from it by an external force, is transformed through a series of extraordinary ordeals and adventures, and finally is again incorporated into his or her original society in a new role.

In Campbell's own words, the basic formula for the hero's journey can be summarized as follows:

> A hero ventures forth from the world of common day into a region of supernatural wonder: fabulous forces are encountered and a decisive victory is won: the hero comes back from this mysterious adventure with the power to bestow boons on his fellow man.

Campbell's inquisitive and incisive intellect was not satisfied with the recognition of the universality of this myth over time and space. His curiosity drove him to ask what it is that makes this myth universal. Why does the theme of the hero's journey appeal to cultures of all times and countries, even if they differ in every other respect? And his answer has the simplicity and unrelenting logic of all brilliant insights: the monomyth of the hero's journey is a metaphor for the inner experiences during a transformative crisis, describing its experiential territories. As the transformative crisis is universally relevant, so is the myth.

SPIRITUAL EMERGENCY AS A HERO'S JOURNEY

Campbell himself was aware of the fact that the adventures of shamans during the initiatory crisis and those of neophytes during rites of passage were special examples of the heroic journey. In 1968 he met the Jungian analyst John Perry, who over the years had done extensive psychotherapeutic work with young clients who would traditionally be labeled as psychotic. In the course of his work, Perry had not used any suppressive medication. As a result of his contact with Perry and his material, Campbell recognized the deep similarities between the symbolism of the hero's journey and the imagery occurring in many spontaneously occurring nonordinary states of mind and extended his application of the monomyth to include certain forms of psychoses.

A typical myth of the heroic journey begins when the ordinary life of the protagonist is suddenly interrupted by the intrusion of elements that are magical in nature and belong to another order of reality. Campbell refers to this invitation to adventure as a call. In psychological terms, we can think of it as the emergence of elements from the deep unconscious, particularly from its archetypal levels, into everyday consciousness. If the hero responds to the invitation and accepts the challenge, he or she embarks on an adventure that involves visits to strange territories, encounters with fantastic animals and superhuman beings, and numerous ordeals. After the successful completion of the journey, the hero returns home and lives a full and rewarding life as a deified being—worldly leader, healer, seer, or spiritual teacher.

Like the hero of the monomyth, the person in a spiritual emergency receives a call. The subtle film that separates our everyday lives from the amazing world of our unconscious mind becomes transparent and finally breaks down. The deep contents of the psyche that we are ordinarily unaware of erupt into consciousness in the form of images, powerful emotions, and strange physical feelings. A dramatic visionary odyssey into the depths of the psyche has begun. Like the heroic stories that we know from mythology, it involves dark forces and terrifying monsters, dangers of all kinds, and encounters with supernatural beings as well as magical interventions.

When the challenges of this inner journey have been accepted and the vicissitudes successfully overcome, the experiences become increasingly rewarding and reach a positive resolution. This often includes a recognition of one's own divine nature and insights into the universal order. Experiences of an encounter with the archetypes of the Great Mother Goddess and of the Divine Father can help one attain a better balance between the masculine and feminine (yang and yin) aspects of the individual's personality. One can see clearly the misconceptions and erroneous strategies of the past and get a sense of how a more fulfilling and productive life might be possible in the future.

If the experience is allowed to reach a natural completion and adequate support and validation are available, such a person can return to ordinary life radically transformed. Many emotional and psychosomatic difficulties have been consumed and eliminated in the transformative process, self-image and self-acceptance are noticeably improved, and the ability to enjoy life is increased. There can be a significant enhancement of intuition and of the capacity to work with other people as a counselor or a guide in times of emotional crisis. All of this can lead to a strong need to include the element of service to others as an important component of one's own life. Although the results might not be as glorious as the outcome of the mythological hero's journey, they are of a similar kind, and the metaphor is quite appropriate.

However, there are many instances where something that began as a visionary adventure does not reach a successful completion. In some instances, one can refuse the call and manage to hold on to ordinary reality, with all its old problems and limitations. Another possibility is a failure to complete the journey; in that case, one delves deep into the abyss of the unconscious and is unable to return to full functioning in ordinary reality. This, unfortunately, is the fate of many people in our culture who have to face a spiritual emergency without proper understanding and support.

DEATH AND REBIRTH OF GODS AND HEROES

One theme that is particularly powerful and recurs with remarkable frequency in the mythology of the hero's journey is the encounter with death and subsequent rebirth. Mythologies of all times and countries include dramatic stories about heroes and heroines who have descended into the realm of the dead and, having overcome undreamed-of obstacles, have returned to earth endowed with special powers. The legendary shamans of various cultures, the twins from the Mayan epic Popol Vuh, and the Greek heroes Odysseus and Hercules are salient examples of such mythic personages.

Equally frequent are tales about gods, demigods, and heroes who have died or been killed and subsequently return to life in a new role, exalted and immortalized through the experience of death and rebirth. The central theme of the Judeo-Christian religion, the crucifixion and resurrection of Jesus, is just one example. In a less obvious symbolic form, the same motif is sometimes represented as the experience of being devoured by a terrifying monster and then regurgitated or making a miraculous escape. The examples here range from the Greek hero Jason and the biblical Jonah to Saint Margaret, who was allegedly swallowed by a dragon and saved by a miracle.

Considering how universal and important these themes are in world mythology, it is interesting to realize that sequences of psychological death and rebirth are also among the most frequent experiences observed in nonordinary states of consciousness induced by various means and occurring spontaneously. They play an extremely important role in the process of psychological transformation and spiritual opening. Many ancient cultures were well aware of this fact and developed initiation procedures that were closely linked to the myths of death and rebirth.

THE MYSTERIES OF DEATH AND REBIRTH

In many parts of the world, myths of death and rebirth served as the ideological basis for sacred mysteries—powerful ritual events in which neophytes experienced psychological death and rebirth. The means for inducing these altered states of consciousness were similar to those used in shamanic procedures and rites of passage: drumming, chanting, and dancing; alteration of the breathing rhythm; exposure to physical stress and pain; and seeming or actual life-threatening situations. Among the most powerful tools employed for this purpose were various plants with psychoactive properties. In some instances, the mind-altering process of these rituals is not known; either it was kept secret or the information was lost over time.

The powerful and often terrifying and confusing experiences induced in the initiates were seen as opportunities to make contact with deities and with the divine realms; they were seen as necessary, desirable, and ultimately healing. There are even indications that voluntary exposure to these extreme states of mind was considered a prevention of and protection against true insanity.

This can be illustrated by the Greek myth of Dionysus, who invited the citizens of Thebes to join him in the Lesser Dance, the rapture of the Bacchanalia—an orgiastic ritual that involved wild dancing and the unleashing of various emotions and instinctual drives. He promised them that this event would take them to places they never dreamed were possible. When they refused, he forced them into the Greater Dance of Dionysus, a spell of dangerous madness in which they mistook their prince for a wild animal and killed him. As this popular myth indicates, the ancient Greeks were aware of the fact that the dangerous forces that we harbor in our psyche need to be given an opportunity for expression in the proper context.

The powerful psychological events that the initates encountered in the death-rebirth mysteries undoubtedly had a remarkable healing and transformative potential. Here, we can refer to the testimony of two giants of ancient Greek philosophy, Plato and Aristotle. (The fact that this testimony comes from Greece, the cradle of Western civilization, is of special relevance here, since it is all too easy for Westerners to ignore the evidence from shamanism or rites of passage, coming as it does from cultures alien to our own tradition.)

In his dialogue entitled "Phaedrus," Plato distinguished two kinds of madness, one resulting from human ailments, the other from divine intervention or—as we could rephrase it in terms of modern psychology—archetypal influences originating in the collective unconscious. In the latter variety, he further differentiated four types, ascribing them to specific gods: the madness of the lover to Aphrodite and Eros, that of prophetic rapture to Apollo, that of artistic inspiration to the Muses, and that of ritual ecstasy to Dionysus. Plato gave a vivid description of the therapeutic potential of ritual madness, using as an example a less-known variety of the Greek mysteries, the Corybantic rites. According to him, wild dancing to flutes and drums, culminating in an explosive emotional release, resulted in a state of profound relaxation and tranquillity.

Plato's great disciple, Aristotle, was the author of the first explicit statement that the full experience and release of repressed emotions, which he called *catharsis* (meaning, literally, "purification" or "purgation"), represented an effective treatment of mental disorders. He also expressed his belief that the Greek mysteries provided a powerful context for this process. According to Aristotle, through the use of wine, aphrodisiacs, and music, initiates experienced extraordinary arousal of passions followed by a healing catharsis. In agreement with the basic thesis of the members of the Orphic cult, one of the most important mystical schools of the time, Aristotle was convinced that the chaos and frenzy of the mysteries were conducive to eventual order.

This understanding of the relationship between intensive emotional states and healing is very close to the concept of spiritual emergency and corresponding treatment strategies. Dramatic symptoms are not necessarily indicative of pathology; in certain contexts, they are better understood as manifestations of various disturbing contents and forces that preexisted in the unconscious. From this point of view, bringing them into consciousness and confronting them is considered desirable and healing. The popularity and wide distribution of the mysteries in the ancient world indicate that participants considered them psychologically relevant and beneficial. The famous mysteries in Eleusis near Athens were conducted every five years without interruption for a period of almost two thousand years.

We would like to mention briefly the most important mysteries of death and rebirth that were performed in the ancient times in various parts of the world. The archetypal themes that were enacted in these rituals regularly emerge in the experiences of modern Westerners undergoing deep experiential therapy or spiritual emergencies. For these people, and for those who are assisting them in their process, knowledge of the mythology encountered during the inner journey can provide important guidelines.

Among the oldest mysteries of death and rebirth were the Babylonian and Assyrian rites of Ishtar and Tammuz. They were based on the myth of the Mother Goddess Ishtar and her descent into the underworld, the realm of death ruled by the terrible goddess Ereshkigal, in search of an elixir that could restore to life her dead son and husband, Tammuz. According to the esoteric interpretation, the myth of Ishtar's journey into the underworld and successful return symbolized the imprisonment of consciousness in matter and its release through the liberating effect of secret spiritual teachings and procedures. By opting to go through an ordeal similar to Ishtar's, initiates could reach spiritual liberation.

In the temples of Isis and Osiris in ancient Egypt, initiates underwent complex ordeals under the guidance of high priests in order to overcome the fear of death and gain access to esoteric knowledge about the universe and human nature. During this procedure, neophytes experienced identification with the god Osiris, who according to the myth underlying these mysteries was killed and dismembered by his evil brother, Seth, and then brought back to life by his sisters, Isis and Nephtys.

In ancient Greece and its neighboring countries, mystery religions and sacred rites were abundant. The Eleusinian mysteries were based on an esoteric interpretation of the myth about the goddess Demeter and her daughter, Persephone. Persephone was kidnapped by Pluto, the god of the underworld, but was released at the intervention of Zeus with the condition that she return to Pluto's kingdom for one-third of each year. This myth, usually considered an allegory about the cyclical growth of plants during the seasons of the year, became for the Eleusinian initiates a symbol for the spiritual struggles of the soul, periodically imprisoned in matter and liberated.

Other examples of Greek mysteries include the Orphic cult, which revolved around the legend of the deified bard Orpheus, the incomparable musician and singer who visited the underworld to liberate his beloved Eurydice from the bondage of death. The Dionysian rites or Bacchanalia were based on the mythological story of the young Dionysus, who was dismembered by the Titans and then resurrected when Pallas Athene rescued his heart. In the Dionysian rites, the initiates experienced identification with the murdered and reborn god through drinking intoxicating beverages, orgiastic dancing, wild running through the countryside, and eating raw animal flesh.

Another famous myth about a dying god was the story of Adonis. His mother, Smyrna, had been turned by the gods into a myrrh tree. After a wild boar had facilitated his birth from the tree, he was assigned to spend one-third of each year with Persephone and the rest with Aphrodite. Mysteries inspired by this myth were annually celebrated in many parts of Egypt, Phoenicia, and Byblos. The closely related Phrygian mysteries were held in the name of Attis, a deity who emasculated himself and was resurrected by the Great Mother Goddess Cybele.

These examples are by no means an exhaustive account of ancient mysteries and mystery religions. Similar procedures centering around death and rebirth can be found in the Mithraic religion, in the Nordic tradition, among the Druids, and in the pre-Columbian Mayan culture; they are also present as elements of initiation into various secret orders and societies and in many other contexts.

SACRAL KINGSHIP AND THE ROYAL DRAMA OF DEATH AND REBIRTH

Before we leave the realm of myth and ritual, we would like to make a brief reference to one phase of cultural development that was made particularly relevant to the study of spiritual emergency by the work of John Perry. In the evolution of great cultures of the world, even those that to our best knowledge did not have any contact with each other, there is a period that can be referred to as the era of sacral kingship or, in Perry's terminology, the "archaic era of incarnated myth." During this time, which roughly coincided with the emergence of cities, the King was seen by the culture as being literally an incarnation of god. This type of society can be found in the history of Egypt, Mesopotamia, Israel, Rome, Greece, the Nordic lands, Iran, India, China, and Mesoamerica (the Toltecs and Aztecs).

Quite independently of each other, these cultures celebrated elaborate New Year's festivals, at which time a ritual drama was performed that revolved around the person of the king and had certain standard themes. After the place of the ritual was established as the center of the world, dramatic sequences portrayed the death of the king and his return to the beginnings of time and the creation. This was followed by his new birth, sacred marriage, and apotheosis as a messianic hero.

All this happened in the context of a cosmic conflict involving a dramatic clash of opposites—combat between the forces of light and darkness, and confrontation of good and evil. An important part of the royal drama was the reversal of sexual polarities, expressed by the participation of transvestites. The symbolic performance ended with a portrayal of a renewed world and revitalized society. These rituals were considered to be of critical importance for the continued existence and stability of the cosmos and nature, and the prosperity of society.

During systematic psychotherapeutic work with clients experiencing spontaneous episodes of nonordinary states of consciousness, Perry came to an astonishing conclusion: many of these states revolved around the same themes as the New Year's dramas described above. As we mentioned in chapter 4, he labeled this important form of transformational crisis the renewal process. The fact that the experiences that constitute it have such amazing historical parallels has far-reaching significance. It is a critical challenge to the view of these states as indications of mental disease. Their archetypal themes are clearly meaningfully related to the evolution of consciousness on a collective scale, and possibly on an individual scale as well, and it is highly unlikely that their rich and intricate content could be the product of a distortion of mental processes due to a pathological impairment of the brain.

Dramatic mythological sequences portraying death and rebirth and other themes are extremely frequent in experiential psychotherapy, as well as in episodes of spiritual emergency. In nonordinary states of consciousness, this mythological material emerges spontaneously from the depths of the psyche, without any programming and often to the surprise of everybody involved. Archetypal images and entire scenes from the mythology of various cultures often occur in the experiences of individuals who have no intellectual knowledge of the mythic figures and themes they are encountering. Dionysus, Osiris, and Wotan, as well as Jesus Christ, seem to reside in the psyche of modern Westerners and come alive in nonordinary states of consciousness.

Spiritual Legacies of the Great Religions

> *The demons attack,*
> *some throwing mountain tops the color of flames;*
> *some throwing uprooted trees and shafts of copper and iron;*
> *some throwing camels and elephants with frightening eyes,*
> *snakes and dreadful reptiles with venomous glances,*
> *and other demons with heads of oxen.*
>> Buddha's confrontation with Kama Mara, *The Lalitavistara Sutra*

The study of the history of the world's great religions and their sacred scriptures is highly relevant to the understanding of spiritual emergencies. Even a cursory look at this material reveals that all the religious movements that have shaped human history were inspired and repeatedly revitalized by visionary experiences of transpersonal realities.

The mystical traditions and monastic orders of many religions have left cartographies of the states of mind encountered during important junctures of spiritual practice, including the various pitfalls and vicissitudes. People in spiritual emergencies encounter many of the same difficulties, and their process often follows the same stages. For this reason, these charts represent important guides for individuals in crises of transformation and for those who assist them. In many instances, the experiences actually involve the archetypal forms specific to a particular religious system, such as Hinduism, Buddhism, or Christian mysticism. In the following pages, we will look at some of the cartographies that can be particularly useful to those who deal with spiritual emergency.

HINDUISM

The Vedas, the sacred scriptures of the oldest religion of India and the starting point of Hinduism, although not associated with any specific person, are known to be based on divine revelations of ancient seers. Together with the Upanishads, later texts that further developed and refined the Vedic philosophical and spiritual message, they have been an inexhaustible source of inspiration not only for India and the Far East but for spiritual seekers all over the world.

The different schools of yoga offer sophisticated practices by which individuals seek to achieve union with their divine essence, or Atman-Brahman. Indian mystical literature is a true gold mine of information based on many centuries of profound transpersonal experiences of countless accomplished spiritual masters. The very essence of Yogic teachings has been summarized in the Yoga Sutras of Patanjali, the legendary Indian philosopher and grammarian. A map for inner experiences that is of special interest for people in spiritual emergency is the Indian system based on the concept of seven centers of psychic energy, or chakras, and cosmic energy, referred to as Kundalini. We have already mentioned that one of the most common forms of psychospiritual crisis shows a close correspondence to the descriptions of Kundalini awakening. For people in this form of transformation crisis, teachings about the chakras can provide invaluable understanding and guidance.

According to Kundalini Yoga, the chakras are located on a line along the spine, between the sacral area and the top of the head. Although they have functional connections with important organs of the body, they are not material in nature, but belong to the energetic or "subtle" body. Each chakra is associated with a specific way of seeing the world and with characteristic attitudes and behaviors. Each of them is also related to specific mythological realities and archetypal beings. During spiritual awakening, Kundalini or Serpent Power, an aspect of cosmic energy that normally lies dormant at the base of the spine, becomes activated and flows upward, opening, cleansing, and lighting up the chakras. While this is happening, the person involved often has rich and dramatic experiences that take characteristic forms depending on which chakra the process is focusing on at the time.

BUDDHISM

Like many other great religious systems, Buddhism started with a dramatic "spiritual emergency" of its founder, Gautama Buddha Sakyamuni. According to the scriptures, his arduous search for enlightenment was replete with visionary adventures. During his meditation, he experienced the visitation of Kama Mara, the master of the world of illusion, who tried to detract him from the spiritual path. First, Kama Mara tempted the Buddha with his three voluptuous and seductive daughters, Discontent, Delight, and Thirst. When he did not succeed, he sent an army of demons who threatened to kill him with various ominous weapons, torrential rains, storms, flaming rocks, boiling mud, and hot ashes.

That same night, while sitting under the Bo tree, the Buddha experienced profound insights into his previous incarnations and acquired the "divine eye," the gift of inner vision. When he achieved enlightenment, "the ten thousand worlds quaked twelve times, as far as the ocean shores. Lotuses bloomed on every tree. And the system of ten thousand worlds was like a bouquet of flowers sent whirling through the air." This story might sound like a naive fairy tale; however, work with people experiencing nonordinary states of consciousness shows that under certain circumstances the human psyche of an ordinary person can generate powerful and convincing sequences of a similar kind.

In addition to the accounts of the visionary experiences of the Buddha, Buddhist literature contains numerous descriptions of the states of consciousness that occur during spiritual practice. Perhaps the broadest and most detailed of these is the encyclopedic text Abhidhamma, based on forty years of Gautama Buddha's discourses, as recorded by his disciples. The centuries-old tradition of Vajrayana, the Tibetan version of Buddhism, offers meticulous and sophisticated maps of the spiritual path, such as the Six Yogas of Naropa.

Zen is a school of Buddhism that refuses to follow doctrines and scriptures and claims to mediate direct transmission of the spirit or essence of Buddha's teachings. It is well known that in Zen practice a variety of disturbing, as well as ecstatic and tempting, experiences can arise during meditation; these range from biographical material to mythological visions and past-life memories. However, Zen masters have shown little interest in cataloguing these phenomena and refer to them by the general term *makyo*. Disciples are encouraged to not pay them special attention, but simply to sit, observe them, and move experientially through them and beyond them.

However, Zen students are not left entirely without maps for their practice. Instead of specifically describing different types and levels of experiences, Zen maps refer to major transformations of consciousness and stages of inner development. The best known of these are the so-called ox-herding pictures, where the stages of the spiritual path are represented by a series of simple drawings depicting different situations involving a man and an ox. The ox-herding pictures represent ten stages or "seasons of enlightenment," from the moment when the seeker becomes aware of the possibility of enlightenment to the time when he returns as a sage to the world of everyday life, having renounced personal liberation in order to help others.

Another, similar map is the Zen Circle, a simple diagram where the changes in consciousness during spiritual practice are symbolized by movement along the circumference of a circle. The starting point, at zero degrees, symbolizes the state of mind in which one identifies with the world of names and forms and perceives it in terms of polarities, such as pleasant-unpleasant or good-bad. The 90-degree position on the circle represents the level of consciousness evolution where one perceives that everything comes from nothingness and disappears into nothingness; at this point, form and emptiness become interchangeable. The 180-degree position stands for the state of consciousness where the entire world of forms appears as illusory and nothing really exists. The 270-degree point represents a realm of magic and miracles; the mind seems to have transcended all limitations, and everything conceivable is possible.

The end of the journey is symbolized by the 360-degree point of the Zen circle, which is also zero degrees. This situation has a psychological correspondence to the fact that this state is in some ways the same as at the beginning of the spiritual journey, yet in another sense also distinctly different. One returns to the ordinary world but sees it without attachment and value judgments, just as it is. At this point, even the distinctions between the states represented by the different positions on the circle disappear and one realizes that the entire cartography was just a teaching device.

The same situation is expressed even more succinctly in a Zen saying: "When you embark on the journey, mountains cease to be mountains and rivers cease to be rivers. When you complete the journey, mountains are mountains again and rivers are rivers." This principle illustrates the basic thesis underlying the concept of spiritual emergency: on the path toward greater clarity and sanity, one often has to pass through stages that involve strange and disorganizing states of mind. When the crisis is successfully completed, one returns to everyday reality, which is much the same as before yet radically transformed in a subtle but profound way.

THE JUDEO-CHRISTIAN TRADITION

Direct visionary experiences have also played a very important role in Judeo-Christian religions. In the famous episode from Exodus, Yahweh appears to the bewildered Moses in a burning bush. He introduces himself as the God of Moses' fathers and reveals his intention to deliver the people of Israel from Egypt and settle them in the land of Canaan. There are literally hundreds of episodes in the Old Testament described as visions of God or hearing his voice. The line that began with Moses continues with Solomon, Samuel, Daniel, Elijah, Ezekiel, Jeremiah, Isaiah, John the Baptist, and others.

Powerful visionary states were also of critical importance in early Christian history. The New Testament describes many situations where Christ communicated with God, as well as numerous instances where his disciples and followers had experiences of heaven, discarnate beings, angels, and the Holy Ghost. During Christ's stay in the desert, the devil appeared and subjected him to painful temptations, offering worldly power and trying to instill in him doubts about his divine origin.

As he was traveling to Damascus, the Roman citizen and strict Pharisee Saul of Tarsus had a shattering encounter with blinding light, supernatural sound, and the presence of Christ. It transformed him from a sworn enemy of the Nazarene sect to a passionate follower of Jesus and the most important figure in the history of the Christian church.

A classical example of a spiritual emergency from the history of Christianity is the life of Saint Anthony, who during his solitude in the desert endured many visionary temptations and combats with the Devil. In these visions, the Devil appeared to him in the form of an innocent young boy, a devoted monk bringing him bread during his fasts, and sensuous women, as well as various terrifying monsters and wild beasts. At times, the Prince of Darkness had brutally beaten Anthony and left him for dead. Anthony emerged from these psychological struggles as a sane, sensible, and noted Christian father.

Visionary experiences, both ecstatic and agonizing, can be found in the lives of Saint Hildegard von Bingen, Teresa of Avila, Saint John of the Cross, and many other Christian saints. The literature of the desert fathers, such as Evagrius—who all underwent austere practices in extreme physical conditions—is a rich source of information on the vicissitudes of the spiritual journey.

Some Christian writers tried to describe in a systematic and comprehensive way the stages of the path and the difficulties that the seekers might encounter. Among the most famous Christian maps of this kind is the Ladder of Divine Ascent, written in the seventh century by Saint John Climacus, a hermit and the abbot of the Saint Catherine Monastery on Mount Sinai. It sums up the teachings of the desert fathers on spiritual development, defining thirty distincts steps, from renunciation of worldly life on the first rung to faith, hope, and charity on the topmost one.

The Pilgrim's Progress, the famous allegory written by the Puritan minister and writer John Bunyan, describes the evolution of the human soul as various arduous adventures on the way to the celestial city through many specific dangers and obstacles. The author drew on his own shattering spiritual emergency, which took the form of a profound psychological death and rebirth and completely transformed his life.

Probably the most famous of the Christian guidebooks for the spiritual journey is *The Interior Castle*, written in the sixteenth century by Saint Teresa of Avila. The castle is a symbol of the progress of the soul from the earliest imperfect state to the final achievement of mystical marriage. It is portrayed as a fabulously rich building consisting of seven mansions or apartments, the seventh and central one being the dwelling place of the Blessed Trinity, residing in the depth of the soul. The way of the mystic is described as turning away from external reality and entering into the inner world to find oneself in the embrace of God.

ISLAM

The prophetic mission of Mohammed began when he was meditating in a grotto on Mount Hira near Mecca. Here he had a vision of the Archangel Gabriel, who delivered a scroll revealing to him that Allah had chosen him as his prophet. Several years later, he underwent what is known as "the miraculous journey of Mohammed." Guided by Gabriel, he visited the seven heavens, the gardens of paradise, and the infernal regions of Gehenna. He had many additional experiences of communication with the divine realms through visionary states, by hearing the spoken word, and in dreams.

The various Sufi orders, the mystical branches of Islam, have amassed through the centuries a profound knowledge of consciousness and the human psyche, including the obstacles and vicissitudes of the spiritual path. This knowledge was made possible by the Sufi emphasis on personal encounter with the Divine and on the union with God, which they share with mystics of all countries and ages. The simple methods that the Sufis have developed to achieve this state involve whirling or rhythmic movements of the body, chanting, and breathing.

One of the most famous Sufi maps of consciousness is al-Harawi's treatise *The Stages of Pilgrims toward God*. It describes the spiritual path from its beginning to the union with the absolute in terms of ten stages or houses, including the virtues required for each of them and the specific difficulties that one might encounter. Another famous spiritual cartography comes from Simnani. According to him, the creation of the cosmos proceeds from the divine essence to the world of man and nature and happens in seven stages. On the return, one passes through the same stages in reverse order, ascending through seven subtle, nonphysical aspects of self. An especially beautiful parable of the quest is Attar's Conference of the Birds, where the spiritual journey is represented as the search of a group of birds for Simurgh, the legendary king of birds.

There are many additional examples in the history of various religions and in their sacred scriptures illustrating the critical role of visionary experiences in the spiritual life of humanity. However, this selection should be sufficient to demonstrate the fact that at the cradle of all great religious systems are the mystical revelations of their founders, prophets, saints, and important disciples. It also shows that the mystical branches of religions and their monastic orders have honored such experiences, developed powerful methods to induce them, and left for posterity intricate cartographies of the inner journey.

A deep awareness of the fact that such profound transpersonal states are possible, that they are available to all of us, and that they reveal authentic dimensions of existence is very likely the vital force behind all religious systems. The descriptions of the stages of the spiritual path and its vicissitudes that we have inherited from the past are as relevant today as they were centuries ago. They are invaluable sources of information for a better understanding of modern spiritual emergencies.

The common denominator in the areas we have explored here is a deep cross-cultural conviction that there exist nonordinary states of consciousness that are healing, transformative, and revelatory. Although challenging at times, they can be very beneficial if they occur in the right context and if those participating have sufficient knowledge of the processes and of the states involved. It is also important that those experiencing spontaneous episodes of this kind be protected and supported. And it seems worthwhile to develop methods that can induce such transformative experiences in socially sanctioned and supportive ritual frameworks.

From a practical point of view, the historical and anthropological data show clearly the need to give people in spiritual emergencies a nonpathological context for their experiences and general maps for the territories of the inner world they are traversing. These elements are usually painfully missing when Westerners confront transformational crises; most have to face the difficult realms of the psyche completely unprepared and with the complication of stigmatizing psychiatric labels.

More specifically, observations from other times and cultures indicate the necessity to create social support systems—therapeutic teams, treatment centers and retreats, informed circles of families and friends, communities, and special-interest groups sharing a philosophy based on a genuine understanding of nonordinary states of consciousness. Western culture is beginning to raise its level of sophistication in regard to these states; perhaps in the near future people in psychospiritual crises will find understanding, compassionate, and intelligent support.

CHAPTER 7

MODERN MAPS
OF CONSCIOUSNESS

> Like the giraffe and the duck-billed platypus, the
> creatures inhabiting these remoter regions of the
> mind are exceedingly improbable. Nevertheless they
> exist, they are facts of observation; and as such, they
> cannot be ignored by anyone who is honestly trying
> to understand the world in which he lives.
> ALDOUS HUXLEY, *Heaven and Hell*

We saw in the preceding chapter that cultures of all times have shown a profound interest in nonordinary states of consciousness. They developed effective ways of inducing them and described the different stages of the spiritual journey. For centuries or even millenia, this knowledge was passed from generation to generation, becoming increasingly refined and perfected in the process. At the beginning of the modern era, when Western science was still in its infancy, this wisdom of ages was rejected and replaced by models of the psyche based on a strictly materialistic philosophy of nature. When the new discipline of psychiatry applied its principles and criteria to human spiritual history, mystical states and great religious personages were relegated to the realm of psychopathology.

During the first half of this century, academic psychiatry was under the influence of three major orientations: the biological school of thought, behaviorism, and psychoanalysis. Each offered its own interpretation of the human psyche and culture, reducing the complexity of mental life to organic processes in the brain, simple physiological reflexes, and primitive instinctual impulses, respectively. None of these systems had any place for spirituality and its role in human life.

Dramatic developments in the 1950s and, particularly, the 1960s brought serious challenges to such a limited understanding of psychology. The critical element was the firsthand experience of many professionals and lay people with powerful technologies of the sacred from various cultures and their modern analogs. This led to the recognition that in the course of our determined pursuit of logic and sober rationality, we had overlooked the many powerful tools and invaluable empirical knowledge of our ancestors.

Key to this realization were several influences: the mass interest in various meditative practices from Eastern and Western mystical traditions, experimentation with shamanic techniques, psychedelic research, and the laboratory development of mind-altering methods, such as biofeedback and sensory isolation. Honest personal reports of a new generation of anthropologists about their experiences in shamanic cultures and scientific studies of near-death experiences provided additional challenges to traditional psychiatry and psychology. Many researchers who systemically explored these new areas of interest came to the conclusion that the perennial wisdom deserves to be reexamined and that Western scientific concepts and beliefs in this regard have to be revised and expanded.

Psychedelic Therapy and Holotropic Breathwork

As Stan mentioned in his prologue, his clinical research with psychedelics convinced him that the territories of the human psyche are not limited to the Freudian unconscious and memories from postnatal life. Psychedelic sessions repeatedly took people to experiential domains that were known from various perennial maps of consciousness but were not included in the models of traditional Western psychiatry. These early observations showed the necessity to develop an extended cartography of the unconscious that included not only the biographical level, but also two additional domains—the perinatal and transpersonal. Later it became obvious that this cartography was, in fact, a modern version of the perennial maps, enriched by the data from twentieth-century consciousness research.

Although the new map of the psyche was based on observations from psychedelic work, there were strong indications that it was relevant not just for psychedelic sessions, but for all nonordinary states of consciousness and for the human psyche in general. It was becoming increasingly evident that LSD and similar substances did not produce any psychological contents by their pharmacological effects. They were best understood as unspecific catalysts—agents that energize the psyche and facilitate the manifestation of previously unconscious contents. This was further confirmed by the fact that such experiences could also be found in various perennial maps of cultures that used not psychedelics but powerful non-pharmacological methods for changing consciousness.

However, it was difficult to completely exclude the possibility that the experiences were in fact produced by the psychedelic substances. Our last shadows of doubt were radically dispelled in the mid-1970s, when we developed a method of deep experiential self-exploration and therapy that we now call Holotropic Breathwork™ and started using it systematically in our workshops.

This method, combining simple means, such as faster breathing, music and sound technology, and a certain form of body work, can induce the entire spectrum of experiences that we used to see in psychedelic sessions. These experiences are generally gentler, and the person has more control over them, but their content is essentially the same, although no drugs are involved. The main catalyst here is not a powerful and mysterious psychoactive substance but the most natural and basic physiological process imaginable—breathing.

The experiences elicited by Holotropic Breathwork™ have a very powerful healing and transformative effect. Since essentially the same types of experiences occur during various forms of spontaneous psychospiritual crises, the observations from holotropic sessions have great theoretical and practical importance for the concept of spiritual emergency. They suggest that such crises are genuine expressions of the human psyche rather than artificial products of a pathological process and that they are spontaneous efforts of the organism to heal itself and simplify its functioning.

Many holotropic sessions bring to the surface difficult emotions or unpleasant physical feelings of various kinds. Their full emergence makes it possible to free oneself from their disturbing influence. The general rule in holotropic work is that one gets rid of a problem by confronting it head-on and working it through. This is a process of purging and clearing old traumas; it often opens the way to very pleasant or even ecstatic and transcendental experiences and feelings.

It is remarkable that such elementary means as faster breathing and music can elicit an entire spectrum of powerful experiences that are very similar to, if not identical with, those occurring during psychedelic sessions as well as spiritual emergencies. Because of the deep similarity that exists among these three conditions, a new cartography of the psyche is a useful guide for all of them. An intellectual knowledge of the inner territories and an understanding of the stages of the transformational process can be of great help to individuals experiencing nonordinary states of consciousness, whether planned and induced by known means or unsolicited and spontaneous.

A Map of the Inner Journey

The experiential spectrum of nonordinary states of consciousness is extremely rich; however, all the experiences seem to fall into three major categories. Some of them are biographical in nature, related to various postnatal traumatic events from one's life. A second group revolves primarily around two issues: dying and being born. They seem to be deeply connected with the trauma of biological birth. The third large category includes experiences that can be referred to as transpersonal, reaching far beyond the limits of ordinary human experience; they are closely related to the Jungian collective unconscious.

BIOGRAPHICAL EXPERIENCES: RELIVING POSTNATAL MEMORIES

When the unconscious psyche becomes activated, the first experiences that are readily available are recollections of events that happened in people's lives after birth. As long as the process remains on this level, various emotionally unfinished issues from the past emerge into consciousness and become the content of the experience. It is known from traditional psychotherapy that access to this level of the unconscious is important for therapeutic work. This domain has been thoroughly explored and mapped by biographically oriented therapists.

However, it is important to note here that unfinished biographical issues are not necessarily limited to psychological traumas. One can often relive memories of physical insults, such as diseases, operations, or near-drowning, during which one encounters extreme emotions and physical sensations. Memories of physical traumas are often the source of serious emotional and psychosomatic problems, such as depression, various phobias, asthma, migraine headaches, and severe muscular pains. These problems can be dramatically alleviated or even disappear when the individual brings the underlying memories into consciousness.

PERINATAL EXPERIENCES: THE PROCESS OF PSYCHOLOGICAL DEATH AND REBIRTH

Since under ordinary circumstances we do not remember the details of our birth, most professionals and lay people have difficulty in accepting that these could be psychologically significant. However, recent research has repeatedly confirmed and further developed the original ideas of Freud's disciple Otto Rank about the paramount role that the birth trauma and even prenatal influences play in human life. These findings have inspired an entire new field: prenatal and perinatal psychology.

As nonordinary states of consciousness deepen, the experiences typically move beyond postnatal biography to two critical aspects of human life—its beginning and end. On the perinatal level, birth and death are very intimately interwoven, which seems to reflect the fact that human birth is a difficult and potentially life-threatening event. Many of us got a taste of death as we were struggling in the birth canal to start our existence in this world. When someone is reliving the memory of birth, he or she often confronts extreme forms of fear of death, loss of control, and insanity; as a result, he or she may behave in most unusual ways, and the condition can have a psychoticlike character.

When the material from the perinatal level of the unconscious emerges into consciousness, the individuals involved become preoccupied with death. They can be overwhelmed by an intense fear of death, see death-related imagery, and become convinced that their lives are actually biologically threatened. These experiences alternate or even coincide with a dramatic struggle to be born or to free oneself from a very uncomfortable form of confinement. In this situation, one can relive the trauma of one's biological birth. However, this process can also feel like spiritual birth—a powerful mystical opening and reconnection with the Divine.

These experiences are often interspersed with mythological motifs from the collective unconscious, which C. G. Jung described as archetypes. Some of them can be figures of deities representing death and rebirth; others portray the underworld and hell, or, conversely, paradise and the celestial realms. The concrete symbolism associated with these archetypal themes can be drawn from any culture of the world and is in no way limited to one's previous intellectual knowledge of the areas involved. The perinatal level of the unconscious thus represents the interface between the individual and the collective unconscious.

Once the perinatal level becomes activated, a complex psychological process of death and rebirth is begun. It involves certain distinct experiential patterns characterized by specific emotions, physical feelings, and symbolic images. A closer examination reveals that these patterns are related to the stages of biological birth, from the state preceding the onset of delivery to the moment of emerging into the world.

It would be beyond the scope of this book to discuss in detail all the specifics of these connections. However, we will briefly outline them here, since they are important for the understanding of many aspects of spiritual emergencies. A more complete and detailed discussion can be found in Stanislav Grof's *The Adventure of Self-Discovery*.

The amniotic universe. Prenatal intrauterine life can be referred to as "the amniotic universe." The fetus does not seem to have an awareness of boundaries or the ability to differentiate between the inner and outer. This is reflected in the nature of the experiences associated with the reliving of the memory of the prenatal state. During episodes of undisturbed embryonal existence, people can have feelings of vast regions with no boundaries or limits. They can identify with galaxies, interstellar space, or the entire cosmos. Or one may experience being the entire ocean, floating in the sea, or identifying with various aquatic animals, such as fish, dolphins, or whales. This seems to reflect the fact that the fetus is essentially a water creature. One might also have visions of Mother Nature—safe, beautiful, and unconditionally nourishing like a good womb, such as luscious orchards, fields of ripe corn, agricultural terraces in the Andes, or unspoiled Polynesian islands. The images from the mythological domains of the collective unconscious that often appear in this context portray various celestial realms and paradises.

The persons reliving episodes of intrauterine disturbances, or "bad womb" experiences, have a sense of dark and ominous threat and often feel that they are being poisoned. They might see images that portray polluted waters and toxic dumps, probably reflecting the fact that many prenatal disturbances are caused by toxic changes in the body of the pregnant mother. Sequences of this kind can be associated with visions of frightening demonic entities. Those who relive more violent interferences with prenatal existence, such as an imminent miscarriage or attempted abortion, usually experience some form of universal threat or bloody apocalyptic visions of the end of the world. This again reflects the intimate interconnections between events in one's biological history and Jungian archetypes.

Cosmic engulfment. Individuals reliving the very onset of birth typically feel that they are being sucked into a gigantic whirlpool or swallowed by some mythic beast; they might also experience that the entire world is somehow being engulfed. They can actually see images of devouring archetypal monsters, such as leviathans, dragons, giant snakes, tarantulas, and octopuses, and their experience of an overwhelming vital threat can lead to intense anxiety and general mistrust bordering on paranoia. Others have a sense of descending into the depths of the underworld, the realm of death, or hell.

No exit. The first stage of biological birth is characterized by a situation where the uterine contractions periodically constrict the fetus and the cervix is not yet open. Each contraction causes compression of the uterine arteries, and the fetus is threatened by lack of oxygen. Reliving this stage is one of the worst experiences a human being can have. One feels caught in a monstrous claustrophobic nightmare, exposed to agonizing emotional and physical pain, and has a sense of utter helplessness and hopelessness. Feelings of loneliness, guilt, the absurdity of life, and existential despair reach metaphysical proportions. A person in this predicament often becomes convinced that this situation will never end and that there is absolutely no way out.

Reliving this stage of birth is typically accompanied by sequences that involve people, animals, and even mythological beings in a similar painful and hopeless predicament. One experiences identification with prisoners in dungeons and inmates of concentration camps or insane asylums, and senses the pain of game caught in traps. He or she may even feel the intolerable tortures of sinners in hell and the agony of Christ on the cross or of Sisyphus rolling his boulder up the mountain in the deepest pit of Hades.

It is only natural that someone facing this aspect of the psyche would feel a great reluctance to confront it. Going deeper into this experience seems like accepting eternal damnation. However, this state of darkness and abysmal despair is known from the spiritual literature as a stage of spiritual opening that can have an immensely purging and liberating effect.

The death-rebirth struggle. Many aspects of this rich and colorful experience can be understood from its association with the second clinical stage of the delivery, the propulsion through the birth canal after the cervix opens. Besides the elements that are easily comprehensible as natural derivatives of the birth situation, such as sequences of titanic struggles involving strong pressures and energies or scenes of bloody violence and torture, there are others that require special explanation.

There seems to be a mechanism in the human organism that transforms extreme suffering, particularly when it is associated with suffocation, into a strange form of sexual excitement. This explains why a large variety of sexual experiences and visions often occur in connection with the reliving of birth. One can feel a combination of sexual arousal and pain, aggression, or fear, experience various sadomasochistic sequences, rapes, and situations of sexual abuse, or see pornographic images. The fact that, in the final stages of birth, the fetus can encounter various forms of biological material—blood, mucus, urine, and even feces—seems to account for the fact that these elements also play a role in death-rebirth sequences.

These experiences are often accompanied by specific archetypal elements from the collective unconscious, particularly those related to heroic figures and deities representing death and rebirth. At this stage, many people have visions of Jesus, the Way of the Cross (Jesus carrying the cross), and the Crucifixion or even actually experience full identification with Christ's suffering. Others connect with such mythological themes and figures as the Egyptian divine couple Isis and Osiris, the Greek god Dionysus, or the Sumerian goddess Inanna and her descent into the underworld.

The frequent appearance of motifs related to various satanic rituals and the witches' Sabbath seems to be related to the fact that reliving this stage of birth involves the same strange combination of emotions, sensations, and elements that characterizes the archetypal scenes of the Black Mass and of Walpurgis Night: sexual arousal, aggression, pain, sacrifice, and encounters with ordinarily repulsive biological material— all associated with a peculiar sense of sacredness or numinosity.

Just before the experience of (re)birth, people often encounter the motif of fire. This is a somewhat puzzling symbol. Its connection with biological birth is not as direct and obvious as are many of the other symbolic elements. One can experience fire either in its ordinary form or in the archetypal variety of purifying flames. At this stage of the process, the person can have the feeling that his or her body is on fire, have visions of burning cities and forests, or identify with immolation victims. In the archetypal version, the burning seems to have a purgatorial quality; it seems to destroy whatever is corrupted and prepare the individual for spiritual rebirth.

The death-rebirth experience. One often experiences death and rebirth when the memory that is surfacing into consciousness involves the moment of one's biological birth. Here one completes the preceding difficult process of propulsion through the birth canal and achieves explosive liberation as he or she emerges into light. Such a person often relives various specific aspects of this stage of birth as concrete and realistic memories. These can include the experience of anesthesia, the pressures of the forceps, and the sensations associated with various obstetric maneuvers or postnatal interventions.

To understand why the reliving of biological birth is experienced as death and rebirth, one has to realize that what happens is more than just a replay of the original event. Because the fetus is completely confined during the birth process and has no way of expressing the extreme emotions and sensations involved, the memory of this event remains psychologically undigested and unassimilated. Much of our later self-definition and our attitudes toward the world are heavily contaminated by this constant reminder of the vulnerability, inadequacy, and weakness that we experienced at birth. In a sense, we were born anatomically but have not caught up with this fact emotionally.

The "dying" and the agony during the struggle for rebirth reflect the actual pain and vital threat of the biological birth process. However, the ego death that precedes rebirth is the death of our old concepts of who we are and what the world is like, which were forged by the traumatic imprint of birth. As we are purging these old programs by letting them emerge into consciousness, they are becoming irrelevant and are, in a sense, dying. As frightening as this process is, it is actually very healing and transforming.

Approaching the moment of the ego death might feel like the end of the world. Paradoxically, while only a small step separates us from an experience of radical liberation, we have a sense of all-pervading anxiety and impending catastrophy of enormous proportions. It feels as if we are losing all that we are; at the same time, we have no idea of what is on the other side, or even if there is anything there at all. This fear drives many people to resist the process at this stage; as a result, they can remain psychologically stuck in this problematic territory.

When the individual overcomes the metaphysical fear encountered at this important juncture and decides to let things happen, he or she experiences total annihilation on all levels—physical destruction, emotional disaster, intellectual and philosophical defeat, ultimate moral failure, and even spiritual damnation. During this experience, all reference points—everything that is important and meaningful in the individual's life—seem to be mercilessly destroyed.

Immediately following the experience of total annihilation—hitting the cosmic bottom—one is often overwhelmed by visions of light that has a supernatural radiance and beauty and is usually perceived as divine. The survivor of what seemed like the ultimate apocalypse experiences only seconds later fantastic displays of rainbows, peacock designs, and celestial scenes. He or she feels redeemed and blessed by salvation, reclaiming his or her divine nature and cosmic status. At this time, one is frequently overcome by a surge of positive emotions toward oneself, other people, nature, and existence in general. This kind of healing and life-changing experience occurs when birth was not too debilitating or confounded by heavy anesthesia. If the latter was the case, the individual has to do psychological work on the traumatic issues involved.

TRANSPERSONAL EXPERIENCES

Beyond the biographical and perinatal domains in the psyche lies the transpersonal realm. This is a modern term for a broad variety of states that are in other contexts referred to as spiritual, mystical, religious, magical, parapsychological, or paranormal. In the past, this entire area has been subject to many misinterpretations and wild distortions. A knowledge of the nature and basic characteristics of transpersonal phenomena, free from popular misconceptions, is extremely important for the understanding and treatment of spiritual emergencies.

The remarkable nature of transpersonal phenomena becomes obvious when we compare them with our everyday perception of the world and the limitations we consider mandatory and inevitable. In the ordinary, or "normal," state of consciousness, we perceive ourselves as solid material bodies and our skin as the boundary and interface with the external world. In the words of the famous writer and philosopher Alan Watts, an interpreter and popularizer of Eastern spiritual teachings in the West, this leads us to believe that we are "skin-encapsulated egos."

We are usually limited in our perception of the world by the range of our senses and the configuration of the environment. We cannot see ships beyond the horizon or objects from which we are separated by a solid wall. It is impossible for us to observe and hear the interaction of people in distant locations. We cannot taste food that is not in our mouths, smell a flower if the wind is blowing away from us, or feel the texture of objects without touching them. With our ordinary senses, we can experience only what is happening here and now—in our momentary geographical location and at the present moment.

In transpersonal states of mind, all these limitations appear to be transcended. We can experience ourselves as a play of energy or a field of consciousness that is not confined to a physical container. This can further develop into identification with the consciousness of other people, groups of individuals, or even all of humanity. The process can extend beyond human boundaries and include various animals, plants, and even inorganic materials and events. It seems that everything that can be experienced in everyday life as an object has in nonordinary states of consciousness a corresponding counterpart in a subjective experience. What we ordinarily perceive as elements separate from us—such as persons, animals, trees, and precious stones—we can actually become and identify with in a transpersonal state.

Time and space cease to be limits; one can experience various historically and geographically remote events as vividly as if they were happening here and now. It is possible to participate in sequences that involve one's ancestors, animal predecessors, and people in various cultures and periods of the past who are not at all genetically related to us. In some instances, this might be associated with a sense of personal remembering.

The world of transpersonal phenomena offers yet another intellectual and philosophical challenge. Frequently, they involve entities and realms that in the Western worldview are not considered to be part of objective reality, such as deities, demons, and other mythological personages from various cultures, or heavens, purgatories, and hells. These experiences are as convincing and real as those that include elements we are familiar with from our everyday life. The transpersonal states thus do not differentiate between the world of consensus reality and the mythological world of archetypal forms.

At this point, it seems appropriate to address a question that probably has arisen in the minds of many skeptical readers who share the traditional Western scientific worldview. Why should so much importance be attributed to transpersonal phenomena, and what relevance does this discussion have for the problem of spiritual emergency? After all, the fact that the human psyche produces such experiences and that the people who have them find them subjectively real and convincing does not mean that they should be taken seriously as authentic connections with various aspects of the universe.

A most common argument of those who refuse to pay attention to transpersonal phenomena is that they are random and meaningless products of a brain affected by an unknown disease process. Acording to this view, their rich content comes from our memories. We live in a culture in which we are exposed to an enormous influx of information of all kinds through newspapers, magazines, television, radio, movies, school education, and the books we read. Everything we experience is stored in our brains with photographic detail. Under certain circumstances, erratic cerebral activity creates out of this rich material countless imaginary sequences; these are meaningless, without any relevance, and of no value for the understanding of the human mind.

This might seem a reasonable explanation for those who have only a superficial acquaintance with the facts and data. However, a careful and systematic study of transpersonal experiences indicates that they are extraordinary phenomena that seriously challenge the Western scientific worldview. Although they occur in the process of deep self-exploration, often following memories of childhood events, birth, and intrauterine life, they cannot be explained solely in terms of processes occurring in the human brain. They can often provide, without the mediation of the senses, direct access to information about the universe that the individuals involved could not possibly have acquired through conventional channels.

In sequences from the lives of ancestors and the history of the race, from other cultures, and from "past lives," people often learn new and accurate details about the costumes, weapons, rituals, architecture, and social structure of the cultures and historical periods involved. We have observed many instances in which individuals experiencing identification with various animals acquired amazing insights into their psychology, instinctual behavior, and specific habits, or even enacted in spontaneous movements their courtship dances. This information was often far beyond their knowledge in the areas involved. On occasion, new information can also emerge from experiences of identification with plants or inorganic processes in nature.

It is even more amazing that people who in nonordinary states "visit" various archetypal realms and encounter mythological beings residing there can often bring back information that can be verified by research into the mythology of the corresponding cultures. Observations of this kind led Carl Gustav Jung many years ago to the idea of the collective unconscious and the assumption that each individual can under certain circumstances gain access to the entire cultural heritage of humanity.

If the above observations leave any doubts about the authenticity of the information acquired in transpersonal states, these are easily dispelled by data from the study of out-of-body experiences, where consciousness detaches from the body, "travels" to remote locations, and accurately observes what is happening there. This occurs during spiritual emergencies, in sessions of experiential psychotherapy, and particularly often in near-death situations; thanatologists have confirmed this in carefully controlled studies.

Another important aspect of transpersonal states—besides their authenticity—that challenges the disease model is their remarkable healing and transformative potential. Anybody who has witnessed the process of spiritual emergency under favorable circumstances will find it difficult to believe that it is not an intelligent move on the part of the psyche. Many emotional and psychosomatic disorders seem to have as their source—besides biographical memories and perinatal material—transpersonal constellations that lie close to the surface. These can have the form of past-life memories, identification with various animals, and demonic archetypes, among others. When such unconscious contents emerge fully into consciousness during a transformational crisis or in experiential psychotherapy, they lose their disruptive influence on everyday life; this can result in dramatic healing of various emotional and even physical problems.

Transpersonal experiences associated with positive emotions, such as feelings of oneness with humanity and nature, states of cosmic unity, encounters with blissful deities, and union with God, have a special role in the healing and transformative process. While various painful and difficult experiences cleanse the psyche and open the way to more pleasant ones, the ecstatic and unitive states represent the very essence of true healing.

In spiritual emergencies, the experiences we have described here— biographical, perinatal, and transpersonal—appear in various specific combinations that constitute the different forms or varieties of transformational crises described earlier. The cartography that we have just explored can thus be seen as the general matrix for spiritual emergencies; it can be and has been of great help to people undergoing this challenging and demanding process.

PART THREE

LIVING IN TWO WORLDS

CHAPTER 8

STRATEGIES FOR EVERYDAY LIFE

The two worlds, the divine and the human . . . are actually one. The realm of the gods is a forgotten dimension of the world we know.

JOSEPH CAMPBELL, *The Hero with a Thousand Faces*

Imagine going to your job on a typical day. You just spent a restless night, bombarded by vivid dreams in which you were dying. You felt piercing pain and overwhelming fear as you saw blood streaming from your wounds. The faces of the people surrounding you were vivid and menacing. It all seemed very real, as though it were actually happening. You wakened breathlessly several times, relieved to find that you were safe, only to drift into more tortured sleep.

As you drive to work on this bright spring day, all of the physical distress and the wrenching emotions from the dream follow you. It seems as though your waking state is simply a continuation of the night's activity; it is difficult to separate them. Although the content of the dreams varies, you have felt haunted by the nocturnal adventures of your mind for a while. You are exhausted by the end of the day, and you have started to get depressed.

You notice that if your resistance is down, the experiences become stronger; it happened during the flu you had last week and after a few sleepless nights. Sometimes, you see brief visions of scenes from other times and places or of mythological figures. And you have been doing what you can to try to hold down the waves of anger and fear that have been unexpectedly hitting you.

You have also been bothered by strange physical sensations; sometimes, when you are quiet, your body shakes automatically, and you feel some kind of electricity pulsing through your limbs. Sometimes you feel a pressure on your chest, and you have started to have frequent, immobilizing headaches. At times you feel driven and anxious, even though from the outside you appear to be managing everything efficiently. You feel as though you are leading a double life: the deceptive facade of normalcy and cheerfulness that you present to the world, and a secret, troubled reality that is difficult to talk about. You are beginning to shy away from social activities, since you never know when these strange experiences are going to hit you.

Today, you have a major presentation for your company's board of directors, and you are worried: you are not sure that you can keep yourself together. You keep getting flashes from your dream that seem to be as real as the activity in your office, and you are having trouble concentrating. Your headache has returned, and you feel excessively fearful, as though this meeting is a life-or-death situation.

This is what it is like to be in the middle of a spiritual emergency and still try to operate as usual in your ordinary life. This is how it feels to attempt to live in two worlds. One world is the ordinary, familiar reality in which you have certain expectations to fulfill, roles to play, and obligations to meet. The other is the domain beneath the everyday layer, the vast pool of the unconscious, which contains unknown possibilities. When the inner realm becomes increasingly available, it intrudes into ordinary awareness, and the separation between the two domains begins to crumble.

It is this gray area that presents problems to the individual in a transformational crisis. You are neither here nor there, fully present neither in the outer reality nor in the internal regions, and the tension that results can create great discomfort. If you identify with the person in the above example, you may discover that your intense inner process has a disorganizing impact on your everyday functioning and that your concern about your effectiveness in the world can add to the anxiety that is already prominent as part of the emergence process. If your awakening is relatively mild, you may be content to live with the passing inconveniences that arise when you are trying to balance these realities. Or you might become more actively involved and feel impelled to *do* something to relieve the situation.

This section will focus on practical ways of living through and working with spiritual emergency. Many of the approaches have resulted from the personal knowledge gained during Christina's daily struggle to endure the manifestations of the Kundalini awakening and Stan's experience of living with and helping her. Others were gleaned from Stan's many years of clinical research into nonordinary states as an experimental psychiatrist. We have also learned a great deal during our joint work with thousands of people in our workshops and training seminars and through regular contact with the Spiritual Emergence Network. We have had many discussions with individuals who have had some form of spiritual emergency, and when we compared their strategies for living with our own, we discovered that our solutions were the same or very similar.

Much of what we describe can be done at home during the course of everyday life, often with the assistance of family, friends, and open-minded professionals. (We have included in appendix III some suggestions for professionals, therapists, and counselors who may become involved along the way.)

Your Attitude Toward Your Spiritual Emergency

It is important for you to know that many of the problems that arise during the course of your spiritual emergency, such as those involving your relationships, home, professional life, and health, will be relieved as part of the transformation process—and not solely through your own forceful efforts. It is impossible for us to give you tips on or solutions to such difficulties in themselves. Instead, we can offer the reassurance that if the emergence process is allowed to progress, if the inner world that is causing the discomfort is fully expressed, you will reconnect with the daily world; in addition, you will most likely have an increased capacity for effective functioning and an insight as to why the apparent problems were necessary for your development.

You may feel as though your spiritual emergency has a mind of its own, arriving in your life uninvited and proceeding on its own course, without regard for timing or convenience. In spite of the fact that existence during this period can be a major challenge that consumes a great deal of time and energy, you can live more comfortably in everyday life by cooperating and actively working with this healing process. Your attitude toward such an event is critical: as long as you are limited by fear, resistance, disbelief, or denial, a potentially life-changing opportunity can be severely hampered or even interrupted.

In our experience, once an emergence process is set in motion, it will not stop until it has run its course. The intense period of awakening may take quite some time, ranging from a few months to a number of years. There may be times in which the transformation process is more troublesome or obvious than others, but generally it is continuous until it is finished. Approaching it fearfully or attempting to stop it prematurely is counterproductive. You will most likely find that a resistant attitude makes this natural process more difficult; as a result, it will take much longer.

If you are able to maintain a general sense of cooperation with and even enthusiasm about your spiritual emergency, the entire process will be easier and, most likely, shorter. And you have a good chance of emerging from your journey with a feeling of accomplishment and victory rather than shame and discomfort. So how can you learn to work with this important process?

Often, people in spiritual emergencies will intuitively know what is right for them but have trouble translating these insights into action. We have found it helpful to utilize two general strategies. The first and preferable one is to create a situation in which you can fully confront the inner experiences that are trying to surface, thereby moving through them and learning from their content. The second is to take measures that will inhibit the emergence process and temporarily lessen its impact on daily life when circumstances require it. We will look at each in turn.

Facing Your Spiritual Emergency

When unconscious emotions and experiences become available, they are on their way toward being cleansed or released from the body and mind. For example, a man who has carried a lifelong fear of enclosed places may relive his birth during a spiritual emergency, complete with intense feelings of suffocation and colorful visions of narrow channels; afterward, his claustrophobia can disappear and he may have gained the insight that it was his birth memory, for years just under the surface of his daily awareness, that had kept him out of elevators and airplanes. By fully facing this memory, with all of its complexities, he purges it from his unconscious. Once fully eliminated, it will never return.

You will most likely find it valid and necessary to work with the great range of emotions, experiences, and energies that can surface during a spiritual emergency. Sometimes you have no choice but to face them as they come up; you may feel completely consumed by them, unable to control their fluctuations. Or you may find that when the process is not particularly overwhelming, it is helpful to find some nonintrusive method to assist you in confronting the experiences and expressing the energies and emotions associated with them.

There are many ways in which you can actively work with the elements of your spiritual emergency as they arise. Some of these approaches include becoming involved in effective therapy or counseling, joining a support group, participating in regular spiritual practice with a knowledgeable teacher, and working with a skilled body worker. This kind of help is *extremely important* and often *very necessary*, and we will offer advice on how you can find and select such assistance in chapter 10. For now, we will focus on what you can do for yourself.

The following suggestions are particularly useful when your process is not so overwhelming that you cannot provide your own support. If you find yourself at the mercy of very strong emotions and experiences, we recommend instead that you find a sympathetic person to help you.

Play evocative music and express the emotions and experiences through sound and movement. Choose music that enhances the experiences you are having. Lie down on the bed or the floor, and allow the feelings to express themselves. You might find yourself crying or screaming, shaking, singing, or moving in various ways. This often brings significant temporary relief. You might find that the same effect can be accomplished through approaches such as dance or yoga; it is important to keep your attention focused internally during the movement so as not to confuse inner experiences with external surroundings.

Actively work with your dreams. This can give you insights into your own internal world, how it works, and what is contained there. Sigmund Freud, the father of psychoanalysis, called dreams "the royal road to the unconscious." During a spiritual emergency, your dreams are frequently continuations or completions of the experiences that occur during your waking hours. Sometimes answers that you have been struggling to find appear during your sleep. Often, dreams can be instructive or predictive. Try keeping a pad of paper by the side of the bed, and regularly write down your dreams in the morning or if you wake up in the middle of the night. Then reserve a quiet period during the day in which you can play with dream imagery, perhaps even doing some drawing. Ask yourself questions about the imagery, or conduct a dialogue with the figures in your dream. Inquire within yourself about the meanings and origins of the feelings involved and look at the answers you come up with.

You might find another person with whom to regularly share dreams; this works best with someone who is caring but has an objective perspective. There are a number of good books that offer instructions about working with dreams, among them Patricia Garfield's *Creative Dreaming*.

Use artistic expression. This will help you understand and process your experiences by exteriorizing them. Drawing, painting, and sculpting also allow you to channel strong physical and emotional energies, and as you do so, you may well discover some new aspects of yourself. The great Spanish artist Francisco Goya described his sense of increased mastery over his dramatic inner life that came from putting the images within him on canvas.

The use of artistic expression in this context does not require personal talent. It is simply a powerful tool to help to gain insight into a very dynamic and often confusing process. Since vivid visual imagery often plays a large part in a spiritual emergency, you may find it extremely valuable to externalize your visions through drawing or painting. It does not matter whether the images that appear are figurative representations, abstract shapes, or plays of color. Sometimes your creations will seem to make no sense at the moment, but after a period of time they may offer an important aid in understanding your experience. Some people keep a journal of pictures, much as others write in a diary, beginning or ending each day with a painting or drawing.

Working with clay can be a very satisfying way to express some of the emotional and physical movement of the process. This malleable, tactile material can provide a wonderful outlet for intense feelings and energies, and its three-dimensional qualities may give you an additional perspective on your inner images. As with any other form of artistic expression, if you work with clay during a spiritual emergency, try to focus on the process of using the material and the insights that this activity brings you rather than worrying about the finished product.

It is a good idea to keep on hand a supply of tempera paints, brushes, magic markers (including gold and silver, frequently used to convey the radiance of mystical states), oil crayons, paper, and clay.

Practice focused meditation. Concentrating on the experiences that you have been having will help you gain insight into specific areas of your process. Many meditators concentrate on the breath, a candle flame, or a sacred phrase or mantra in order to quiet the mind and open themselves to deeper realms within. This approach, although related, is somewhat different: here you can use physical and mental relaxation to deepen, amplify, or refine your understanding of a particular issue, image, emotion, or problem that has arisen as part of your spiritual emergency or to move past a place where you may feel stuck. It might also help you to complete an experience that you could not fully finish.

While resting in bed after a night's sleep or while lying on the floor, play some quiet music, relax, and allow yourself to wander mentally through some of the visual images, physical sensations, emotional states, and memories that have been prominent in your inner process. If you want to clarify some aspect or theme of your journey, gently guide yourself to that part of the experience, instructing yourself to pass through it and asking, "What do I see around me? How do I react to it physically and emotionally? What is it telling me?" As the information starts to become available, allow it to lead you to new insights and furthe understanding.

When it is time to finish your meditation, gradually lead yourself back to everyday reality, giving yourself plenty of time to complete your experience. As you begin to sense the room around you, gently move your body and stretch. After you have opened your eyes, you might try drawing or writing about what you have just seen or felt.

This practice is based on principles similar to "active imagination," an approach to dream work that was developed by C. G. Jung. In working with active imagination, you are asked to go back into a dream and continue it experientially; the content of this process is then analyzed with the help of a therapist. A good book describing this method is *Encounters with the Soul: Active Imagination* by Barbara Hannah.

Develop simple personal rituals. Many people do this to help them through the difficult stages of a transformation process, often using approaches that are practiced in various spiritual traditions. These are often very personal and may not work for everyone. For example, you might try this simple cleansing meditation during a long shower: while standing under the stream of water, imagine that the water is flowing all the way through your mind and body, clearing out any negative emotional debris and washing it down the drain. This can also work with the image of fire. While watching the flames in a fireplace, envision the heat and power of the fire pouring around and through you, consuming the troublesome obstructions within.

You may find it helpful to meditate on relieving yourself of difficulties by giving them to some form of higher power or by asking for help from a larger force. For example, you might visualize yourself offering your problems to huge, primal regions such as the desert, the ocean, the earth, or the infinite space of the universe. Imagine yourself standing on a cliff above a vast expanse of ocean, holding a large bundle that represents all of your pain and all of your obstacles; then watch yourself forcefully throwing your burden into the sea, with the injunction, "Please, take this from me." Another approach is to practice surrounding yourself with imaginary white or deep blue light as a shield that protects you against intrusions by unwelcome elements.

Be creative in finding ways to facilitate the situation. No matter what you come up with, if you believe strongly that it will work, it usually does. Perhaps this is because you feel a sense of mastery or cooperation when actively participating in a process that can feel overpowering or unmanageable at times.

Temporarily Containing a Spiritual Emergency

It would be ideal to have an ongoing situation in which you could focus on your spiritual emergency without having to do anything else. But the reality is that, for most people, there are important relationships to attend to, daily tasks to accomplish, work to do, people to meet, and airplanes to catch. And work on the issues, emotions, and sensations during a spiritual emergency must be limited to designated periods of time. The question then becomes, How can I slow down my inner activity so that I can somehow balance it with my daily pursuits?

In the following pages, we offer some ideas that have worked for us and for others. Again, we must emphasize that slowing down the emergence process is not the ideal strategy, and it is certainly not the solution. These are temporary measures that will serve to provide interim relief and periods of balance. As long as extreme interventions—such as the ongoing use of tranquilizers and other repressive approaches—are avoided, these measures are not harmful. They may prolong the length of the crisis period, but they will not completely arrest an already active transformation impulse.

Temporarily discontinue active inner exploration. You may want to stop experiential therapy or dream work for a while if you feel that too much is going on already. You might not want to stir up any more of your unconscious if you are somewhat shaky. If at this point you have an ongoing relationship with a therapist, it is important for you to discuss with him or her your reasons for discontinuing deep experiential work, so that you will have his or her support. You will most likely find it helpful to continue seeing your therapist in order to discuss some of your daily problems, but with the understanding that further active exploration is inappropriate at this point. When you are ready, you can resume using approaches that will allow you to work further with your emergence.

Temporarily discontinue any form of spiritual practice. Various sacred approaches are designed to awaken spiritual energies and experiences in people. So instead of participating in intense prayer, meditation, or chanting, eliminate them altogether. Discontinue yoga, tai chi, and any other form of movement meditation. Stop attending spiritual retreats, and set aside any inspirational reading for a while. It is useful to avoid any activity that is very focused on internal introspection. Again, this is a temporary measure, and you will find that as your inner process becomes smoother, you will often intuitively know when to return to the practices that are important to you.

Change your diet. Food can be a very important consideration during a spiritual emergency. There are many current theories concerning nutrition and diet, and we do not wish to compete with any of them. Certainly, each person is different and must find what works for him or her. Here we simply offer some of our observations and experiences; they have been useful for us and have been echoed by other people.

It is well known that fasting and other dietary manipulations are practiced in spiritual disciplines to refine the functioning of both body and mind in order to allow for greater access to meditative realms. So if you want to slow down an intense emergence process, you might avoid such approaches.

During your crisis, you may find yourself developing a craving for heavier food and might even gain weight. We have known devout vegetarians who suddenly find themselves yearning for meat. A friend of ours related a story of how his spiritual awakening eventually took him to McDonald's for his first hamburger in years. He humorously described the radiance of the familiar golden arches at the restaurant, which for him became a mystical symbol of this step in his journey.

Another person describes a similar situation: "I would drive by the deli and impulsively end up ordering a half-pound of rare roast beef. Chicken or fish was not enough. It had to be red meat, and not too well done. Once I devoured that, I felt much better."

Often after a period of needing animal protein you will find that substantial grains and cheese will have the same effect. People have told us that the heavier food seemed to bring them "back to earth," making them feel physically more solid and less absorbed in their inner drama.

In addition, you may suddenly find yourself constantly thinking about chocolate, cookies, ice cream, and other treats, even though you may never have thought of yourself as a sweets lover. You may be shocked as you watch yourself making trips to the candy store specifically to satisfy your sudden urges, especially as you see the scales reflecting your newfound passion. Yet the ingestion of sweets, or glucose, can actually help one return to everyday activities.

Glucose is the main nutrient of the brain; other carbohydrates, proteins, and fats must be converted into glucose before the brain can use them. Deep experiences with strong emotions and intense physical activity require a great deal of energy and deplete the nutrients in the body, thus lowering blood sugar. An inadequate supply of sugar to the brain, in turn, tends to induce unusual experiences, thus creating a vicious circle in someone who is already susceptible to nonordinary states of mind. In this situation, glucose is a quick and immediate nutrient that helps to interrupt this cycle.

In order to slow down intense states during your spiritual emergency, experiment with various foods to see what works for you. Try eating heavier foods such as red meat or other sources of protein: poultry, fish, beans, cheese, or other dairy products. Incorporate nutritious grains and hearty whole-grained breads into your diet. And keep some sugar or honey on hand. We should stress that if you were committed to a successful dietary regime previous to your spiritual emergency and find yourself straying from it, your new cravings are most likely temporary and will not necessarily commit you permanently to a new eating style.

A good medical checkup with a sympathetic physician is important if you are concerned about issues such as diabetes or hypoglycemia. In addition, cravings for certain foods may indicate a real deficiency in the diet. On the other hand, certain passing physical manifestations that occur during a spiritual emergency simulate true medical problems but are in reality rooted in old memories, emotions, or other experiences that are surfacing. Medical tests and evaluations will help to distinguish which is which.

A number of people have told us that they have found themselves suddenly craving alcohol or tobacco during a period of intense inner activity. Taking a drink or puffing on a cigarette somehow helped to bring them back to earth, and they found that the compulsion disappeared in a short time, after their spiritual emergence had progressed further. We have heard similar reports about strong coffee; in contrast to its usual stimulating effect, it can be relaxing for some individuals.

Caution: While in some people this craving for tobacco or alcohol is only a stage in a multifaceted process and passes without any apparent effect, for others, especially those with a propensity toward chemical dependency, it can be disastrous. Use of such chemicals can lead to long-term substance abuse, which can serve only to complicate an already complex situation. It is very easy for someone who is addicted to add to an already intricate system of denial a rationalization such as, "I am drinking this bottle of wine because this is what my spiritual process needs right now." For this reason, we recommend that anyone involved in a spiritual emergency exercise *extreme caution* when using possibly addictive substances.

Become involved in very simple, calming activities. Complicated and focused projects often become difficult. The attention required for such activities is akin to the introspection required in spiritual practice and can accelerate the process. Sometimes the feelings of uncontainable energy that accompany a spiritual emergency make it impossible to sit still for long. You might find it difficult to read, sew, paint, or write letters without feeling a surge of symptoms. The same can be true when watching movies, television, or videotapes. You may find it challenging to drive a car or have trouble with too much verbal input during conversations.

If you find that you are having difficulties with activities such as these, discontinue them for a while if possible. Temporarily suspending favorite pastimes such as reading and creative work does not mean they will be eliminated from your life forever. It simply means that for a while, your inner world is so complex that you find it necessary and helpful to simplify your involvement in your surroundings.

Try replacing more complicated or focused activities with simpler ones. Working in the garden can be a wonderful way to literally ground yourself, as well as participating in uncomplicated tasks such as washing dishes, cleaning the house, waxing the floors, or chopping and stacking wood. In many ashrams or monasteries, the same person sweeps the same floor day after day after day. This is not just a tedious chore; it is a very straightforward way to balance the tension between worlds.

Participate in regular exercise. Running, walking, dancing, and swimming can all can be helpful in bringing you back to earth and providing channels of release for complex pent-up energies. These are different from activities such as movement meditations, yoga, or active self-exploration, which require introspection and are designed to enhance or accelerate the process.

Some doctors prescribe jogging as an effective antidote for depression, often with great success. The same approach applies here: instead of turning the energies, emotions, and sensations back on yourself, allow time for regular movement that serves to let off steam. As you run, dance, or swim laps, use the exercise as a way to simply feel your body, your connection with the earth or the water, and your muscles as they move. This can be particularly helpful if you are so busy with inner experiences that you tend to forget about your physical well-being.

Discover which environments and people stimulate your process and avoid them for a while. After years of living relatively easily in the world, you may find that there are suddenly certain situations that seem to accelerate your spiritual emergency. If you live in the country, you may find that the noise and mechanical vibrations of a large city activate unusual physical energies, strong emotions, and unexpected experiences. You might be set off by the perpetual sound of heavy machinery or even the subtle but regular movements of an airplane or train. The noise and activity of a crowd can have the same impact. It is important to find out which situations have an such effect and avoid them for a while.

In addition, the presence of people with particularly strong person-alities can feel overwhelming, whether you feel negatively or positively about them. During a spiritual emergency, personal boundaries often seem tenuous and you may become very sensitive to the world around you. As a result, you might feel that you easily absorb the emotional attitudes of others. If an individual exudes love and compassion, being around him or her may seem nourishing and soothing. But if the same person is also vigorous and dynamic, even the most positive contact may be too overwhelming for a while.

We have heard stories of people who found it temporarily difficult to be near a highly developed spiritual teacher, priest, or shaman because their process seemed to be stimulated by his or her presence. The same can be true if you find yourself around someone who is hateful, angry, or oppressive. In your receptive state, his or her negativity might feel extremely forceful and even harmful to you.

Be aware of your reactions to various people and environments. If you want to slow down your spiritual emergency, temporarily avoid sit-uations in which you are overstimulated emotionally, physically, or men-tally or in which you feel uncomfortably sensitive to the world around you. Chances are that when your transformational crisis passes, you will not be so easily affected.

One general suggestion to those who wish to slow down the emergence process: keep it simple. Eliminate the activities and situations that disturb you, and focus on an uncomplicated lifestyle. This does not mean that the complex world and involvement in activities that used to excite you will become forever unavailable. You can return to them after the intense period of change is completed.

Living in two worlds is a challenge. Many shamans and healers have trained themselves to travel between worlds at will. But most of us are not that skilled, and for a while we may end up in a confusing interface between everyday reality and the extraordinary depths of our uncon-scious. It is very reassuring to know that this experience is transitory, that there are ways in which we can live more easily with this phase of our transformation, and that we can get help when we need it.

CHAPTER 9

GUIDELINES FOR FAMILY AND FRIENDS

Emboldened by the thin light
She strained for more
Until her mold shattered,
Releasing her exuberantly.
Floating now on high,
Shimmering in the sun,
She scorns the earth.
Will she see, one day,
That the light is also here,
Illuminating the earth,
Her children, friends and lovers,
The here and now?

THE MOTHER OF A YOUNG WOMAN
IN A SPIRITUAL EMERGENCY

Living with someone who is going through a spiritual emergency is often very demanding for everyone involved. Those close to that person, as well as the person himself or herself, spend much time and energy on the changes that are being brought into their lives, and friends and family are regularly confronted with their own emotions and limitations. Seemingly normal and stable relationships become threatened by abrupt shifts in one person's interests and behavior that often require an unwelcome adjustment on the part of others.

Just as the intensity of the transformation process varies greatly, so do its effects on the people surrounding the one going through it. Those close to someone who is engaged in a gentle metamorphosis may not even notice the subtle changes as they occur and perhaps may naturally accompany the person into new and interesting territories. It is only in retrospect that they realize that their understanding, values, and way of relating to themselves and to the world have evolved and that the growth process that has fostered these changes has had an understandable progression.

However, if the emergence is more evident, and especially if it occupies everyone's daily attention, it can be challenging for family members and friends to witness and participate in it. And when spiritual emergence becomes a spiritual emergency, the stress on those who are emotionally connected to the individual can be immense indeed.

Because of the demanding nature of the situation and of the inter-actions involved, however, people do not usually maintain a positive, accepting attitude and tend to react with emotions ranging from fear, helplessness, and confusion to denial and rejection. In the following pages, we will specifically address the friends and family members of those who are going through a spiritual emergency.

We will not give specific advice for dealing with the interpersonal problems that may arise, since each situation is different and the nature of the relationships varies. However, it can be helpful merely to know what sort of behavior to expect from those in a transformational crisis as well as what kinds of problematic responses tend to arise in the people close by. Simply knowing in advance what issues are likely to come up can help family members and friends deal with them.

Before moving on to some concrete examples of the ways that the emergence process can affect one's behavior and, consequently, imme-diate relationships, consider the following story:

Diane is your daughter. She is very outgoing, sociable, and pretty. She has quietly gone through her life, easily accomplishing whatever tasks have been put before her, and she has always been very dependable and thoughtful toward those around her. She did well in school, and during her teenage years she participated in the activities enjoyed by most young people, but she never became involved with drugs or did anything she could not discuss with her family. After college, she married Jim, her high-school sweetheart, and together they presented you with your first grandchildren. You are still very close to her, and you see each other regularly on weekends.

Suddenly, something very strange begins to happen. After her best friend's death in a car accident, Diane starts to change. She begins to talk about all kinds of things that never interested her before and that are very unfamiliar to you. She has even brought you some of the books she has been reading that she says are changing her life. One is about the death experience, another deals with life after death, and a third one talks about reincarnation. Diane's conversations are now peppered with words such as *karma, energy, unity, God,* and *consciousness,* and she becomes impatient when you tell her that you really do not know what she is talking about. You have noticed that she is moodier than ever before, feeling ecstatic one day and quite depressed the next.

Diane has excitedly told you that she is taking Hatha Yoga, and she shows you a corner in her sewing room at home that she has changed into some sort of altar with a pillow nearby, where she sits to practice her meditation. She has also stopped wearing much makeup and jewelry and is spending time with new friends from her yoga class; they seem very personable and candid, but they discuss subjects that are foreign to you. Since she met them, Diane has seemed strangely aloof from the family, saying that she is afraid you will not understand.

In a recent telephone conversation, Diane expressed a lot of dissatisfaction with her marriage, with Jim, and with her role as a mother. This is very unlike her; she has always loved her family and has thrived as a parent. According to her, Jim has been unwilling to join her in her newfound activities and is even reluctant to discuss her current ideas and insights, often escaping into the newspaper or going out to play tennis with his friends. She has recently felt lonely in the relationship and guilty that she cannot do anything about the diverging paths she and Jim seem to be traveling. She worries that since she is spending more time away from home, she is not as fully involved with the kids as she was in the past.

Privately, Jim has confided to you that he is very worried, that he does not know what to do or how to communicate with Diane; she seems to be off on some solitary tangent with her new interests, activities and friends that do not include him. You are concerned that something is terribly wrong with your daughter, and in your worst moments you worry that perhaps she is going crazy. You feel helpless in dealing with her, and you feel that she should see a psychiatrist.

This is a scenario that, in some form, has been played out many times. A family member or a friend abruptly changes his or her behavior and interests and starts to interact in unfamiliar ways. If he or she expresses new individual needs and no longer meets the usual expectations, the people close by might feel concerned, helpless, frustrated, judgmental, or rejecting. We will describe some of the specific behaviors with which people who surround someone in a spiritual emergency might be confronted.

Behaviors and Attitudes That Affect Family and Friends

As a result of new insights and awarenesses, someone in a transformation process often *changes his or her daily habits or outward appearance*. For example, a person who has been known as a late riser may suddenly start setting the alarm at an early hour in order to wake up for meditation practice or prayer. In other cases, invididuals who have always been fairly conservative dressers may suddenly adopt new habits, trading button-down shirts or linen suits for jeans and casual clothes as expressions of their new inner freedom. In the extreme, they may begin wearing strange spiritual garb and shave their head or adopt an unusual hairstyle.

People who come upon the insight that everything in life is interconnected may develop a new ecological awareness. They might impulsively trade in the family station wagon for a more economical vehicle or take a sudden interest in recycling the household trash. Longtime meat-and-potato lovers can turn into vegetarians and might try to impose their newfound dietary regimens on others, becoming judgmental of those who remain true to the old ways. Many other forms of new behavior are more subtle but are still noticeable to those whom they affect.

An individual who may have been extremely outgoing and social may abruptly *become introspective, avoiding social activities or acting in an asocial way*. He or she may spend days alone, reading, meditating, or taking long walks. The emotional reactions of such a person may swing from one extreme to another for no apparent reason. On a given day, one's husband seems very peaceful and accepting; the next day he is extremely agitated and angry. He may talk a lot about his fears, or he may isolate himself and become completely uncommunicative or depressed.

Sometimes people become so intrigued with their new experiences and insights that they *reject the ordinary world as trivial and mundane*. They may wish to spend their time engaged in activities that will allow them to move away from daily reality. Their colorful visions and cosmic insights might seem alluring and exotic compared with mundane and familiar pursuits, and they may feel for a while that these new areas deserve their exclusive attention. This is usually only a passing phase, a well-known diversion on the spiritual path, which will either pass on its own or be resolved with the help of an understanding guide.

When people enter a transformation process, their interests often change and they may want to *discuss their new insights and ideas with anyone within range, becoming judgmental or impatient with others who do not share their concerns*. These are usually concepts or beliefs that resonate with their experiences, sometimes explaining or validating what might at first have seemed to be a mysterious event. Naturally, because these ideas are so meaningful to the individuals going through the emergence, they assume that those who are close to them will also find them beneficial.

Such people often discover books that they find so important that they feel impelled to spread the word, at times becoming somewhat messianic. Confused relatives and friends suddenly receive unsolicited volumes as presents, accompanied by urgent notes instructing them to read and digest their wisdom. These same people might suddenly be invited to attend lectures conducted by a teacher or guru, on topics that seem peculiar and sometimes threatening to their well-established belief systems. Conversations may suddenly become uncomfortable as the enthusiastic family member regularly steers the subject matter away from familiar topics such as the news of the day to issues of cosmic and universal significance.

Those around such an individual may already have worldviews that work for them, may be content to stay where they are, or may feel threatened by anything new. They may turn down the enthusiastic urgings. Their loved one may easily accept that what is right for him or her may not be suitable for others, and proceed quietly along the path. But those who already feel lonely in their experiences or have trouble with issues of rejection may take their family's lack of interest as a statement about them. As a result, they may become judgmental toward those who are neither willing nor able to accompany them on their new journey, feeling that they have been shown the light of truth and that others are still in the dark.

Individuals in a transformation process may *project or blame their difficulties on others or on the circumstances around them*. Projection occurs when one disowns his or her own feelings or attitudes and attributes them to other people or situations. A person struggling with strong aggressive feelings can perceive others as threatening or experience his or her fears as a justified response to external circumstances or alleged activities of other people. Similarly, the individual may externalize emotions such as blame or guilt as a way of defending against the real issues that are coming from within.

Projection does not always involve negative emotions; one may also disown positive feelings and ascribe them to others. For example, someone who is swept by a strong sense of love may project it on a person nearby and become convinced that this means there is a special bond between them, rather than realizing that he or she has discovered a source of compassion within.

In this confusion between the inner psychological process and outer reality, the individual might perceive other people or the environment in a way that reflects what is happening inside, and even act on those perceptions, a process that is called "acting out." The individual who has discovered love may feel that he or she needs to approach the person who is the object of the projection and form a permanent relationship with him or her. Mixing the internal and external worlds in this way can result in problematic situations.

One common negative projection is blame. Especially when difficult emotional material is surfacing from within, it is easy to hold the people at hand or the surrounding circumstances responsible for the unpleasant feelings involved. For example, a person who becomes claustrophobic may blame those nearby for asking him or her to stay in a room rather than face the experience of being trapped in the birth canal. Or he or she may blame the room itself for the discomfort, complaining that it is too small and suffocating.

Sometimes, people in a transformation process *use their family or friendships as symbols of the restrictions they are shedding.* They confuse freeing themselves from internal limitations with actually moving away from the family. They are dissatisfied with ways of being that are no longer compatible with their new worldview, and they blame their discontent on some of the closest or most caring people in their lives.

This kind of behavior can be particularly prominent during the phase of spiritual emergence in which one faces issues of detachment. Here, people have the insight that their pain and restriction in life have to do with the degree to which they are emotionally clinging to roles, relationships, and material possessions. In order to become free of suffering, these attachments must be severed. It is important to know that this does not necessarily mean that they need to physically move away from their attachments. The process of detachment can be completed internally, through meditation or other experiential methods, without jeopardizing one's external world.

It is common, however, to interpret this realization as an indication about how one should behave in life. A person who experiences persistent impulses to let go of old attachments may not have the insight that this can be done inwardly. He or she may feel that the only way to follow this strong inner urging is to leave parents, children, spouse, friends, job, or home. Individuals in this stage may give away money or possessions and attempt to live a spartan lifestyle.

People *may become preoccupied with the issue of death* during spiritual emergence. Whether one encounters memories of near-death situations, confronts his or her mortality and the transitory nature of existence, or experiences death as part of a death-rebirth cycle, this issue is often profound and shattering. Because of the authenticity of the feelings and the convincing physical manifestations, the person who is having the experience may become convinced that he or she is literally dying or needs to die. This stage can sometimes be confusing and frightening if everyone involved lacks understanding about the nature of the encounter with death during spiritual emergency. (We have discussed this phenomenon in depth in chapter 2.)

Persons involved in a transformation process can *change their sexual responses*. They may have new experiences and insights that can dramatically alter what used to be a predictable and "normal" sexual relationship. These changes can be very distressing and confusing to the partner. Perhaps someone feels that his or her true goal is a union with God, not with a mortal such as a wife, husband, or lover, and that the only choice is to remain celibate.

Someone who has easy access to mystical experiences or likes to escape into those realms might try to use the sexual situation to reach them. The emotion and force of a powerful sexual encounter can propel such people into transpersonal experiences that remove them from usual personal interaction. This can be very exciting and insight provoking if both people are engaged in a similar spiritual journey, but if only one of them is moving in such a direction this change can occur at the expense of the partner. He or she feels lost, left out, left behind, or perhaps used merely as a vehicle for the partner's transcendent states.

With forms of spiritual emergence such as the Kundalini awakening, one feels enormous physical and spiritual energies that use any channel to express themselves, the sexual outlet being a very obvious and powerful possibility. The energies feel so strong that a person may feel that if he or she lets go into orgasm, something catastrophic will happen: he or she will die, the partner will die, the world will explode, the universe will collapse.

If someone with these feelings does allow the orgasm, his or her body may explode with powerful energy that courses up the spine and throughout the limbs, often creating violent tremors and involuntary breathing rhythms. Often, women experience multiple orgasms simply as a way of releasing the intense Kundalini force. Obviously, this does not provide for a familiar, romantic sexual situation. The strange movements, shaking, and automatic breathing, as well as the often strong emotions, can be very frightening for an unsuspecting partner.

Another difficulty occurs when a person undergoing a spiritual emergency projects unresolved sexual problems onto the partner. Often, the process stirs up a lot of old memories, and as with other issues, it is easy to mistakenly blame the partner for whatever one is feeling at the time. For example, if a woman is working on incest, she can, within the very open and vulnerable context of lovemaking, easily project the qualities of her molester onto her mate. Since most relationships have inherent problems anyway, couples feel added stress when they have to cope with the strange sexual developments that are part of a person's spiritual emergence. If a relationship is already seriously in trouble, frequent projections and unfamiliar sexual expressions might exaggerate existing difficulties.

Often, during a period of psychic opening, people *may become ex-*

tremely intuitive or psychic when relating to those close to them. They may suddenly report clairvoyant dreams and insights or demonstrate an unsettling intuitive knowledge of issues in the lives of other people. Relatives or friends who have no prior understanding of such phenomena can feel very confused if a loved one brings up certain secrets for discussion or accurately tells them beforehand what will happen to them. Someone who is very open intuitively might show an acute understanding of the feelings, personality traits, and patterns of interaction demonstrated by family members and friends.

People in a transformation process *may feel guided by meaningful coincidences (synchronicities) that involve those close to them.* They suddenly see such connections everywhere, and may find that some of them intersect with the lives of those around them. Some people are excited about synchronicities, attributing tremendous importance to them and benefiting from their guidance. Others feel frightened by them, fearing that their well-structured cause-and-effect world is in danger.

How Family and Friends Respond

Family and friends can have a wide range of responses to one who is going through a dramatic transformation process. Their feelings can range from the very positive to the extremely negative. Some people feel caught up in the excitement of such an event and, without necessarily knowing why, are eager to cooperate, feeling they are gaining something significant from the experience. Those who helped a young woman through a dramatic episode of spiritual emergency made such comments as: "I feel deeply grateful and awed by what she has given to me"; "I am so moved by Karen and thankful for the opportunity to be with her . . . It's hard to leave"; "Thank you, Karen, for reminding me how much I need to show people that I care, for reminding me to trust the process that I am here to witness and support."

Unfortunately, many responses to such a process are not so positive. If you are unprepared for the advent of such a disruption in your life or have no idea what is happening to your child, parent, mate, or friend, you might find yourself responding with denial, confusion, fear, guilt, or judgment. Let us take a closer look at some possible reactions.

You may deny that anything is wrong. When people do not want to recognize a situation and the feelings that accompany it, they often protect themselves in this way. Such individuals might be untruthful with themselves about what is really going on in order to reassure themselves that everything is under control. Or they might ignore the situation, hoping it will go away.

Denial is common in many relationships in connection with a variety of problems, such as interpersonal conflicts, emotional, sexual and physical abuse, alcoholism, and drug addiction. Some people will not admit that anyone in the family has any kind of a problem until it becomes so obvious that it can no longer be ignored.

This can also occur when someone in the relationship has a spiritual emergency. Perhaps it is too painful to watch your mother struggling with the emotional swings inherent in a transformation process, so you pretend that it is not happening or tell yourself she is simply overworked or premenstrual. Or you do not believe in the spiritual experiences that your friend is telling you about, so you ignore them and hope that they will pass.

Kurt is a young man who had a spiritual emergency that was unacknowledged by everyone in his family until it was almost too late. Engulfed by feelings and experiences related to death, he had no understanding of why they were happening to him and no idea that facing them could be an important turning point. Whenever he tried to talk with his parents about his despair and fear, they assured him that everything would be all right and that perhaps he was not getting enough sleep.

He knew only that something in him had to die, and, becoming very suicidal, he overdosed on his mother's sleeping pills. Fortunately he survived, and after some family counseling his father admitted, "I simply had not allowed myself to see the problems Kurt was having. My love for him wished them away until he made them so obvious I could no longer ignore them." This kind of denial can have serious or even fatal consequences.

You may feel confused. If you have been used to relating to someone in a particular way, you may become very unsettled when confronted with his or her new behavior, beliefs, lifestyle, or worldview, which can seem unfamiliar and foreign to you. You might even find yourself changing your long-established ideas about how things should be or facing emotions that have been kept well hidden for a while. As a result, you may feel temporarily disoriented, perhaps even wondering about your own sanity, and your usual clarity of thought and your ability to make simple decisions may become clouded.

You may feel helpless. You likely sense that there is nothing you can do to help. Some people react to this by trying to control the situation. Your loved one is involved in a process that moves of its own accord, with a prescribed trajectory and timing. His or her emotions, experiences, and revelations are often unexpected, and the person going through it may feel completely at the mercy of the situation.

A normal reaction of a caring friend or family member is to want to help make things easier, to bring the difficulties to a conclusion. However, because the process has to run its own course, much like the flu, only so much can be done. When one becomes aware of this fact, a natural feeling of helplessness often ensues.

You may feel afraid. The intense emotions (depression, anger, fear, ecstasy), emotional expressions (crying, raging, screaming, laughing), and physical manifestations (shaking, writhing, frantic dancing) that may occur during a spiritual emergency can be scary if you have never seen them before or allowed them in yourself. In addition, unusual experiences such as a dramatic reliving of birth, a realistic sequence of dying, or an identification with a monster can be alarming to an unprepared observer.

Even those situations in which the outward mainifestations are relatively mild can be frightening; if someone close to you is constantly talking about death and detachment or becomes involved in some unknown spiritual practice, you might feel alarmed. And the fact that you can do very little about altering the course of the process can be scary if you are used to being in control.

Relatives can also be afraid that if something is wrong with a family member, something could be wrong with them. If they perceive the person as sick, they can become concerned that his or her condition has been caused by family history or latent genetic abnormalities. They may secretly wonder, "If she is ill, does this mean I could be, too?" And they sometimes try to prove the other person weak and unstable, in order to appear "normal" by contrast.

You may feel threatened. Someone else's intense experiences may elicit unwanted emotions and reactions in you. If a man has a deep mistrust of his own sanity, seeing his son behaving in a fashion that he considers crazy can stir up his own feelings of madness. Spending time with a loved one who is frequently talking about dying and the afterlife is extremely distressing to someone who is struggling with his or her own fear of death.

People express concerns such as these in many different ways. Those who have had therapy or have participated in spiritual practice might recognize their responses and will openly discuss them and willingly work on them. Others may not have the insight that their reactions reveal anything about themselves and may become increasingly defensive as a way to avoid looking at their own painful feelings.

Sometimes, friends or family members are threatened because their loved one is moving in a direction that they are afraid of or are unable to follow; they are left with the question, If he keeps changing, what does this mean about me? And the relationship? Will I be left behind? They may feel left out or even envious of the other person's process.

You may react with guilt. When faced with someone in a spiritual emergency, parents might suspect that the fact that their son or daughter is having such experiences is a direct reflection on their inadequacies during child rearing. A father who was present during a portion of his daughter's crisis felt partly responsible for it and later apologized to her for not having been available enough during her childhood. Although this was partially true, he was later able to see that his occasional absence was not the basic reason for her episode.

A wife can feel guilty about the disagreements and tensions that have been part of the relationship, wondering if her husband's new interests, experiences, and emotional swings are the result of problems she has caused. A boss who has just confronted one of his salesmen may feel responsible when he learns that his employee has taken time off to deal with a spiritual crisis.

You may feel shame. This is often connected with guilt. If you feel guilty that your loved one's spiritual crisis is the result of something you have done or not done, you may also feel that the situation reflects poorly on you, on your character, or on your family. You may be concerned that if other people find out about it, they will criticize and dislike you. This may lead you to avoid contact with people who might in fact be helpful to you during a time when you need some emotional support; and you may be needlessly hard on yourself.

You may become judgmental. Some people attempt to insure the safety and stability of their own worldview by defining their loved one as weak, unstable, ill, or crazy, thus defending themselves against feelings of guilt, fear, and shame and allowing themselves to maintain a position of relative strength and solidity. In this way they can avoid the possibility of having to change in response to the crisis.

Marsha was a sensitive young woman who lived with her family in an oceanside town in California. One day, she returned from a walk on the beach and told her parents of a beautiful mystical revelation that had come to her as she stood by the ocean. She had been flooded with white light and had experienced the unity of all of existence. She was ecstatic, very deeply moved by what had happened to her, and eager to share it with her loved ones. After a brief consultation, her family decided that Marsha had obviously lost her mind and should be hospitalized. Her spiritual awareness was unacceptable to those who were dedicated to protecting their own definition of reality.

We have seen families that retain a judgmental attitude even after a person has successfully moved through a spiritual emergency and is functioning perfectly adequately in the world. They maintain the position that because he or she has had such an episode, his or her life will never return to "normal." They may occasionally ask such questions as, "Tommy, are you still involved with that crazy psychic stuff?" and they are extremely alert to any indication that something is wrong. If, for example, their son has difficulties in getting along with his father, the parents immediately attribute such problems to the fact that he has been "sick," thereby conveniently escaping their own contribution to the situation.

You may find someone or something to blame. Friends or family members may blame the person who is having the transformational crisis ("He must have done something to deserve it"), his or her friends or partner ("This never would have happened if she hadn't met that man at church"), or certain activities ("It must be the result of that class he's taking"). Or they might blame themselves or even God.

You may reject both the individual and the process itself. Some people want nothing to do with something that is so foreign and so frightening, and they prefer to have it handled by someone else. It is this attitude that frequently drives family or friends to immediately hospitalize the one in crisis, without regard for the way in which that person is handling the experience.

What Family and Friends Can Do to Help

Many of us take on responsibilities with the idea of carrying them out perfectly. Since the process of a spiritual emergency is out of our control, any illusions we might have regarding our abilities to direct the course of such an occurrence are quickly shattered, and we are forced to be content with the sense that we are doing the best we can. It is both relieving and exciting to realize that by its very nature a transformation process cannot be outguessed or pinned down and that we cannot possibly exert impeccable control in relation to it. And we soon understand that if we offer help, we must grow and change along with the person we are supporting.

Following are some guidelines that have been helpful to us and to others who have worked with spiritual emergencies. Although these suggestions are designed to assist the person in crisis, we hope they will make the situation easier for everyone involved.

Become aware of your own motivations for providing support. This may seem simple, but often it is not. Some people offer assistance because of selfish reasons: they like drama, they are curious and want to study the phenomenon, they are afraid of their own craziness and need to try to control another person's unusual experiences, they need to show off their effectiveness as individuals with training or knowledge, they have an unsatisfied need to mother someone, they arrive at their self-definition by being "helpful."

Make sure that your own motives are clear and that even though you will most likely receive satisfaction and love in return, this is not your primary goal in offering your help. Be there because you genuinely care about the other person and want to assist his or her journey.

Allow the transformation process to unfold, and be willing to support it with trust and patience. Whatever assistance you offer must not interfere with the natural trajectory of the experience. Your task is not to control or manipulate but to support the emergence with sensitivity, to help the person past the obstacles if he or she gets stuck, and to offer a loving presence. Be available for discussion and frequent hugs, give back rubs, and offer other caring gestures.

It often takes some time to develop the trust necessary to put this attitude into practice completely, but it is helpful to start with the understanding that spiritual emergency has happened many times to many people, with very productive outcomes. Keeping in mind that the resolution will most likely not come overnight, lend your emotional aid, and watch your confidence develop as you see both the minor and major changes that take place. If you really do not have faith in the positive outcome of the process, remind yourself of the many others who have lived through it, and try familiarizing yourself with it until you accumulate enough evidence for such trust to develop.

A few words about patience: many of us are used to instant gratification, to having what we want when we want it, and we bring this attitude into the spiritual realm. We expect to achieve objectives and to arrive at certain stages according to our own timetables, which usually means sooner rather than later. This goal-oriented approach has caused many Westerners frustration as they become involved in spiritual pursuits. For everyone who is part of a transformative crisis, it is very humbling to learn that the process will take the time it needs to complete itself, and that one of the best things that we can do is to add patience to our sense of trust.

Be honest with the other person and yourself. People in spiritual emergencies are often extremely perceptive and are able to see through any dishonesty in those around them. To maintain a relationship of trust, the people around them need to remain truthful. This does not mean you need to be brutally forthright or relate every perception or feeling. Just honestly answer questions and, when possible, keep your loved one informed about the situation, what is happening around him or her, what you are doing, and who is involved.

Suspend your judgment. One way of doing this is to acknowledge that the transformation process is guided by a deeper wisdom. As long as we are judgmental, whether we judge the other person or ourselves, we are putting barriers between ourselves and the individual in crisis. We are experts, and the person in a spiritual emergency is sick; we are sane, and he or she is insane; we have our world in order, and his or hers is obviously falling apart. Or we judge ourselves negatively, telling ourselves that our loved one has something special that we lack. It is essential to suspend this kind of judgment and to develop an attitude that the two of you are on an exciting adventure, a hero's journey, together. It has its challenges and its peaks. Your loved one is the adventurer, and you are his or her partner. This is a journey that you might take yourself at another time.

An approach that involves such an acceptance of the other person and of his or her experiences will melt the barriers between you and greatly ease the journey. This does not mean that you have to enthusiastically embrace all that happens; this may not be possible during the most difficult passages. However, it is essential that you maintain the attitude that each step is part of a larger unfolding whose meaning will become clear when it is complete.

Offer frequent reassurance. Often people in spiritual emergencies feel that they are the only ones who have ever been through such an experience. They feel isolated and fearful, or perhaps elevated and grandiose. A good general strategy is to explain that this is a transformational journey that is ultimately evolutionary and healing, even though it may not feel that way at the time. Explain that it has many stages, some of which are uncomfortable and challenging, but that it is possible to move through them. Remind the person that the states of mind involved are temporary and can often be understood as stages in the cleansing of the psyche, which is taking him or her to a new, healthier way of being. Let the person know that the fastest way out of a difficult experience is to face it fully, and that this often takes courage. Remind him or her that by confronting the feelings and sensations fully and with support, they will dissipate and he or she can then gain insight into their origins.

For example, if the individual you are helping is discouraged, feeling that the struggle will never end, remind him or her to allow the process to continue without resisting it too much and that it will be completed naturally. If your friend or loved one experiences fear, offer reassurance that such reactions are common and acceptable, and, if possible, gently guide him or her to face the frightening feelings and memories.

It is important for you to tell people who feel alienated that they are not alone, that many others have had similar experiences. Remind them that these states of mind have been well documented throughout history and are highly respected and sought after by those who pursue spiritual practice. On the other side of the feeling of separation is a sense of unity; behind detachment is a sense of greater connection.

If your friend or loved one is facing an experience of insanity, let him or her know that these feelings are familiar and natural aspects of personal transformation and will ultimately lead to a higher degree of sanity. In a state of disorganization, limitations and narrow-mindedness are often destroyed. After moving through it, the person will find a new order.

You can use a similar approach with someone who is facing the experience of death. Be sure that the person is healthy, and request a medical checkup if there is any question. Tell him or her that symbolic dying in the process of transformation is one of the major turning points, perhaps mentioning the well-charted death-rebirth cycle. On the other side of a complete experience of death is a new life, a new way of being, a new self. After such assurances, you can then say, "Go ahead and die inwardly," reminding the individual that this psychological experience can feel very real.

Use your intuition. This is the part of you that has hunches and is able to discover direct knowledge or understanding without rational thought. Being around someone who is engaged in a nonrational experience such as a spiritual emergency requires a great deal of intuition:

because there are no firm solutions, spontaneous responses are often required. Even those who have had a great deal of exposure to spiritual emergencies have to remain open to all possibilities, since each person's experience is unique.

A good starting point is to take clues from the ones in crisis and be willing to experiment; very frequently, in their intuitive state, they know what they need. Certain foods are right and others are wrong, physical contact may or may not be helpful at different junctures, people or objects in their environment may be appropriate one day and inappropriate the next. Be willing to listen to such suggestions and honor them.

Avoid giving inappropriate messages. Since people in a spiritual emergency are often very open and intuitive, they readily receive both verbal and nonverbal communications from those around them. If they have their own doubts or fears about what they are going through, they may be acutely sensitive to any confirmation of these feelings from those they respect.

Be careful of your language. If you use words such as *crazy, sick, psychotic,* or *manic,* your loved one will most likely perceive them as verdicts confirming the hopelessness of the situation. Avoid obvious labels, classifications, or negative evaluations. For example, when appropriate, talk about manifestations rather than symptoms, opportunity or adventure rather than crisis, excitement rather than fear, episode rather than illness.

Watch the language of your actions; many responses contain hidden messages. If you are afraid of the process and want it to end, you will probably do things that relay just that message: you might try to prematurely return those in spiritual emergency to daily activities, asking them to pull themselves together at a time when they are moving toward an important experience of disintegration. Or if someone is very focused on the inner world, you might try to ask him or her to make eye contact rather than allowing him or her to focus on what is happening within. Your loved one may believe these messages, or he or she may know that they are not true and protect himself or herself by withdrawing from you or becoming agitated and difficult to reach.

Become open, receptive, and willing to listen. Very often, people in a transformation process need a sounding board, someone with whom they can share their new insights. If we have too much to tell them about what they are experiencing, offering our analyses and giving suggestions as to what should be done, there is a good chance that we will complicate the situation. In the more extreme forms of spiritual emergency, people often have difficulty handling too much verbal input. It is important, as we suspend our judgment and sense of control, that we learn to listen, offering our ideas only when appropriate or when asked for.

During an intense spiritual emergency, people frequently experience such an outpouring from their unconscious that they need to vent the experiences and emotions through words, sounds, songs, or poetry. Be available, quietly listening from a meditative and patient place within yourself. If you resonate empathically with what is being expressed, the other person will often be aware of this feeling without your having to say or do much.

If what you are hearing is offensive or threatening, quiet yourself and try to observe the situation as a witness, without being drawn into the emotional drama. This is more difficult if you are the target of such expressions. In this case, remind yourself that your loved one's assertions are most likely colored by emotions and memories that have little to do with you. This is obviously not the time to become involved in an argument; relationship issues should wait until after the spiritual emergency has been completed for resolution.

To help you to get through these difficult junctures, you might try imagining yourself as vast, empty space that has the capacity to absorb anything without negative effects. Or imagine that you are invisible and that the other person's words are moving right through you.

Be willing to offer physical comfort. People in spiritual emergencies will often tell you when they need to be touched, hugged, or held. Perhaps they feel very vulnerable and need to feel protected, or very tender, wishing to express their love through touch. After reliving birth they often experience themselves as tiny infants and want to be nurtured. Those who had very little emotional warmth in their childhood may want to be held as a corrective measure, to heal the void they feel inside. Or they may feel out of touch with the world and need the reassurance of contact with an earthbound friend. Because of this, it is essential that the people around them be willing to offer physical contact when it is asked for.

Many of us have our own reservations and inhibitions about touching, but it may be necessary to suspend our personal considerations for a time and respond to the need when it is expressed. Offering a warm body to comfort and nurture someone else can be very healing to the person in crisis if you are at ease.

In order for you to feel comfortable, it is important that you set your own limits. Sexual interaction of any kind is not appropriate if you do not already have an intimate relationship with the person, and should be temporarily avoided at some stages even if you are the person's spouse or lover. If someone is regressed, vulnerable, or working through a difficult memory, introducing your own sexual concerns could be confusing and hurtful. In addition, if the individual is dealing with powerful sexual impulses, he or she may try to engage someone nearby in erotic activities as an attempt to focus on the outer world in order to avoid the depth of his or her own internal experience.

It is perfectly acceptable to firmly but lovingly establish your boundaries. Then, remind the person that it is important and beneficial to face the emotions and feelings internally and help him or her to focus on the inner experience rather than on you. If you have difficulty in obtaining cooperation and the situation becomes uncomfortable, it is helpful to have a backup helper ready to take over, someone who may not be as sexually attractive to the individual.

Allow yourself to be playful and flexible. If you appear to be too stiff and anxious to control your own life, the person who is changing might feel threatened or irritated. If instead you can develop a flexible attitude and become willing to follow his or her experience in any direction, you will most likely feel a greater sense of cooperation and responsiveness from the individual.

Allow yourself to be experimental, since the very nature of the process is enormously creative. If your loved one is having trouble sleeping at night, rather than immediately offering a sleeping pill, suggest a long walk or a hot bath, or do a guided meditation that gently directs him or her within. Try a foot massage or a back rub.

Even though the transformation process is very important and serious, it is necessary to have a sense of humor and to be playful when appropriate. For example, if someone in crisis spends time singing and dancing, he or she might welcome others who are willing to sing and dance, too. By entering his or her world, those offering help can demonstrate their acceptance.

Have both male and female helpers on hand, if possible. There are times when it makes no difference to the person in crisis who is present, as long as they are caring and attentive. At other times, especially during the more demanding forms of spiritual emergency, there may be a specific need for either a man or a woman. If someone has just relived birth or an early childhood memory, he or she may want to be held by a woman who plays the role of mother. If the experience is all about one's father or some other masculine figure, it may be important to have contact with a man. For these reasons, it is always preferable to have both a male and female available if possible.

It can be difficult for a parent, spouse, sibling, or close friend to be present if he or she is the protagonist of a memory that the person is reliving. For example, if a woman relives an experience of incest with her father, it goes without saying that the father's presence at that time could be painful and confusing for both of them. If her husband is there, he could become the target of her anger and fear simply because he is the closest male, and this outpouring from his wife might contaminate their future relationship. In instances such as these, is it important to have a helper on hand who is not an intimate relation since such a person can most likely deal more effectively with any emotions that might be expressed.

What Family and Friends Can Do for Themselves

Because of your genuine love and concern for the person in crisis, it is easy for those of you close to him or her to forget about your own needs or to tire yourself by overcommitting your time and energy. To avoid these kinds of problems, what can family and friends do to help to survive and even benefit from the demands of someone else's spiritual emergency? Are there ways in which you can make such an event easier on yourself? We will offer some practical suggestions:

Educate yourself. The most important strategy for family and friends is to develop some understanding of what a spiritual emergency is, how it differs from mental illness, what to expect, and how to react. So much of the fear, confusion, guilt, and judgment that surrounds a transformational crisis comes from lack of knowledge. Read whatever related materials you can find and talk to people who have some personal familiarity with the subject. Because the field of spiritual emergency is relatively new, literature specifically describing the phenomenon is not widely available. This situation will undoubtedly change as an increasing number of books and articles on this subject become available.

At the back of this book we have included a bibliography for those who want more information. Many publications on transpersonal psychology, spiritual practice, mysticism, mythology, and anthropology, while not addressing the issue of spiritual emergency directly, can assist in expanding one's comprehension of this complex phenomenon.

Get support from others. Discuss feelings, worries, and concerns as they arise with someone who understands. This will likely answer some of your questions about spiritual emergency as well as dispel feelings of isolation. Make time to talk with knowledgeable friends, members of spiritual communities, or people you may contact through services such as the Spiritual Emergence Network. Find an insightful therapist or spiritual teacher whose theoretical framework includes the range of experiences in a spiritual emergency and use him or her as a resource.

A good preparation for dealing with the issues that arise during someone's spiritual emergency might be some exposure to experiential self-exploration in therapy or workshops. You can learn a great deal by being around a number of others who are confronting their own emotions and deep personal issues, as well as through having your own experiences.

We would like to see support groups established for families and friends of people going through spiritual emergencies. There, those with similar experiences could air their concerns and receive comfort, information, and effective strategies from each other. A great deal can be learned from twelve-step programs such as Al-Anon, Adult Children of Alcoholics, and Co-Dependents Anonymous, created for people directly involved in relationships with alcoholics and others who demonstrate addictive behavior.

Determine the degree to which you are willing and able to participate in your loved one's transformation. Every friend and family member has his or her own package of feelings about the loved one's spiritual emergency. We feel very strongly that each person needs to recognize how much he or she wants to participate in the process and to honor those impulses. You might find it useful and important to be present during the intense periods of your loved one's experience: you discover that you can be truly helpful and that the empathy and love that you feel in return is your reward for being there.

However, there is no point in pushing your participation if it creates too much stress in yourself. You may have to recognize that you simply cannot handle the things that are happening and, if there is other support available to the one in crisis, gently and lovingly remove yourself, returning when you feel more at ease with the situation. You might quietly and honestly tell your loved one why you are leaving, saying that this in no way reflects your degree of caring. It is rather a forthright acknowledgment of your own needs, which, if not addressed, could add to the already existing tensions. He or she might have felt your discomfort and will be relieved when you withdraw.

Abandon the idea that you can fix or control the situation. This issue is well known in twelve-step programs that deal with families of alcoholics and other addicts: someone in the family has a drug problem, and the others spend a great deal of time and energy trying to fix or control a situation that has its own course and dynamics. The results are frustration, anger, and resentment, which simply feed an already tense environment. Things change only when everyone admits his or her powerlessness (for the addict, powerlessness over the drug; for the family, powerlessness over the addict and his or her disease). Both the addict and the family members surrender to the fact that their egos are not in control of the situation and instead begin to rely on help from a Higher Power of their own definition—another person, a group, one's own deeper wisdom, or God.

Although the analogy is not exact, since a person in a spiritual emergency is not sick, many of the same considerations apply. It is absurd and frustrating for anyone to try to outguess, patch up, or control a process that is larger and wiser than any individual. On the other hand, no one in this situation is entirely helpless. As long as we know that our rational selves are not the experts in the situation, that a deeper influence is in control, it is possible to lend love and assistance in the same way a midwife supports a mother giving birth.

Use the situation as an opportunity to work on yourself. The emotions and experiences of someone else may activate parallel emotional and psychological issues in you. If you witness your daughter struggling with fear and anxiety, you may find yourself feeling anxious. If she is moving into a state of expansion and peace, you may discover yourself yearning for your own inner tranquillity. In situations such as these, your feelings might have been hidden for a long time, and the fact that they are now readily available is a wonderful opportunity for you to face them.

If such developments occur, you may want to involve yourself in some form of experiential therapy or spiritual practice. This in no way needs to detract from your loved one's emergence process; on the contrary, it can do a great deal to enhance it by allowing you to feel clearer, and may give you a common bond through shared experience.

Pursue activities that provide strength, inspiration, and relief. These will help you in dealing with stresses during your loved one's spiritual emergency. Some people join a group or participate in a fulfilling creative activity or sport, such as painting or running, which gives them the vitality necessary to handle whatever comes along. Others spend time in nature or engage in some form of spiritual practice, such as prayer or meditation. Find whatever appeals to you and use it regularly. The strength, peace, and acceptance that you find will assist you not only in living with the person in crisis, but in every other aspect of your life as well.

Be kind to yourself. Many of us are used to caring for other people at the expense of our own needs. Be sure you pay attention to your own physical requirements: get plenty of sleep, exercise, and regular nourishing meals. Continue to maintain necessary daily business and domestic responsibilities. Long walks or other forms of exercise, writing in a journal, attending a funny movie, taking a relaxing bath, or receiving a massage can all be wonderfully therapeutic if you have been exposed to the intensity of a spiritual emergency.

CHAPTER 10

WHO CAN HELP AND HOW?

"Curiouser and curiouser!" cried Alice . . . "Now I'm opening out like the largest telescope that ever was! . . . Oh my poor little feet, I wonder who will put on your shoes and stockings for you, my dears? I'm sure I shan't be able! I shall be a great deal too far off to trouble myself about you . . ."
LEWIS CARROLL, *Alice in Wonderland*

A person going through a spiritual emergency, whether mild or all-encompassing, often needs a reference point or support, someone based in everyday reality who can offer reassurance from his or her standpoint that everything is all right. If someone is floating beyond the daily world exploring new territories, he or she may need another person to hold the kite string; those delving into the depths need a lifeline. These experiences and ideas are strange, powerful, awesome, and disorienting. It is reassuring to be able to ask, "Am I still on the right track?" and to hear from a trustworthy, earthbound voice, "You are all right, you are safe, the world is still here and so am I. Go ahead and continue your adventure."

This chapter will discuss who can help to hold this kite string, as well as what to look for and what to avoid when one needs help. But before we move on to practical suggestions, we would like to tell the story of a young woman's spiritual emergency; it provides a vivid example of the kinds of issues that might be faced by someone in such a situation and also by those who wish to help.

Karen's Story

Karen is a graceful young woman in her late twenties, blond and lithe, who exudes a soft, dreamy beauty. Externally, she seems rather shy and quiet, but she is very bright and physically active. She had a difficult childhood; her mother committed suicide when she was three, and she grew up with an alcoholic father and his second wife. Leaving home in her late teens, she lived through periods of depression and struggled periodically with compulsive eating.

She traveled, studied, and fell in love with jazz dancing, becoming an accomplished dancer and occasional teacher. She liked to sing and developed professional competence as a skilled massage practitioner. Karen settled in the country, where she met and began living with Peter, a gentle and caring man; although they remained unmarried, they had a daughter, Erin, to whom they are both very devoted.

Karen's story represents the most dramatic end of the continuum between a gradual, gentle spiritual emergence and the extreme crisis of spiritual emergency. Even so, many of the issues surrounding her experience apply to anyone undergoing a transformational process. Much of what we will describe we were able to observe firsthand.

Five days before her episode, Karen had begun taking medication for an intestinal parasite, stopping it the day the experience started. The warning that accompanied the remedy indicated that a rare possible side effect was "psychotic reactions." It is difficult to accurately assess its role in the onset of this event. Although the medicine was possibly the trigger, the fact that side effects of this kind are relatively uncommon suggests that it could have been only one of many factors that precipitated the onset of her episode. Whatever the source, her crisis contained all the elements of a true spiritual emergency. It lasted three and a half weeks and completely interrupted her ordinary functioning, necessitating twenty-four-hour attention. After she had been in her spiritual emergency for a few days, some of her friends, who knew of our interest in this area, asked us to become involved in her care. We saw her almost every day during the last two and a half weeks of her episode.

KAREN'S HELPERS

As is the case with many spiritual emergencies, the onset of Karen's crisis was rapid and unexpected, and Karen became so absorbed in and overwhelmed by her experiences that she could not take care of herself or her three-year-old daughter, who stayed with her father. Her friends took turns caring for her twenty-four hours a day, under the supervision of a sympathetic physician.

The situation that evolved was a gesture of love and concern from the people who participated, and not a highly developed, well-tested professional effort. Because of Karen's obvious need and the reluctance of these around her to involve her in traditional psychiatric approaches, her care was largely improvised. Most of the people who became involved were not primarily dedicated to working with spiritual emergencies.

During the time of Karen's episode, we learned a great deal about what works and what does not and felt greatly encouraged by what we saw and experienced. It is a fascinating example of the potential of this kind of work as the primary focus of professionals and others with specific training in spiritual emergency.

When it became impossible for Karen to continue without help, a group of her friends decided that they would support her through her journey. Although there were several differing ideas as to how this should be done, there was an agreement that everyone wanted to avoid hospitalization. A close friend who was also an experienced therapist took charge of organizing the helpers and was responsible for many of the decisions that were made with regard to Karen's care.

Karen was moved from her house to a room in the home of several of her friends. It had been carefully prepared: with the exception of a bed, the furniture had been removed, so there were no sharp edges or hard surfaces on which she could hurt herself. The floor and walls were covered with mattresses and large pillows, providing a soft surface. Ajoining the room were a bathroom and a tiny kitchen. The physician, who lived nearby, examined Karen initially to be sure that she was physically healthy and continued to monitor her condition throughout the episode, making sure she received the necessary food, water, and vitamins.

Her friends then set up a "sitters' service": two people at a time signed up for two- to three-hour shifts throughout each twenty-four hours. Many of the helpers had training in various therapeutic approaches and brought with them extensive experience in working with other people. They became involved largely because of their friendship with Karen and because they were genuinely interested in the process of spiritual emergence. Even though most of them were familiar with deep emotional states, very few had ever been in the position of helping someone through such a long and difficult process. As a result, the care was not always consistent but essentially effective.

Everyone who participated understood that while Karen's process was physically and emotionally demanding for her, it would also be strenuous for her attendants. The relatively short sitters' hours were arranged so that Karen could receive high-quality support without her helpers becoming burned out.

A notebook was kept just outside the door so that sitters could sign in and out and write down their impressions of Karen's condition, what she had said or done, what liquids or food she had consumed, and what kinds of behavior the next couple should expect. Each sitter had a different style of being with her. Some actively worked with her, using various therapeutic methods that helped her face the issues and experiences that were emerging. Some simply sat with her as her unconscious flooded her, offering their strength and warmth and being sure that she was safe.

KAREN'S EXPERIENCES

On the first day of her episode, Karen noticed that her vision was suddenly clearer, not as "soft and fuzzy" as it usually was. She heard women's voices telling her that she was entering into a benign and important experience. As she began to slip into the world of her unconscious, she asked a close friend for help. Shortly thereafter, her friend, recognizing the depth and extent of Karen's state, organized and mobilized the sitters' service. She contacted some initial helpers, and others, hearing of the situation, volunteered their assistance.

For many days, tremendous heat radiated throughout Karen's body and she saw visions of fire and fields of red, at times feeling herself consumed by flames. To quench the extreme thirst she felt was brought about by the burning, she drank great quantities of water. She seemed to be carried through her episode by an enormous energy that poured through her, taking her to many levels of her unconscious and the memories, emotions, and other feelings and sensations contained there. Becoming very childlike, she relived biographical events such as her mother's suicide and subsequent physical abuse from her stepmother. Once, a childhood memory of being beaten with a belt suddenly shifted, and she felt herself to be a suffering black African being whipped on a crowded slave ship.

She struggled through the physical and emotional pain of her own biological birth and repeatedly relived the delivery of her daughter. She experienced death many times and in many forms, and her preoccupation with dying caused her sitters to become concerned about the possibility of a suicide attempt. However, such an occurence was unlikely because of the safety of her environment and the close scrutiny of the helpers. Everyone involved kept a particularly close watch on her, staying with her constantly and encouraging her to keep the experiences internalized rather than acting them out.

Periodically, she felt that she was in connection with her dead mother, as well as with a friend who had died in an accident just a year before. She said she missed them and yearned to join them. At other times, she felt she was watching other people die or that she herself was dying.

Telling her that it was possible to experience death symbolically without actually dying physically, her sitters asked her to keep her eyes closed and encouraged her to fully experience these sequences of dying inwardly and to express the difficult emotions involved. She complied, and in a short time she moved past the intense confrontation with death to other experiences.

For a couple of days, Karen was swept by sequences involving elements of evil. At times she felt as though she was an ancient witch, participating in magic sacrificial rituals: at other times she sensed a terrible monster within her. As the diabolical beast expressed its demonic energies, she flooded the room with angry explicatives and rolled on the floor, making ferocious faces. Her sitters, realizing that the outpouring was not directed at them, protected her and encouraged further expression.

Sometimes her experience centered around sexuality. After reliving some traumatic memories from her own sexual history, she felt a strong source of energy in her pelvis. After having regarded sexuality as a lowly instinctual impulse, she had a profound spiritual experience in which she discovered the same insight that is offered by certain esoteric traditions: the sexual impulse is not simply a biological drive, but also a divine, spiritual force. She felt that she was the first woman to have been granted such an awareness, and she expressed a new reverence for her mystical role as a life-giving mother.

During another period, Karen felt united with the earth and its people, both of which she feared were about to be destroyed. She envisioned that the planet and its population were heading toward annihilation, putting forth clear and sophisticated insights about the world situation. She saw images of Soviet and American leaders with their fingers on "the button," and offered accurate and often humorous comments about international politics.

For several days, Karen tapped directly into a powerful stream of creativity, expressing many of her experiences in the form of songs. It was amazing to witness: after an inner theme would surface into awareness, she would either make up a song about it or recall one from memory, lustily singing herself through that phase of her process.

Karen was extremely psychic, highly sensitive, and acutely attuned to the world around her. She was able to "see through" everyone around her, often anticipating their comments and actions. One sitter had been discussing Karen before going in to see her. Upon entering the room, he was amazed by Karen's accurate re-creation of his conversation. Much to the discomfort of those involved, she commented very frankly about any personal or interpersonal games that she saw being played and immediately confronted anyone who was too controlling or rigid, refusing to cooperate with them.

After about two weeks, some of the difficult, painful states started to subside and Karen received increasingly benevolent, light-filled experiences and felt more and more connected with a divine source. She saw within herself a sacred jewel, a radiant pearl that she felt symbolized her true center, and she spent a lot of time tenderly speaking to it and nurturing it. She received instructions from an inner source about how to love and care for herself, and she felt the emotional wounds that she had carried in her heart and body being healed. She said that she felt special, "newborn," having passed through a "second birth," remarking, "I am opening to life, to love, light, and self."

As Karen began to come through her experience, she became less and less absorbed by her inner world and more interested in her daughter and the other people around her. She began to eat and sleep more regularly and was increasingly able to care for some of her daily needs. She wanted to finish her experience and return to her home, and it became clear to her that the people around her were also ready for the episode to end. Many long hours and constant attention had exhausted their resources, and although they were willing to spend some time with her and talk with her, they needed to return to their own lives. An agreement was reached among Karen and her helpers that she would try to resume the responsibilities of daily care for herself and her daughter.

As she became increasingly in touch with ordinary reality, Karen's mind started to analyze her experiences, and she began to feel for the first time that she had been involved in a negative process. The only logical way of explaining these events to herself was that something had gone wrong, that perhaps she had truly lost her mind. Self-doubt is a common stage in spiritual emergencies, appearing when people begin to surface from the dramatic manifestations: they become embarrassed and judgmental about their unusual behavior. Some people have compared this feeling to waking up with a hangover after a night of wild, outrageous partying. With a sinking feeling, they ask, "What did I do?" "Who saw it?" and "Was it all right?" Many of these concerns were compounded by the message that Karen was getting from many of the people around her: now it was time to return to the concerns of daily life.

Karen went home to Erin and Peter, where she had to learn rapidly how to once again operate in the ordinary world. She wrote in her journal:

> *Homework now could be:*
> *Connect with women friends,*
> *Slow down,*

Clean up,
And get my health back.
And—
Stay Open,
Open to heart, heavens,
Earth, life, love,
Plants, dogs, flies, etc.
And allow for my needs.

Karen was still very shaky and at the mercy of some strong emotions and experiences. Fortunately, because she lived in a rural setting, Karen could spend a lot of time in nature, where she continued to confront and express the still-strong physical energies, fragments of memories, and other experiences as they arose. She sporadically spent time with sympathetic friends but lacked any consistent follow-up contact with others who could have helped. Eventually, her inner world subsided and she returned to her familiar, effective ways of functioning.

The attempts of her friends to help Karen had the drawbacks that come with an improvised and limited situation, such as the exhaustion of the sitters' resources. Even so, they were a much healthier alternative than hospitalization and suppressive medication would have been, since she was able to work through many difficult aspects of her past. She was also allowed to undergo a great deal of the episode without being burdened with the notion that she was sick. Immediately after emerging, she described her experience: "I cracked my mirror" and "I cracked my egg." If she had received traditional treatment and had become convinced that she was ill, she might not have been able to develop this attitude, which reflects the breaking of old limitations and the freeing of something new.

Two years later, when we discussed her experience with her, Karen said that she has mixed feelings about the episode. She is able to appreciate many aspects of what happened to her. She says that she has learned a great deal of value about herself and her capacities, feeling that through her crisis she gained wisdom that she can tap anytime. Karen has visited realms within herself that she previously had no idea were there, has felt enormous creativity flow through her, and has survived the previously frightening experiences of birth, death, and madness. Her depressions have disappeared, as well as her tendency toward compulsive overeating.

Difficult emotions do not arise as frequently as they did, and she has developed a relaxed, fuller expression in her singing, a wider range of movement in her dance, and a serious interest in drawing. She told us that she felt energized and excited when talking about the episode and was very eager to learn more that would help to explain what happened to her.

On the other hand, Karen also has some criticisms. Even though she could not have resisted the powerful states during her episode, she feels that she was unprepared for the hard, painful work involved. In spite of the fact that she received a great deal of assistance during the three weeks, she feels that she was not yet ready to venture forth into the daily world when she was required to do so by the exhaustion of the resources of those around her. Since that time, she has lacked contact with people with whom to further process her experiences. She considers herself somewhat "different" for having had the episode (an opinion also indirectly expressed by her family and some of her friends) and has tended to downgrade it by concentrating on its negative aspects.

Many of these problems could have been avoided if Karen had had consistent and knowledgeable support immediately following her crisis, perhaps in a halfway house, and follow-up help—in the form of ongoing therapy, support groups, and spiritual practice—for a more extended period of time.

Who Can Help?

Keeping Karen's story in mind, let us look at the resources that are or could be available for someone like her, as well as for people who are experiencing milder forms of spiritual emergency.

An essential requirement for those who become involved with someone in a spiritual emergency is genuine concern, caring, or love. Without that, it is easy to become engaged in manipulations and controlling games that impede the process and possibly hurt the one in whom it is happening. It is not always imperative for trained professionals to assist someone during a transformation crisis. Some well-prepared families or groups of friends may feel equipped to deal with their loved one's transformation process, especially if it is relatively mild. Ideally, the helpers should have some knowledge, through reading or counseling, of the dynamics of the process, its positive potential, and its healing properties. Sometimes an intuitive individual who has no formal understanding can be helpful, but this solution is definitely second best.

On the other hand, there are times when the knowledge and experience of a sympathetic psychologist, psychiatrist, medical doctor, priest, social worker, or transpersonal psychotherapist is essential. Family and friends may feel comfortable up to a point and then need assistance from someone with knowledge and training in the area. If the situation involves extreme mental, emotional, and physical states and occurs over an extended period of time, it will be necessary to enlist the help of a physician in order to rule out medical complications and of someone who is sophisticated in the knowledge and understanding of nonordinary realities.

We have heard stories of spouses, families, or friends who, with no outside help and no formal training or even understanding of the powerful experiences, intuitively helped a loved one through a spiritual emergency. The ensuing stress and confusion make this kind of solitary approach far from ideal, and is not something we would recommend.

Because the field of spiritual emergency is relatively new, in this transitional period the need for assistance is greater than the number of individuals who can offer it. We feel very encouraged that more and more people are becoming personally and professionally interested in transpersonal psychology and are being trained in approaches that acknowledge and work with deep emotional and spiritual states. But we are also aware that it will most likely take some time before widespread care and understanding of transformative crises are readily accessible.

In the meantime, we can outline what is already available as well as some of the ideas, both general and specific, that may be implemented in the near future. Since each situation involves different experiences with varying degrees of intensity, different personalities, and different environments, it is impossible to offer a definitive prescription to those who want to assist. We encourage you to mold our suggestions to fit your own situation.

A twenty-four-hour care facility. Wherever we have traveled in the world, when we talk about spiritual emergency someone always asks the question, Where can we find a good twenty-four-hour care facility that incorporates the ideas you have been discussing? It has been discouraging to have to admit that there are not many. In appendix 2 we outline our dream for such facilities. The basic concept is a place where people can safely go through a spiritual emergency with support from staff members trained in transpersonal approaches who have had their own experiences as part of the preparation.

We are aware that some hospitals occasionally allow patients to progress through their experiences, not using drugs or other interventions to arrest them. However, this is the exception and often depends on an individual staff member's influence. And it is likely to be done without an understanding of the transpersonal nature of the process and its healing potential. In addition, any hospital setting automatically indicates to the person that he or she is sick.

A sitters' service. During our involvement in the area of spiritual emergency, we have known of several situations in which friends and family arranged to provide the necessary guidance and support during a spiritual emergency by arranging a sitters' service, in the way that one was created to help Karen. This occurred when someone needed twenty-four-hour care and there was no acceptable facility available. Although non-professional sitters' services have worked adequately, there are obvious drawbacks, such as a potential lack of understanding and knowledge of nonordinary realities and the taxing nature of the process for those who are unprepared. Following is our idealized concept of a sitter's service:

Like Karen, the person in crisis remains at home or in a homelike setting. The sitters' service is therefore not set up in a permanent location; rather, those involved make themselves available to the person according to need. The service is organized by a professional or professionals with the cooperation of a sympathetic physician. These professionals have had training in working with spiritual emergencies.

Sitters have a knowledge of deep emotional and spiritual states and have preferably had their own experiences of nonordinary realities through transpersonally oriented therapy, spiritual practice, or their own crises. Although their specific approaches may vary, everyone shares a central theoretical and therapeutic strategy that recognizes and trusts the healing potential of spiritual emergencies and the deep wisdom of the process itself.

During the course of the crisis, the sitters have regular meetings with the coordinator to discuss the issues that have arisen. They also meet after the episode is over to evaluate the situation. When the time comes for the person in spiritual emergency to return to ordinary life, the decision is made by everyone involved, including the person in crisis. Sitters arrange for an effective support system—such as halfway houses, professional help, support groups, and regular contact with others who have had spiritual emergencies—during the critical days or weeks that follow a spiritual emergency. This will help the individual accept and integrate the experiences and proceed with further self-exploration if necessary.

The advantages of a sitters' service, besides the obvious one of eliminating the complications of psychiatric labels and medications, include the fact that the person is allowed to remain in a familiar setting or at home, in a situation that is comfortable, with people that he or she knows and trusts.

Mental-health professionals familiar with spiritual emergencies. There might be times in the transformation process when it becomes appropriate to call upon the professional resources of a social worker, psychologist, psychiatrist, counselor, or other kind of therapist. An ideal therapist serves as a compassionate coadventurer with someone who is engaged in a deep and far-reaching journey that will produce answers and insights often defying ordinary logic. He or she should have a conceptual framework that covers the wide spectrum of experiences that are possible in a spiritual emergency. Such a facilitator recognizes the beneficial nature of the transformation process and treats symptoms as opportunities for healing, not indications of disease, working with them rather than attempting to suppress them. He or she trusts that, with encouragement and support, the client can pass through the difficult stages of the spiritual emergency, finding new strength and greater insight in the process. The therapist also believes that the client, given the right circumstances, can guide his or her own process. He or she knows how to create a safe and supportive context for deep personal transformation and senses when to allow the client to proceed without any intervention and when to offer guidance.

The needs that are addressed by the therapist may change according to the level of experience with which the individual is dealing. For example, if the person is dealing with childhood memories, the professional uses his or her knowledge of biography to help unravel the past. If one is reliving birth, the therapist offers a technique to facilitate that. If the experiences focus primarily on the spiritual, mythological, or archetypal realms, he or she needs to work with those levels.

The problem with choosing someone who is focused on only one area is that if and when the inner process moves to another level, the professional may not know what to do. A therapist whose conceptual framework is limited to postnatal biography may try to return someone who is having an experience of the Divine Mother to his or her childhood memories, ignoring the current situation. The very best facilitator for a spiritual emergency is one who accepts all possibilities of human experience and can easily follow the client from level to level, in whatever direction he or she needs to go. Such a therapist is willing to try new strategies if they are indicated and supports possible involvement in spiritual practice as an adjunct to therapy.

An ideal therapist or team of therapists offers both verbal and experiential therapy, as well as addressing the various levels of experience during a client's emergence. Verbal therapy allows you to meet regularly with an open-minded professional to discuss the personal and interpersonal issues that arise during your life in order to help you discover your own solutions. This can be an extremely effective way of gaining insight, guidance, and reassurance during your journey, and can help those whose spiritual emergency is intense to integrate and absorb it afterwards.

For someone who is engaged in a more active and demanding form of spiritual emergency, however, verbal therapy alone is not enough. He or she often needs to actively work with intense energies, emotions, and experiences that cannot be merely discussed. Overwhelming rage or anxiety cannot be talked away; it needs to be expressed in a safe and supportive atmosphere, as part of a purging process. A number of experiential therapies, such as Holotropic Breathwork,™ offer this kind of situation. To be fully effective, they must be based on a theoretical model that includes the entire range of human experience, including the biographical, perinatal, and transpersonal levels. In the hands of a facilitator who has this kind of understanding, powerful approaches such as Gestalt practice, bioenergetics, process-oriented psychotherapy, and neo-Reichian release work can be very effective.

Open-minded physicians. Since spiritual emergency involves emotional, spiritual, and bodily aspects, there are often periods when you might experience distinct physical manifestations that may resemble biological problems. At these times, it is imperative to consult a medical doctor to be sure that any pains, palpitations, or tremors do not have medical origins. It would be ideal to obtain the services of a doctor who is completely aware of the dynamics of spiritual emergency, its manifestations, and its prognosis. He or she would then be able to distinguish the symptoms common to a transformation process from those that have biological origins and treat them accordingly. However, since this is a relatively new field, there are not yet many physicians with such a background.

A medical professional with a holistic orientation, even though he or she may not be specifically aware of the phenomena inherent in a spiritual emergency, may have an open attitude that will support such a process. When relating to physicians without such a background, it is best to avoid discussions of metaphysical issues, since the experiences might be misunderstood. Limit the interaction to a description of symptoms, focusing on the tests that will discern their origin and significance.

A spiritual teacher. Sometimes a transformation process will take you in a direction that you will eventually identify as belonging to a particular spiritual system. A person who has a certain constellation of physical, emotional, and experiential manifestations might realize that he or she is involved in the Kundalini process, has experienced what Zen Buddhists call a *kensho*, or enlightenment state, or has been undergoing something that resembles a shamanic initiation. If this happens, you might find it valuable, and even necessary, to seek out a good teacher within that tradition who has had the experiences, understands them, and knows how to support them in others. He or she can also offer tools to further expand your own process, work with it, and integrate it into daily practice.

It is important to find a practice in which one's process is supported and honored, rather than treated as something to repress or discourage. Some traditions, such as Siddha Yoga, the approach taught by Swami Muktananda and his successor, recognize, discuss, and accept the emotional, physical, and spiritual experiences that meditators have when they sit. Some charismatic churches actively encourage such states, regarding them as genuine expressions of devotion and manifestations of the Divine.

Other kinds of prayer and meditation practice advise people to observe images and sensations as they arise and allow them to pass. Teachers actively discourage emotional expression and encourage students to quiet their minds rather than become seduced by the inner drama. These effective subtler approaches may be temporarily inappropriate for someone who is swimming in a rich inner world of colorful images and feels impelled to make dramatic physical movements.

The wisdom, guidance, and presence of advanced teachers can be very helpful. If they have done a lot of inner work, the results of their own transformation have become apparent in the way they conduct their lives and relate to themselves and the world. Simply spending time with such teachers can be healing, instructive, and inspirational.

Not all who claim to be spiritual teachers are of high caliber. We will discuss what to look for in a spiritual teacher, as well as in a therapist, later. For now, a general guideline for choosing either is that he or she does not claim to have the exclusive answers to life's problems, but instead is someone who will guide and support you in finding your own solutions.

A spiritual or therapeutic community. Joining a spiritual or therapeutic community does not necessarily mean you will have to dedicate your life to it. However, if you have found an effective spiritual teacher or therapist and discover that he or she is involved in such a group, you might consider spending some time with that group. Traditional spiritual groups include Native American fellowships, Christian contemplative orders, Buddhist communities or *sanghas*, and ashrams. There are also various therapeutic groups that have formed around a particular technique and human-potential centers that offer a variety of approaches.

Again, it is essential that the group be knowledgeable about the experiences you are having and that it be willing to support and work with you if necessary. In such a setting, there are most likely those who have had the same experiences that you are having and can help to guide you. These are also places to learn tools—such as prayer, meditation, group chanting, shamanic practices, and therapeutic methods—that will help to facilitate and integrate your experiences.

However a spiritual discipline might be structured, the freedom given to someone who has a spiritual emergency is often the choice of the teacher. A Zen Buddhist master told us of a young man who had come to study in a *sangha*. When his experiences developed into a crisis, "we told him to stop meditating and we put him in the kitchen, chopping vegetables. When he couldn't any longer focus on that, we asked him to work in the garden. When gardening became too demanding, we just let him run around in the pasture, doing what he needed to do, until he was through. And then he could return to his practice."

The young man was fortunate to have the support of a sympathetic community that was open to the spectrum of experiences he was having. Although their structured Zen practice does not promote this kind of manifestation, they were tolerant and adventuresome enough to follow him through his episode. Unfortunately, this attitude is not standard for all spiritual groups.

Peer support groups. A group of people who have gone through spiritual emergencies could provide tremendously effective help to someone who is in the middle of a critical period. Existing self-help groups for many areas, such as drug and alcohol problems, eating disorders, rape trauma, and others, are comprised of lay people in different stages of their journey who share common experiences and understanding. For a person in crisis, such groups provide a forum for discussing problems and feelings and provide empathy and understanding. They can also help you to develop a sense of how to talk about your experiences and with whom. There is a good chance that you will feel immensely relieved to be in the company of others who viscerally understand you and are willing to listen without being judgmental. With them, you can gain a sense of community and lose some of the feelings of loneliness and isolation that could lead you to believe you are the only one who has ever had such experiences.

Someone like Karen could gain a tremendous sense of confirmation from a support group during the months and perhaps years that follow an extreme crisis. Those in whom the emergence process is less dramatic could use the group as an ongoing, regular base of support. However, although they exist for many other needs, to our knowledge there are none for those who are going through or have been through a spiritual emergency. With the experience gained from other fellowships, such groups could easily be started and would provide a valuable service to a substantial population.

A good body worker. Many schools of body work believe that emotions and experiences are somehow stored in the muscles of our bodies. Someone with training in massage or other forms of physical manipulation can assist in their release. During a spiritual emergency, when feelings, memories, and sensations are already becoming unblocked, someone with appropriate training can facilitate such a process.

As the practitioner works, images, memories, or emotions may be released as muscular tension is relaxed. Many realize that they have physically repressed memories of painful situations, as well as their reactions to them, and that body work helps to free them. An ideal practitioner is willing to encourage a client to move into some sort of expression if it arises naturally during the session.

Someone who has lived through his or her own crisis. Often people come out of their own transformation with the feeling that their next step is to help those who may be just as bewildered, overwhelmed, fearful, excited, or confused as they were. If they have experimental the heights and depths of their own emergence process, they have gained a unique experiential training that can be extremely valuable in assisting others. This does not mean pushing their revelations, insights, or ideology in a messianic way, but simply listening and talking about their own journey without demanding that the other person respond in a specific manner.

Prior experience also enables them to comfortably support another's process in all of its complexity and drama, since they know those territories from the inside out. Because they have been there, they do not feel judgmental or superior. Having experienced their own healing, they have confidence in the positive potential of the situation. This is a very different kind of knowledge from that which comes from reading about such experiences; it is a wisdom that is gained from living through them. Just as recovering drug addicts and alcoholics who continue to participate in their own growth are some of the most effective helpers in the treatment of others with those problems, those who have had spiritual emergencies and have successfully integrated the experiences are very effective in working with others on the same journey.

Close friends and family members. These are people who, simply by virtue of their already-established relationship to the person in a spiritual emergency, often find themselves in the position of helpers whether or not they ask for it. Their deep bond can be either a help or a hindrance. Their trust and love can provide an emotionally healing environment. If they live in close proximity, they may be able to provide a familiar and comfortable sanctuary to the one in crisis.

A combination of the above. An ideal situation for anyone in a spiritual emergency is to have all of these resources available, and to be able to create an individual package to fit specific needs. You can work regularly with a good psychologist who knows and understands your spiritual teacher, providing ways to combine your insights in therapy with the lessons from your practice. In addition, you might attend a weekly support group during which your circle of friends grows to include people who have also experienced what you are going through. You may periodically attend retreats given by your teacher, which deepen and expand your experiences and understanding. When you go to your doctor, you can speak freely about the other elements in your life that may have a bearing on your physical condition. And you may go home to family members who not only understand but are also actively involved in their own spiritual growth.

If you are someone like Karen, who, for a time, could not function effectively in daily life, having a twenty-four-hour care facility available can give you a safe place in which you are temporarily removed from the world. Here you can go through your crisis with understanding and love. And when you return to the world, you will be able to use the resources mentioned above for further healing.

What and Whom to Avoid

Some situations and people get in the way of the transformation process, interrupting it, slowing it down, making it seem something other than what it is, or complicating it in other ways. Again, because each instance is different and each person has individual needs, you may find specific things to add to the list.

Certain routinely applied measures are counterproductive. Tranquilizers and other medications may be useful for dealing with certain psychiatric disorders, but we believe that their widespread usage for undertermined causes is unwarranted. If someone is going through a true spiritual emergency, sedatives will operate against the thrust of the healing process. They often add to the person's confusion and disorientation, and they present the problems of possible side effects and chemical dependency. The regular administration of drugs conveys the message that the individual is sick, rather than acknowledging the possibility that he or she is on the path toward wholeness. For this reason, extreme caution should be exercised in the use of medications and other repressive approaches.

The same applies for psychiatric labels. Although in certain cases such definitions are helpful in categorizing and treating patients, diagnostic boundaries are often fuzzy, and people are frequently mislabeled or given diagnoses that do not really apply. This is certainly the case with individuals going through a spiritual emergency who are routinely mislabeled by well-meaning professionals.

It is important to remember that most of us are products of a culture that sees the transformation process as something to be avoided, so that if it happens to us, we automatically think that it is bad or we are sick. If we then receive labels and medications from experts, our fearful side responds, "I was right. There is something terribly wrong with me." It is essential that both the healing community and people going through this process shift their emphasis to treat such a process for its healthy potential, seeing it as an impulse toward wholeness, an opportunity to expand our possibilities.

In the middle of a spiritual emergency, we often feel helpless and welcome assistance from any source, becoming all too willing to put our lives in the hands of someone who claims he or she can restore us to our usual condition. Many therapists feel that they have the training, technique, and understanding that allow them to "fix" a person, in the way that a mechanic fixes a car. This kind of approach will not work with someone who is in a spiritual crisis, since it shifts the responsibility for the process from the deep healing wisdom contained within each of us to the limited scope of an outside individual. It is therefore important to avoid a therapist or guide who offers himself or herself as an expert, someone who has the answers to all of your problems.

Choosing a Therapist, Teacher, or Guide

When the emergence process reaches a point at which you can no longer manage with your own resources, or when you feel that the situation is too taxing on your usual relationships, it is time to find some outside help. Although the area of spiritual emergency is relatively new and there are not yet many people specifically trained to work with those in a transformative crisis, there are many qualified guides available.

Over the years, we have developed our own biases regarding the choice of a good therapist, spiritual teacher, or transformational guide. Following are some of our suggestions:

He or she should have had sufficient training in the technique or discipline involved; ideally, the guide will have had personal experiential exposure to the territories to which clients are introduced. For example, a Gestalt therapist or Holotropic Breathwork™ practitioner has been well educated in theoretical matters, as well as having done a great deal of personal inner work with the approach, experiencing its power as well as its therapeutic potential. His or her conceptual framework is very broad, including all possible areas of human experience, and he or she is willing to follow a client in any necessary direction.

An effective teacher or therapist has humility and compassion and is dedicated to service, maintaining an ethical stance that will not allow the manipulation of others for personal gain. He or she constantly points clients to their own inner resources as the key to strength and growth, rather than taking the credit for their personal or spiritual development or becoming the ultimate object of devotion.

An important qualification is a sense of humor—the ability to laugh at oneself, at any given situation, or at the entire cosmic game. The teacher or guide who has this quality does not take himself or herself too seriously, although the work and the relationship to the work are very serious.

It is essential that there be a resonance between the student and the teacher or therapist. This resonance has nothing to do with what your mind may tell you is appropriate or what you feel you *should* do; it comes from a feeling of trust and confidence as well as an essential attraction to the person and his or her work. Because a person in a spiritual emergency is often emotionally vulnerable, sometimes his or her decisions are based on unfulfilled desires rather than present needs. For this reason, it is important to discuss your choice of a therapist with an objective person whom you trust.

Perhaps these qualifications sound too stringent, and you may ask, "Can I find anyone like that?" We have described the *ideal* therapist or guide, and it may become necessary to make a few compromises. However, there are many qualified people who are not well-known professionals, shamans, or gurus, who quietly do their work within a very small circle. It may take some effort to find them, through transpersonally oriented groups or institutes, but the extra time and research will be well worth it. There are all too many of us who are willing to give our existence over to just anyone, with the plea, "I can't manage my life. You do it." Unfortunately, such a desperate self-abandonment can result in great confusion and even damage at the hands of an unethical, manipulative, and self-seeking authority.

In all spiritual disciplines, the teacher is one who has studied, practiced, and preferably had personal experiences before he or she is ready to guide others. In some traditions, such a person is chosen only through the direct transmission of a certain lineage that has been developed, refined, and revered over many years. The seemingly simple techniques that serve such adepts are in fact complex practices that take years to master.

The same kinds of concerns apply to some people who call themselves therapists, having started working with people after a very brief exposure to one of the many available techniques. Just as a spiritual teacher has spent a great deal of time developing his or her practice, a good therapist needs to have had sufficient personal and professional exposure to his or her school of therapy. He or she has studied and experienced the approach in depth and thoroughly knows its potentials and pitfalls.

When you are choosing a therapist, interview him or her the way would interview someone for a job. Do not be afraid to ask questions about background, qualifications, the definition of his or her role, and the degree of personal and professional exposure to spirituality, nonordinary states, and transpersonal approaches, as well as about any specific personal concerns you may have.

The same general guidelines apply when looking for a spiritual teacher. There are advertisements in various spiritually oriented journals for a wide range of teachers and disciplines. You might read a book and want to study with the author or someone who comes from that discipline. Ask the same questions of a teacher and the people around him or her as you would a therapist, keeping in mind the qualifications you are looking for. Listen to your own inner voice, be sure that your choice *feels* right, and then proceed, knowing that you can change your mind if there are any indications that you have made the wrong selection or if someone better emerges.

Avoid therapists, spiritual teachers, and guides who are rigid, limited, and dogmatic. Such people are arrogant and exclusive, claiming to have *the* answers or *the* way. Demonstrating little humor, they take themselves and their work very seriously. Such people often have done very little consequential personal work and may have had insufficient exposure to the method they are employing with others. Even if they have received training, it is likely limited to conceptual analysis and theory and has very little to do with real human experience. Psychiatrists in this category are uncomfortable with emotions in other people and themselves and tend to prescribe tranquilizers and other medications as solutions to most of their clients' problems.

Beware of therapists or teachers who frequently tell you about their accomplishments and mention clients or students who are wealthy or otherwise prominent. Avoid guides who take credit for fixing clients or students, using such phrases as "I took care of her fear of heights," and thus accepting responsibility for changes that have taken place. Such individuals may also become dependent on clients or students as a way of claiming their identity, perhaps prolonging the relationship in order to fill their own needs.

It is not always easy to know where to start when looking for a good therapist or spiritual teacher. There is no such thing as a telephone number in the yellow pages or a reference in the local newspaper, though this may change as the importance of spiritual emergencies becomes recognized and accepted.

The Spiritual Emergence Network has served as a resource in providing information and services to people in need. SEN's address and telephone number are listed in appendix I. If you are looking for a therapist, you might also contact the Association for Transpersonal Psychology, in Palo Alto, California, or a college or graduate school that offers courses in transpersonal psychology. Ask if they know of therapists with a transpersonal orientation.

Those trained in Holotropic Breathwork™ have both the experience and conceptual framework necessary for working in this area; lists of certified facilitators are available through the International Association of Holotropic Breathwork™ (4286 Redwood Hwy., Ste. A550, San Rafael, CA 94903; 415/479-4703). A Jungian analyst who is comfortable working with strong emotional and physical feelings can be helpful. In general, the Jungian approach tends to be somewhat intellectual but starts from a broad understanding of human experience that includes a spiritual dimension. Contact your local Jungian organization and explain your needs. If you attend a self-help group, ask if other people know of someone who is open to and accepting of the demands of a transformational journey.

There are always exceptional practitioners in any school of therapy. A woman who was undergoing what was later identified as a Kundalini awakening found a Freudian therapist who told her, "I haven't a clue about what is happening to you, and I don't know where it is taking you, but I am willing to support you in whatever you need to do." With his adventuresome spirit and encouragement, she was able to complete a difficult period of transformation and move on to a healthier relationship with herself and the world.

Often the therapy is as good as the therapist, so do not limit yourself to certain psychological schools or become closed to finding possibilities in unexpected places. For example, someone trained in rebirthing, while accepting the reality of the birth memory, may be completely closed to the possibility of spiritual experiences, while another rebirther might readily support clients in any direction their process takes them.

A few words of wisdom regarding others who might present them-selves as helpers—family members or friends who are not willing merely to serve as facilitators or midwives to a process with its own dynamics. A good way to separate those who really want to be in attendance from those who are inappropriate is to look at their motivations. As we have mentioned previously, those who become involved, whether profession-als, friends, or family members, should be there because they genuinely care about the person in spiritual emergency, believe in the healing po-tential of the process, and want to help. If people are there strictly because of their curiosity, their need to control or show off, or their own longing to be needed, their presence will most likely be restrictive or bothersome.

There are certain environments that are also counterproductive. If possible, avoid sterile institutional arrangements, which emphasize ill-ness, as well as those that operate from an inflexible and dogmatic po-sition, such as some families, schools, religious organizations, and commun-ities. Avoid any environment that offers judgment, anger, and arrogance instead of love, support, and attention. If such settings are all that is available to you, look for individual staff members who may be doing work that diverges from the traditional approach and are sympathetic to your needs.

CHAPTER 11

THE HOMECOMING

The gentle world around me is radiant
    and sparkling.
Thank you for returning me
    to my miraculous home!
Its kindly presence
    welcomes me
    warms me
    envelops me
    like the generous arms of a loving parent.
This familiar home is where I began
    so long ago.
Everything here is different now,
    and yet, it's all the same.
WRITTEN AFTER A SPIRITUAL EMERGENCY

The preceding chapters have addressed what to do during a transformation process, offering suggestions to those who are going through the experience as well as to the people around them. Now comes the period when one returns to daily life, whether after a relatively subtle awakening or an all-consuming crisis. What can one expect to feel during this time of transition? What are the benefits, as well as the challenges, of this time? How can you participate in the further integration of your life-changing experiences? And what lasting changes can you look forward to?

This period is the homecoming. People at this stage frequently experience a new home within themselves, an inner source of comfort and nourishment. They also often discover or rediscover meaningful and comforting elements in the world around them, such as sustaining relationships with those who are close or familiar environments and activities. However, because so much in a person's life can change as a result of a spiritual emergency, this period, too, is not without its challenges.

Some of the general changes include the elimination of many difficult personal problems, the addition of positive elements in one's life, a shift in values, and an increased significance of the spiritual dimension. These are the rewards toward which people have been traveling during the

212

transformational process. They may have a sense of being reborn and rejuvenated; they feel very different than they did at the start of the journey, born into a healthier relationship with themselves and the world.

A sense of renewal may or may not happen all at once. Some people experience a sudden resolution of their emergency and a rapid and easy transition into a new, effective way of being. Most people, however, go through a time of reentry during which they are somewhat unsure of themselves and of their place in the world.

In general, none of the diverse and sometimes dramatic experiences we have described are of any value unless they are brought back into ordinary reality and applied in the behavior and activities of daily life. Many spiritual traditions warn that the transcendental realms can be seductive and that we can be tempted to abandon the world in their favor.

Perhaps it is suitable for some people to turn away from the world in the exclusive pursuit of the spirit. Serious candidates for ashrams and monasteries fit into this category. However, most of us find our true calling in everyday pursuits, work in the world, and relationships with other people. Through our own transformation, we can discover a deep mystical meaning in the activities of our daily existence. And we may develop the insight that any significant spiritual contribution begins with the person next to us.

Coming back into everyday life does not imply giving anything up. Instead, it means bringing what we have gained during our adventures in the unconscious realms back into the domain in which we live twenty-four hours a day. By doing this, we can merge the two worlds and discover that the divine impulse is everywhere. We learn to seek and to see it all around us, in every action we take, in every person we encounter.

Joseph Campbell, in *The Hero with a Thousand Faces*, masterfully describes the reentry problems. As we discussed in chapter 6, the elements of the hero's journey reflect the inner experiences of a person traveling through transformation. The hero has left home, a place of safety and known reality, and has set out on an expedition that takes him or her into lands of mystery and adventure. Here he or she is met by many challenges and initiations. When the final ordeal is completed, the hero returns to the place from which he or she began. The setting and the cast of characters there may be the same; however, the hero is very different. He or she now has the gifts of wisdom and understanding developed by the many experiences along the way. But the hero, filled with new insights, finds difficulty in adjusting to the old world. Campbell's portrayal of the returning hero also depicts some of the reentry experiences faced by people who return to daily life after a spiritual emergency:

The first problem of the returning hero is to accept as real, after an experience of the soul-satisfying vision of fulfillment, the passing joys and sorrows, banalities, and noisy obscenities of life. Why reenter such a world? . . . The returning hero, to complete his adventure, must survive the impact of the world.

For example, someone who returns to a familiar situation may find the culture and the individuals within it unreceptive to his or her new capacities. The reborn hero must enter

the long-forgotten atmosphere where men who are fractions imagine themselves to be complete. He has to confront society with his ego-shattering, life-redeeming elixir, and take the return blow of reasonable queries, hard resentment, and good people at a loss to comprehend.

Because of the magnitude of their transformative experiences, many people find it difficult to accept and embrace the seemingly trivial aspects of ordinary reality. They may also face the very real problem that the everyday world around them is often not very receptive to their newfound discoveries.

We will now explore this transition period between a spiritual emergency and a stabilized existence, offering some practical ideas to make the homecoming easier. We will also offer some suggestions about life after this intermediate period.

From Spiritual Emergency to Daily Life

Many of us are very good at looking after and helping other people, often at our own expense. During the transition period, as well as afterward, meeting your own health-promoting needs should be your first priority. You need to nurture yourself first before you turn your attention outward. Following are some of the challenges you will likely face and general suggestions as to what to do about them. Because your experiences and needs are unique, you will probably find variations or additions that are ideally suited to you.

You may find it difficult to know where you end and the external world begins. After a spiritual emergency, you may feel that because of your exposure to diverse inner states, you are no longer sure how to define yourself as an individual. You may have had experiences of becoming animals, demons, or other people. Perhaps you traveled through time and space, identifying with a priest in ancient Mexico or a soldier in World War I. You might have had psychic experiences in which you flew out of your body or merged with another person. Along the way, you might have succumbed to an experience of the annhilation of the ego. You may have had unitive states in which you melted into the cosmos and felt yourself to be part of an interconnected web of consciousness.

And now these spontaneous, disorienting states have ceased. After such an internal onslaught, it is perfectly natural to feel somewhat tentative about your own boundaries as you return to daily life. After an ego-death experience in which you lose your old self-definition, how could you not wonder what comes next? Who is the new you?

As with many elements in a spiritual emergency, the next step usually happens by itself if you let it. Your new self automatically emerges, and your very best strategy is to cooperate by allowing this to happen. Give yourself time to be quiet, keeping your external world relatively uncomplicated. Each morning make a short list of things you need to do that day, and check them off as you go along. Be careful not to overload yourself with tasks that you think you *should* do, and leave yourself room for unfinished tasks the following day. Gently use your spiritual practice to gain insight and direction. Ask your source of higher wisdom for guidance and clarity as you grow into your new self. Talk to your therapist, and design a therapeutic strategy together that suits your needs.

You may find it important to set some boundaries for yourself. Certain activities, such as intense meditation practice or heavy experiential psychotherapy, may be inappropriate at this stage. Before experiencing more powerful inner states, you may need time to become a more solid, better-defined individual. Further inner exploration may be very helpful and exciting later on, when you feel stronger and more secure.

You might also need to set limits within your relationships. This may be difficult if you are used to being available to others without consideration for yourself. Learn to feel and express what you need from the people around you and from various situations. Draw boundaries for yourself, engaging in activities and relationships that support your sometimes tenuous sense of yourself.

Do not worry that by redefining yourself as a separate individual, by returning to a more ego-centered psychology, you will lose the insight that you are more than your physical self. The vividness of your experience will fade, but its memory and impact will never leave you.

You may feel fragile, vulnerable, or tentative and may need to protect yourself from too much outside input for a while. You are emerging from a demanding adventure in which your former self-image and worldview may have been shattered. You have been exposed to a broad range of unfamiliar experiences, and chances are that you will feel physically tired. A woman said to herself at this stage, "I had the image that all of my tiny nerve endings were frayed and wilted, like an overstressed electrical cord, after so much intense inner activity."

Again, we urge you to allow yourself plenty of time to take care of yourself. Keep your life as simple as possible, temporarily dropping any occupations that are too demanding and complex. Indulge in nourishing activities that make you feel good: relaxing hot baths, soothing body work, and long walks. You might also find it helpful to do uncomplicated, grounding tasks such as working in the garden, cooking, or washing the windows. You may need more sleep than usual as your body recuperates from the stress. Go to bed early, allow yourself time to sleep in the morning, and take naps when you need them.

It is easy to forget about regular eating habits during a spiritual emergency. Experiment with various healthy foods as you replenish your resources. You may find that fresh foods such as fruits and vegetables are particularly appealing.

After having been so involved with your inner world, you may find it helpful as well as amusing to concentrate for a while on your external appearance. Simple though they may be, a new haircut and new clothes may express and enhance your newfound self.

You might feel temporarily protective of yourself during interaction with other people, as well as with the world at large. You may have difficulty exposing yourself to stimulating environments such as large, noisy parties, city streets, busy airports, or a stress-producing job. As much as you can, avoid such situations for a while. The same goes for demanding relationships. You may want to limit your interactions to a small group of supportive friends and family. If you are a parent, get temporary help with the children, and if you work in the helping professions, see fewer clients. Anyone who truly cares about you will respect any temporary boundaries that you need to erect.

Sexual relationships deserve to be treated with special care at this point. Most of us normally feel vulnerable in intimate situations. This sensitivity can be magnified in someone who is just coming out of a spiritual emergency, feeling wide open and extremely receptive. You may be full of a newfound sense of love and connectedness and may want to express them physically to your partner. Yet when you enter into the intensity of a sexual encounter, you may feel fragile and overwhelmed. Once again, you might need to establish a stronger sense of your own boundaries before engaging in such a powerful interaction with another person.

If you already have a comfortable and trusting relationship, ask your partner to hold you and give you frequent hugs. Cuddling can be very nourishing and reassuring at this point. If you feel less sexual than usual, do not be concerned that your intimate life has ended. This is just a stage, and chances are that your developing strength and new sense of self will eventually enhance your future interactions.

A few words of caution to those who, during this stage, enter a new sexual relationship: Because you are often so sensitive and vulnerable, your emotional needs may be more intense than usual. As a result, you may become inadvertently involved in an intimate situation that may eventually become uncomfortable or even harmful. If, for example, someone offers you physical warmth and comfort at a time when you are particularly needy, you might become very attached and dependent on that person, inhibiting your own development and sense of strength. You might find yourself becoming very demanding, or you may find that a partner can take advantage of your fragility by manipulating you into unhealthy behavior or awkward situations.

You may continue to have short-lived and temporary waves of emotions, visions, insights, or other experiences left over from your spiritual emergency. This is a very common occurrence. The dramatic, involving part of the transformation process is over, you are returning your attention to the daily world, and you are profoundly aware of leftovers from your experience. Sometimes you feel a seemingly inappropriate surge of anger or fear—familiar emotions from your crisis, but not as strong.

Physical sensations such as tremors, body heat, or various pains may recur in milder form. Or as you go through your day you might see something that reminds you of a piece of your experience or may even trigger a brief vision. Perhaps a profound insight comes to you at some unexpected moment, taking you away from your daily activities and reawakening you to your depths.

These waves of emotions and experiences do not necessarily mean you are about to plunge again into the depths of your unconscious. They are very likely residual fragments of your transformation process that are being swept away as you further heal yourself. When they occur, you can work with them by using the same strategies that were effective during your spiritual emergency. Experiental therapy, meditation practice, physical movement, and creative expression are all good ways to deal with these leftovers.

For the sake of your relationships as well as your own health, learn to watch for the appearance of these remnants and keep them separate from your external life. Be careful not to project these emotions onto other people or to blame your life circumstances for your unresolved inner experiences. For example, you might find it tempting to project a wave of leftover anger onto your undeserving spouse or collegues, perhaps justifying your emotions by finding something wrong with your marriage or job. A good therapist, spiritual teacher, or support group can help to direct you.

You may be unsure about what to say to people or how to act. Coming out of your spiritual emergency, you might ask yourself, What happened? And it might be a while before you can satisfactorily answer that question. Very frequently, people's experiences occur ahead of their intellectual understanding of them. The logical explanation often develops slowly, as they are exposed to books, teachers, or others who have traveled similar paths. For a while, you might find yourself in a kind of limbo, not even sure how to talk with yourself about what has occurred.

Or you may be very excited about your new perspectives and feel an urge to share them with anyone who will listen. Perhaps you are even hopeful that your new wisdom will help other people. Chances are that there are curious people around you who have observed and helped you in your transformation. They most likely have questions of their own. Your problem now becomes how to communicate something you may not understand yourself.

Add to this the fact that you are still growing into your new self, feeling vulnerable and unsure about your boundaries. You may have some reservations about how to act and feel somewhat confused and uneasy around others. Perhaps you think they are critical of you for your strange experiences or are anticipating that you will continue to behave in an unusual way. Some families or friends, relieved that the dramatic phase of the emergence is over, may state that everyone's lives should now "return to normal." You, on the other hand, feel that you have just begun a lifelong spiritual journey.

In general, others have little idea of the significance of your experiences. If they are commited to a materialistic worldview, they may even be threatened by a new perspective. You, on the other hand, feel that you have emerged from your spiritual crisis with broad insights or creative gifts that can be used to help others. In *The Hero with a Thousand Faces*, Joseph Campbell beautifully describes this feeling:

> How to teach again . . . what has been taught correctly and incorrectly learned a thousand thousand times, throughout the millenniums of mankind's prudent folly? That is the hero's ultimate difficult task . . . How to communicate to people who insist on the exclusive evidence of their senses the message of the all-generating void?

How *do* you discuss your new perspective with people who remain limited by their own ideas about life? *Very carefully*. The problem of communication is one of the trickiest aspects of the homecoming. We have met all too many people who have tried to talk about their experiences and insights with others who are not prepared to hear such things—who have never tasted these realms and are probably very committed to and protective of their way of understanding themselves and the world.

Whatever you tell such people may fall on deaf ears. They simply cannot or will not listen. Or they may react in a way that could be harmful to you. Employers, colleagues, friends, and family members may feel threatened by your reports and withdraw or become actively antagonistic. Professionals with a limited understanding of your process may define you with pathological labels and recommend treatment that is contrary to your further development.

There is a good way to discriminate between those who may respond negatively and those who are sincerely curious about your transformation. Very possibly, without your saying anything, people will notice some external difference in you. Your eyes might look clear and sparkling, your face radiant, and you may exude a new excitement or peace. Someone might exclaim, "You look great!" and ask, "What have you been doing with yourself?" Rather than immediately revealing your deepest experiences, ask them if they would like to spend some time talking about it.

This simple question helps to sort out those who are truly interested. If someone replies, "Sure," and quickly moves on to some other subject, you know that he or she is probably only superficially interested. If, on the other hand, your friend replies, "Oh yes. When can we sit down together? I want to hear all about it," there is a good chance that he or she is serious. Even then, learn to tell your story sensitively, taking your listener only to the depth of detail and insight that he or she is seeking. You can always reveal more in further conversations.

Spiritual disciplines have varying attitudes about whether people should talk about their inner journey. Some schools believe that it detracts from the power of the experience to talk about it and that such discussion may lead to undesirable traits such as pride and self-satisfaction. Many states are ineffable anyway, and even the most eloquent mystics have had difficulty expressing them in words. You will probably find that it is impossible to satisfactorily articulate something as intangible and transitory as an overwhelming death experience or dissolution into the cosmos.

Other traditions encourage expression, however limited, as a way to integrate the inner states into daily life. By talking about your experiences with people who understand, you will further comprehend what happened to you. You also learn how to apply your new insights and lessons to the everyday world.

You will need to choose your own strategy while remaining open to changing it as time goes by. You may want to give yourself some time to be quiet before talking to others about your journey. Or you might feel some urgency about discussing your experiences as a way to help you understand them. Be sure you find people who are receptive—someone who has been through a similar process, a knowledgeable therapist or spiritual teacher, or a support group.

You might try expressing your experiences through painting, writing, poetry, dancing, or singing. The metaphors of these creative forms are close to the symbolic language of your inner world. The culture at large has more tolerance for insights that are expressed artistically than it has for those that are expressed directly.

Whatever you do, do not make the mistake of imposing your insights on people who do not want to hear them. Some of us are so enthusiastic about the changes we have seen in ourselves that we feel we should share them with everyone. We might go so far as to try to convert others. This approach will cause discomfort and interpersonal problems. All of us are at different stages in our own development. We all deserve respect for who and where we are at any given juncture. Each of us has our own journey to travel, and our routes may be very different.

Although it may not feel this way at first, your experience does not mean that you are special or superior. If you have had a revelation of transcendent domains or insights about cosmic workings, remember that this experience is potentially available to anyone. Otherwise it is easy to develop a sense of spiritual pride and grandiosity, very seductive but potentially harmful diversions that are well known in spiritual traditions. If you find yourself believing that you have *the* answers and that you have a special mission to convey your message to the world, be careful. Answers that may be important for you may not be appropriate for someone else. Humility is one of the most important characteristics of a truly developed spiritual person.

You may feel embarrassed, judgmental, or guilty about your behavior during your spiritual emergency. This is especially true for people who have gone through an extreme form of spiritual emergency involving colorful experiences, dramatic movements, and emotional expression. You may not remember some of the things you might have said or done. Once you start coming out of your crisis, you might suddenly wonder, "Oh, no. What have I done? Who was there? And what did they think?"

This kind of attitude is very common and confounds your further healing. The mind is our worst enemy during a transformation process. During a powerful experience, your logical world was most likely subsumed by the irrational realms of your unconscious. You probably did and said things that seemed perfectly appropriate at the time in the context of your emergence. However, once you start to return to your rational existence, such behavior seems out of place and even unacceptable.

Now that the charge and the consuming involvement have diminished, the vividness fades into memories. Your mind steps in and tries to justify your unusual, seemingly illogical behavior. People in this stage regularly attempt to deny the scope and significance of their experience. You may even try to talk yourself out of experiences and perspectives that were tremendously important to you. Or you may try to minimize their impact by trying to explain them away, saying, "I had been under a great deal of stress and just wasn't being myself."

If you have not yet understood what happened to you and feel isolated, you may even try to convince yourself that you were indeed crazy. You are so shattered by the experience that you want desperately to return to "normal" life. You were so out of control that you need to return to a carefully monitored existence. You cling to your concept of normalcy, wanting to be acceptable again to yourself and to the culture around you. You feel guilty and become your own worst judge.

This is another place where a good community of understanding people can assist you. A knowledgeable therapist, a spiritual teacher, a support group, and fellow travelers can all help you realize and honor the profound nature of your life-changing experience. They can help you accept whatever form it took and move on.

Continue to educate yourself about the dynamics of spiritual emergency. You will find that many transformative experiences are dramatic. Read the descriptions of the spiritual experiences of the saints and prophets and of Christ's forty days in the desert. They were full of explosive challenges. Listen to the evocative, emotional music of charismatic churches. Learn about cultural rituals of transformation. These devotional displays are almost all expressive, passionate, and powerful. They demonstrate the enormous, elemental spiritual force that is active during a world-shattering awakening experience. They have nothing to do with the polite, controlled veneer that smoothes most social interactions.

Once you have accepted that your experiences were a necessary aspect of your emergence, you will become grateful for their forceful appearance in your life. And you can continue to honor them for their role in your development. But move on. Do not dwell on what has happened. There are many more exciting steps ahead.

With so much else happening to you, the last thing you need is an extra layer of guilt and self-judgment. Be easy on yourself. Use a meditation practice to quiet your mind and to develop your ability to witness its mental gymnastics without being influenced by them.

You may have difficulty digesting your experience intellectually and philosophically or reconciling it with your old worldview. This is another common challenge. Think of the way in which your worldview was constructed before your transformation started. Perhaps you believed you were nothing but your body, that your life began at birth and will end at death. Developing your potential meant developing your mind and mechanical skills as well as getting ahead in the world. Your perception was related to what you could see, taste, touch, hear, and smell. Love was based on sex and security. And your aspirations were connected to material success.

Then, during your spiritual emergency, you relive your birth and confront death, and you realize that there is more to life than you thought. You have several out-of-body experiences and learn that you are more than a physical being. Perhaps you become a samurai warrior in a vivid scene from ancient Japan and begin to think about the possibility of reincarnation. Visiting new realms within yourself, you are suddenly imbued with creative ideas and new insights and find that your potential seems limitless. After many clairvoyant dreams and intuitive perceptions you realize that you have more available to you than just your five senses. Experiencing the mystical unity of all of creation, you discover a new meaning of love. And having seen all of this, you become dedicated to the pursuit of a truly spiritual life.

As if this were not enough, imagine that you are Jewish and your most important mystical visions happen in the context of the Arabic Sufi tradition. Or you are a staunch Catholic, and your significant transformative states are Hindu. Or you are a Buddhist having vivid Christian experiences.

How do you even begin to think about these radical departures from your old worldview? Do they make sense? How can you conceptualize them for yourself? Does this mean that you must leave your familiar identity as well as the relationships based on that identity?

These kinds of questions are often answered automatically for many people. As they emerge from their experience, they feel accepting and complete, without much need to question what happened. The experience often makes sense on a gut level and speaks for itself. Other people struggle with these questions. They have a whole lifestyle and set of values constructed around their old way of being and are reluctant to give them up.

A helpful way to digest your new insights is to educate yourself. Read books and talk to others. If you have had experiences involving another culture, look specifically at its history, art, and literature and see if these resonate with your new awareness. If a specific symbol, such as a swan or a circle, keeps reappearing, find out the cross-cultural meaning of swans and circles. Perhaps you will find some clues to help you to understand their significance in your life.

Surround yourself with people who have an understanding similar to the one that is developing within you. Become involved in a meditation or prayer group that offers practices from a tradition that you might have encountered internally. This does not mean you must immediately accept what they might be teaching. But by being there, you may find further clues to your own inner direction. This may or may not mean temporarily or permanently dissociating yourself from friends or organizations that represent your old worldview. Some people can easily maintain their new direction while remaining in their old environment. Others cannot.

Having a spiritual emergency does not mean you are automatically required to leave your old way of life. Although a great deal has changed internally, you can still maintain the same activities and relationships. You simply connect with them in a different way. However, you may find that your life circumstances are incompatible with your new perspectives and values. You want to be in surroundings that are more congruent with who you are becoming. And you need to be around people who understand.

The same goes for religious traditions. You may have grown up in a devout family or community. When your transformation began, you suddenly had significant experiences of a different faith. You may have begun to question your own belief system, wondering if you must now leave it. Especially if you feel considerable pressure from the people around you to remain where you are, this can be a very difficult dilemma.

You do not necessarily have to throw away beliefs that have been important for you. However, some people choose to. They may adopt another tradition, finding a deep resonance that they had never experienced in their own background. Many people become interested in the mystical dimensions of all religions, realizing that it was the mystical core of their own religion that held their attention. They might see each faith as a different path to the same goal and develop a universal, ecumenical attitude, a kind of planetary spirituality.

Others only temporarily move away from their own tradition, returning to it later with a new attitude. A friend of ours, who was raised in an Orthodox Jewish household, experienced her awakening in a Hindu context. She spent a number of years with an East Indian teacher, where she gained knowledge and learned practices that were valuable to her development. She realized that her problems with her own tradition came from the dogmatic and exclusive approach of her family. In her mystical states, she had learned the value of a life based on her new inclusive, unitive perspective. Still yearning for her own tradition, she finally returned to Judaism, but this time she was attracted to its mystical aspects found in Hassidic practice and the Kabbalah.

You may alternately feel strong waves of relief, humility, awe, grace, gratitude, and wonder. Now we come to some of the most pleasant challenges. As well as the surges of leftover emotions such as anger or fear, you might begin to notice waves of positive emotions or experiences. As many of the disruptive states fade, your whole being may sink into a state of relief. The pressure of the intense inner states is gone, and you feel more relaxed and balanced.

Perhaps you looked at some of the most elemental aspects of yourself, such as your fear of death or your destructive impulses. Or you may have been humbled in the face of profound inner radiance. As a result, your false pride has softened and you feel a new humility. Many barriers between you and the rest of humankind have been removed.

You may feel awed by the scope and quality of your experiences and blessed by a larger force that has guided you through the rough spots. You are grateful not only to be through with many of the difficulties, but to have been awakened to new dimensions and potentials within. Returning from your journey, you may be filled with wonder at the immensity of your experience and at the newly discovered riches of your daily life.

Ordinary moments yield extraordinary feelings. During a walk in the woods, you notice a nest full of baby birds and feel a strong surge of connection with the creativity of the universe. A sparkling window in a skyscraper catches your eye and you once again feel an experience of exceptional clarity. Listening to a powerful piece of choral music, you are transported by feelings of awe and reverence for the vast dimensions of the creative spirit. As you and your child share a quiet moment, you are flooded with a sense of grace.

A new, positive place within you has broken through. Although the states emanating from it are nourishing and healing, they are usually transitory. You can learn to work with them, developing and broadening them. Give yourself time for reflection and creative activities, such as writing and painting. Take walks in nature if possible. Expose yourself to situations and activities—such as listening to elevating music or caring for your garden—that stimulate these feelings.

Again, meditation, prayer, and regular therapy can all help to promote these states and turn them into more consistent parts of your life.

You may have difficulty accepting the unfamiliar positive experiences that are coming into your life and may not know how to deal with a new source of strength. Many of us are so used to struggling that we do not know what to do when we start to feel better. We have spent so much time feeling inadequate and fighting our fears and fantasies that we know little else. Suddenly feeling a fairly consistent stream of positive emotions can be a shock. Many of us react by holding on to whatever pains and problems might still exist because they are familiar. We may even find activities—such as militant political causes or troublesome relationships—that will ensure our continued struggle and unhappiness. It is often difficult to break this lifelong pattern.

Further inner exploration, when you are ready, will assist you in removing the doubts and finding the roots of your hesitancy. Experiential therapy will help you discover the old restrictive programs ("I do not deserve to feel good"; "Life is suffering and I live to suffer"; "If I feel too happy, I am not working hard enough") and eliminate them. You will find that as you clear these old feelings out of the way, your new source of strength will become increasingly potent.

You will learn that you do indeed deserve to feel happy, peaceful, and fulfilled, and that this is a very natural goal for everyone. With time, you will learn to accept and welcome this new core of yourself and use it in your daily life.

You may catch yourself expecting the bottom to drop out of your newfound state. For months and probably years, you may have been used to extreme emotional highs and lows. You had glimpses of expansion and serenity, but they never lasted very long and were overshadowed by your problems. Repeatedly, when you were convinced that you had finally achieved happiness, something happened and your world seemed to fall apart once again. You became so used to this pattern that you assumed that this unreliable roller-coaster ride was standard for everyone.

Soon after your spiritual emergency, you might start noticing that the positive changes in your life are not going away. More time passes and you realize that you have been tiptoeing through your days waiting for an abrupt reversal that has not happened. For most people, once enough barriers have been removed between them and their positive potential, that strong and vital source does not diminish. It is as though the dam has broken and the ocean that was contained behind it pours through.

This does not mean your existence will be constantly smooth and happy. You will continue to meet all kinds of challenges as part of life. But because of your new inner peace and clarity, your perspective as to the significance of these junctures has changed and your reactions to them are milder and more balanced. As one person told us, "Problems used to be obstacles as I stumbled through life; now they are hurdles in my spiritual path."

You are no longer at the mercy of your emotions. Consequently, the emotional highs and lows are not as extreme. Someone in this stage said, "I know I am not enlightened, but there is a lot more light in my life now."

As with other aspects of the homecoming, give yourself plenty of time to watch and enjoy your newfound gifts. You will eventually learn to accept them as part of your renewed self and find ways of using them in the world.

You may have a sense that though there is more work to do, you need to concentrate on nourishing activities for a while. Many people who embark on a journey of self-exploration develop the insight that our inner dimensions are bountiful and endless. Our continued spiritual journey will take us into ever deeper and broader aspects of ourselves and the mystery that surrounds us. Perhaps the state of final liberation described in mystical texts is waiting for you. But you become aware that there is much to do before realizing it. After your spiritual emergency, you may be left with the sense of an immense inner domain waiting to be explored. There are leftover feelings such as anger, fear, and resentment that still need healing. Perhaps you need to deal with an unhealthy pattern with your parents, spouse, or friend. You know that you need to do more work on yourself in order to become even clearer. But you have done so much for so long that you are tired.

Unless your emotions or experiences are getting in the way of your daily life, further therapeutic work may not be the best approach at this point. With the knowledge that you will need to do more at some point, you can freely allow yourself a period of rest and recuperation before plunging into further deep effort. You have just been through a major transformative experience, which is most likely one of the most important phases in your life. You need to give yourself enough time to soak in the lessons from your experiences, to reflect, and to recharge yourself.

Find out what nourishes you, and reserve a part of each day to allow yourself those activities. Perhaps you feel nurtured by a luxurious bath or a swim, reveling in the healing qualities of the water. A period of quiet meditation or a long run in the early-morning hours might do the same thing. You might take special care as you dress, finding some favorite articles of clothing that make you feel good inside and out. Whatever it is, take the time you need to continue your healing process. You will most likely know when you feel ready to continue more active work on yourself.

As you move toward full participation in daily life, you will find it helpful to continue some of the strategies we have suggested. Create a lifestyle for yourself that includes simplicity, reflection time, and activities that nourish you. Continue your spiritual practice and/or some form of transpersonal therapy. Include people in your life who share the same worldview and values.

And when appropriate, use your experience to help others. Service to others does not have to mean anything more than truly listening to your children when they need someone to talk to or helping your partner do something that is important to him or her. It might involve being available to others who are going through a crisis or volunteering to work with a service-oriented organization such as the Spiritual Emergence Network.

Perhaps you will feel drawn to give talks about the lessons you have learned or to write an article to educate others. Whatever the form, service is just as beneficial to the one who offers it as it is to the one who receives it. It is a wonderful way to counteract any tendency you might have to dwell on your own daily problems and frustrations. By focusing on someone else for a while, very frequently your own preoccupations fade away.

Heed the familiar saying: "you cannot truly have something until you give it away." Give away your new wisdom and the benefits of your healing, and you will add great meaning to your life.

The Rewards of the New Self

In *Lalleshwari: Spiritual Poems by a Great Siddha Yogini*, we find the following:

> *When your impurities are burned*
> *through suffering,*
> *you will become more lustrous*
> *than a mirror in the sun,*
> *more pure than*
> *the most perfect of pearls.*

During spiritual emergence, many of the screens that obscure who one really is are removed, and one can begin to sense a personal positive essence. These barriers were the emotional, psychological, and physical experiences that were stored within. With the dissolution or purging of these blockages, new dimensions of oneself break through and become stronger. Through further development and nurturing, the essential spiritual core grows increasingly potent, available, and prominent in an individual's life.

Many people who reach this stage may temporarily think that they have "arrived." But very quickly they often find themselves moving again and realize that self-exploration and transformation are ongoing processes. Once they feel reborn, they realize that there are many more opportunities for death and rebirth. They see that the further they go, the more there is to do; the more they know, the more there is to know. But rather than being discouraged by this insight, they often become excited about the dance of life, its mysteries and challenges, and about their roles as participants. Through their struggles, they have gained a new ease, strength, and sense of mastery that accompanies them on further life adventures.

Each person's life circumstances are different, and each spiritual path is unique. While some people enjoy dramatic resolutions and sudden access to some of these rewards, many others taste them only briefly. They now know that these promises exist, and they continue to develop slowly with continued self-exploration. Many of us discover these elements as a goal toward which we continue to strive during spiritual practice. At a certain point, they become constant and available. Although we are more in touch with them during some periods than others, these harmonious feelings and attitudes usually return. With this in mind, let us look at the possibilities waiting on the other side of personal transformation.

Many people discover new, positive elements in their daily world. They develop a general sense that the life process is trustworthy, rather than something to be wrestled with or resisted. They might feel quieter, more relaxed and satisfied with what they have, and appreciative of life in general. After having met numerous difficult areas within themselves during their crises, such individuals frequently emerge with a deeper appreciation of life. If they have looked closely at death, life often becomes more valuable by contrast and they are able to recognize and savor aspects of it that they had previously missed.

After a transformative crisis, many individuals become more centered in the present moment. Previously, they may have spent a great deal of time living in the past or preoccupied with the future. They might have felt driven, competitive, or goal oriented. They often have taken themselves very seriously, needing to constantly demonstrate their worth or get ahead. Having reached success, they were most likely dissatisfied, feeling that there was always more to do.

Now they may feel less of an impulse to prove something to the world, since their inner needs are more satisfied. Because they have become freed to enjoy the present moment and its offerings, their obsessive goal orientation is diminished. Cleansed of frenetic energies and bothersome emotions, many people feel happier with whatever is available to them and are attracted by the simple, uncomplicated aspects of their lives.

One may develop a new interest in cultivating serenity and peaceful pursuits in life. In the past, a person may have thrived on excitement and drama. Now he or she discovers what real peace of mind feels like and becomes interested in nurturing and increasing it. Such a person is often more able to enjoy solitude, as well as to feel an enhanced appreciation for other human beings. Time alone is qualitatively different than the painful isolation and loneliness they may have felt previously. Such individuals can now enjoy quiet times of reflection, meditation, and creativity. This solitary time may become a necessary and an important element, a time when they can reconnect with themselves and their positive attributes.

Feeling more accepting and comfortable within themselves, many people also more fully enjoy contact with others. They are less concerned with issues such as whether people will approve of them, how they present themselves, or whether they will be successful. Instead, they often operate out of a basic sense of contentment and positive self-image, and they are more able to accept others and to relate to their positive qualities.

They might also feel that their perception has been cleansed and that they have a greater sensory appreciation of the surrounding world. They might find that they are able to experience their environment more clearly, as though their senses are keener, with a greater appreciation for detail. The world appears to be alive and full of riches. Music suddenly seems to have added dimensions, and food tastes especially good. Previously, if one visited the desert, one could see and feel only death and barrenness; now, the same person might be selectively aware of the multitude of life forms, the exquisite spectrum of sounds, the eternal quality of the rocks, and the vastness of space.

Some individuals find that they can think more clearly and that they suddenly have access to untapped sources of creativity within themselves. They might find new and imaginative ways of conceptualizing and conveying ideas or feel a new stream of artistic inspiration within. They may be drawn to activities such as writing, painting, dancing, or singing, or may find new creative outlets within their jobs.

Personal values may change and new ones become essential ingredients in life. These values have become obvious as the person has evolved, and to exist without them would be contrary to his or her present insights and understanding. For example, many people discover a new self-acceptance, a tolerance for others, and an appreciation of differences. After having delved deeply into the experience of extreme loneliness and separation during a spiritual emergency, they frequently arrive at previously unknown feelings of unity and connectedness with everything and everyone around them. Previously, they might have felt that their world revolved around them and were constantly preoccupied with their own personal process and problems. With the resolution of their crisis, this self-centered tendency often relaxes and they naturally redirect their focus to include others. They may feel special and full of grace and at the same time realize that others are equally unique and blessed.

Some people discover the need for honesty as well as feelings of love and compassion for themselves, for others, and for the world. Now that they have moved through their crisis, they often feel a poignant respect and caring for the "old self" that for years bore a heavy load of problems, as well as for the "new self" that struggled courageously to come into being. Through their own hardships, many people feel a deeper connection with the suffering of others.

In addition, they might have had a mystical experience of unity with all of life and realize that they cannot hurt others without hurting themselves. They might feel a deepening commitment to ease someone else's life and discover that by doing so they are also easing their own. They may become interested in using their newfound strength and insight to help others.

For many people, spirituality becomes a desirable and necessary part of life. They realize that the spiritual element has been missing from their lives. As part of their emergence process, they may have had transcendent experiences that have made them aware of previously hidden areas of existence. Others find this expanded dimension only after they have confronted certain difficult aspects of themselves. Whatever the route, most individuals want to stay in contact with the nourishing and inspirational dimensions they have discovered. These extensive, new spiritual impulses within themselves are expressed in their lives in a number of ways:

Many people discover a deep connection with an inner source, higher self, or God, and they might experience the world as an expression of the Divine. Previous to their awakenings, they most likely had their own ideas of God. This notion may have come from their families or religions, from their intellectual analyses of philosophy and literature, or from their own speculations about the ways in which the universe operates. Perhaps their concept of God had to do with something that is unattainable, externalized, or unknowable. The Divine was beyond them and superior to them.

People often have their first taste of a direct personal connection with this source during their spiritual emergency. They often have firsthand experiences that take them beyond what they had been thinking or talking about. They contact a potential greater than those afforded by their ordinary means. This source provides answers and inspiration, guidance and strength, protection and assistance. When the crisis has resolved itself, this connection abides more or less continuously, and they often have the sense that, unbeknownst to them, their Higher Power has guided them through the challenges and problems of their crisis.

Their God has become immediate and available within them, and it becomes an important and necessary part of their daily existence. They might even begin to see the whole life process as a miraculous cosmic drama that is carefully orchestrated by a divine creative force. They can also feel that everything in the world around them is an exquisite display of God's handiwork.

One of our favorite stories illustrates the importance of a true experience of the Divine. A reporter from *Time* magazine interviewed the famous Swiss psychiatrist C. G. Jung toward the end of his life. At one point the journalist asked whether Jung believed in God. He replied: "I

ıot say that I believe. I know! I had the experience of being gripped
ıething that is stronger than myself, something that people call
God."

As a result of discovering the wise force that guides them, many
individuals develop a trust in the life process as it unfolds. They increasingly experience a deep faith that their existence is developing as it should,
perhaps as part of some greater plan. They often stop trying to struggle
against the momentum of life, finding that their resistence to its dynamics
usually introduces unnecessary pain. They find that things work better
if they abandon their need to control their situation, allowing the deeper
wisdom to guide them.

Once people have experienced the spiritual dimension growing in
their lives, they often learn that their lives without it were futile and
impoverished. Previously, they may have managed adequately but un-
happily, unaware of the seemingly endless realms that have since enormously enriched their existence. They discover that spirituality is a
necessary element that enhances their lives and sense of well-being.

Such individuals often become interested in actively developing their
spiritual nature. Their well-being may have improved in so many ways
since their discovery of their Higher Self that they become interested in
cultivating that dimension in their lives. They may feel pulled to develop
a regular, daily spiritual practice that serves to enhance their contact with
their deeper nature, bringing it into daily activities. These people learn
that they can connect with the spiritual source during walks in nature,
or through prayer, meditation, or other devotional practice, and that they
can depend upon its wisdom and benevolence. In their best moments,
they can sense that everything that they do during the day is a form of
meditation, an offering to God or the Higher Power.

As we come to the end of this volume, let us look back on our journey.
We have examined the potential of spiritual emergence, focusing on the
times when this very natural unfolding becomes a crisis. For some of us,
the nature of this crisis is quite dramatic and disruptive, an emergency;
for others, it is not. Are the problems and challenges, the drama and the
disruption, the heights and the depths worth living through? We believe
so, and so do many others who have tasted the benefits of this adventure.

And what does such a transformation mean for our lives? The famous
story of the Zen student and his teacher beautifully captures the answer.
The disciple asked the master, "What did you do before your enlightenment?" The teacher answered, "I chopped wood and carried water." "What
did you do after enlightenment?" To which the master replied, "I chopped
wood and carried water."

During a spiritual emergency much, perhaps everything, changes. The path is often rough and difficult to navigate, but it eventually leads to peace and inner freedom. Coming home, you may still chop your wood and carry your water, but in an entirely new way. And though you may very well be aware that enlightenment still awaits you, you experience increasingly more light along the way.

SPIRITUAL EMERGENCE AND THE CURRENT GLOBAL CRISIS

The only devils in the world are those running in our own hearts. That is where the battle should be fought.

MAHATMA GANDHI

If there be righteousness in the heart,
  there will be beauty in the character.
If there be beauty in the character,
  there will be harmony in the home.
If there be harmony in the home,
  there will be order in the nation.
If there be order in the nation,
  there will be peace in the world.

CONFUCIUS, "The Great Learning"

The twentieth century has been a period of unprecedented triumphs for the human species. Modern science discovered nuclear energy, developed sophisticated rockets that can carry astronauts to the moon and leave the solar system, cracked the DNA code, and started genetic engineering. An electronic network combining radio, telephone, television, satellites, and computers is rapidly transforming the fragmented mosaic of disconnected human communities into a global village.

However, the dark side of twentieth century's history is equally overwhelming. Unimaginable sums of money have been wasted in the insanity of the arms race, and a minuscule fraction of the available arsenal of nuclear weapons could destroy all life on earth. Tens of millions of people have been bestially tortured and killed in the Holocaust, in the purges and labor camps of Stalin's Russia, and in the prisons of other totalitarian regimes of the world. Many additional millions have died in the two world wars and in countless other violent confrontations.

Humanity lives in constant fear of an atomic war that would mean

234

radical extermination of life on this planet. Several other doomsday scenarios are already relentlessly unfolding: industrial pollution of soil, water, and air; the threat of nuclear accidents and waste; destruction of the ozone layer; the greenhouse effect; possible loss of planetary oxygen through reckless deforestation and poisoning of the ocean plankton; and the dangers of the toxic additives in our food.

While the technologically developed countries are realizing their dream of unlimited growth, hundreds of millions of people are living in misery, dying of starvation or of diseases for which known cures exist. Together with the progressive accumulation of wealth, industrialized nations are showing a rapid increase in emotional disorders, suicides, and criminality.

It is not an exaggeration to refer to this situation as a global crisis; this dangerous development threatens not only homo sapiens—if under these circumstances we still deserve that name—but all other species as well. It is a matter of life and death to correctly identify the causes of this dangerous situation and to find effective remedies.

Considering the available resources and the progress of science, the problems of hunger, poverty, and most disease-related deaths in the world are unnecessary. In addition to the psychological absurdity of wars, statistics clearly show that no modern nation has ever become richer as a result of a war; senseless destruction of economic values as well as of lives is the rule. There is no real need for plundering nonrenewable reserves and polluting vital resources. Humanity has the means and technological knowhow for feeding the population of the planet, guaranteeing reasonable living standards for all, combatting most diseases, reorienting industries to inexhaustible sources of energy, and preventing pollution.

Diplomatic negotiations, administrative and legal measures, economic and social interventions, and other similar efforts have had very little effect, and it is becoming increasingly clear why they have failed. Today, many people are realizing that the problems we are facing are not really political, military, technological, or economic in nature. Such approaches are extensions of the same attitudes and strategies that have created the global crisis to begin with.

Though the problems in the world have many different forms, they are nothing but symptoms of one underlying condition: the emotional, moral, and spiritual state of modern humanity. In the last analysis, they are the collective result of the present level of consciousness of individual human beings. The only effective and lasting solution to these problems would, therefore, be a radical inner transformation of humanity on a large scale and its consequent rise to a higher level of awareness and maturity.

The task of creating an entirely different set of values and tendencies for humanity might appear to be too unrealistic and utopian to offer any hope. What would it take to transform contemporary mankind into a species of individuals capable of peaceful coexistence with their fellow men and women regardless of color, language, or political conviction— much less with other species? How could humanity be imbued with profound ethical values, a sensitivity to the needs of others, and an awareness of ecological imperatives? Such a task appears too fantastic even for a science-fiction novel.

Fortunately, nature seems to have provided the necessary means and conducted pilot experiments in this regard. The study of spiritual emergence and emergency, as well as modern consciousness research and new forms of psychotherapy, provide the necessary information and clues. We have described in this book the changes that occur in people who have had powerful mystical experiences and have successfully overcome a spiritual crisis. We have also suggested that changes of a similar kind can be observed in the course of systematic spiritual practice and deep experiential self-exploration. Let us now look at this transformation and its possible relevance for the planetary crisis.

Among the psychological forces that characterize the current condition of humanity and contribute to the global crisis are a strong readiness for violence, an insatiable greed and acquisitiveness, and a habitual dissatisfaction that tends to breed limitless ambition and the pursuit of irrational goals. In addition, most people suffer from a severe lack of awareness that we are intimately interconnected with nature; they do not have the ecological sensitivity that is essential for continued survival. In the last analysis, all these characteristics seem to be symptomatic of severe alienation from inner life and loss of spiritual values.

People who gain access to deep domains of their unconscious in various experiential psychotherapies, as well as those for whom this happens spontaneously during crises of transformation, are given the opportunity to find the roots of such ultimately destructive and self-destructive aspects of human nature and to overcome them by bringing them fully into consciousness. They also are often able to become aware of the transpersonal dimensions of their being and their spiritual core or self.

People who connect experientially to the transpersonal domain of their psyche tend to develop a new appreciation for existence and a reverence for all life forms. The spontaneous emergence of deep ecological concerns is one of the most striking aftereffects of profound mystical experiences. As self-acceptance improves, this leads to much greater tolerance toward others. Differences among people now appear to be interesting and enhancing rather than threatening, whether they are related to sex, race, color, language, political conviction, or religious belief.

Following deep mystical experiences, the interests of humanity as a whole, all of life, and the entire planet tend to take priority over the narrow interests of individuals, families, political parties, classes, nations, and creeds. What connects us and what we have in common become more important than the ways in which we differ. As the ability to enjoy the present moment increases, the unfulfilling pursuit of grandiose projects and goals as means of achieving satisfaction becomes less and less compelling. As a result, life is less a struggle and more a fascinating adventure or play.

Because of the positive transformation it induces, spiritual emergence might play a significant role in the world if it could occur in a sufficiently large number of people. Many researchers in the field of transpersonal psychology believe that the growing interest in spirituality and the increasing incidence of spontaneous mystical experiences represent an evolutionary trend toward an entirely new level of human consciousness. Some go even further and seriously consider the possibility that this accelerated spiritual development reflects an effort on the part of the forces of evolution to reverse the current self-destructive course of the human race.

This possibility throws new light on the need to create supportive networks for people undergoing crises of spiritual awakening. The fact that the new strategies honoring the transformative potential of spiritual emergencies are beneficial for people in crisis, their friends, and families would be more than sufficient to justify this work. But the possibility that such efforts could make an important contribution to the relief of the global crisis adds an exciting dimension and a strong motivation. In conclusion, we hope that this book will help to increase interest in the spiritual dimension of existence and to ease the lives of those who are encountering difficulties during their journey to the next stage of personal evolution.

THE SPIRITUAL EMERGENCE NETWORK

Christina founded the Spiritual Emergence Network (SEN) in the spring of 1980. Over the years, it has grown into an international organization that offers a referral service, education, and information to people going through transformational processes, as well as to the families, friends, and professionals around them. Currently located at the Institute of Transpersonal Psychology, (250 Oak Grove Ave., Menlo Park, CA 94025; 415/327-2776), SEN is based on an expanded understanding of human experience offered by transpersonal psychology and is dedicated to helping people live through a process that is often misunderstood and mistreated in our culture.

In 1978, having had intimate exposure to spiritual emergency through our own experience, we began, in our workshops and seminars, to discuss the lessons we had learned. With some hesitancy, Christina described her own experiences and Stan outlined the theoretical insights he had developed during his years of working with nonordinary states of consciousness. Time and again, the people in the room responded with their own evocative stories and questions.

We began to realize that there was a sizable group of people who had had transformative experiences that they had never talked about with anyone, for fear of being considered crazy. Many others said that they had made the mistake of telling the wrong people about their experiences: they had been hospitalized, medicated, and given psychiatric labels, even though deep within themselves they felt they had not been involved in a pathological process. Mental-health professionals, physicians, and clergy repeatedly told us of their dissatisfaction with professional limitations and of their own often lonely work, which departed from traditional approaches. They were interested in locating like-minded collegues for mutual support and the exchange of information.

Soon we began to become known for our ideas and hopes of providing alternative understanding and treatment of many nonordinary states that are automatically labeled psychotic. During this period, we were suddenly flooded with mail and telephone calls from people both asking for and offering help.

At one point, when we were feeling quite overwhelmed by the huge response, Christina had a meditative image of the globe, encompassed by a large interconnected web. At each intersection, a point of light sparkled. This beautiful experience made her feel that we had to start systematically putting people in touch with one another. People wanting help needed to contact those offering assistance, and vice versa. Those already working with approaches compatible with the new understanding of spiritual emergence should be connected with others who shared the same worldview. But how to do it?

The Spiritual Emergency Network was the answer. We talked to our friend Dick Price at the Esalen Institute in Big Sur, California. Because of his own unhappy excursion into the world of psychiatric hospitals, he had been eager for some time to help initiate some tangible, viable alternative. Dick offered us a place at Esalen for our first network coordinator, as well as a small grant. Without his enthusiastic support, SEN would never have gotten off the ground.

The original name, Spiritual Emergency Network, was chosen very consciously as a play on words, the term *emergency* inferring both "crisis" and "emerging." It was later renamed the Spiritual Emergen*ce* Network as a way of focusing more on the positive aspects of the phenomenon.

Rita Rohen became our first coordinator. A wonderful, nurturing woman who had raised six children, Rita had lived for years with a schizophrenic husband. She brought her life experience, combined with her professional skills as an organizational development consultant and a family counselor, to the job. Together, we began a Spiritual Emergency Center in a house that we rented practically next door to Esalen.

Here, assisted by two or three students who had a special interest in spiritual emergency, we started a fledgling training program for potential facilitators and developed an international referral and information system. We created a file with names, addresses, and other relevant information about people offering help and began putting people in need of assistance in touch with nearby helpers. International regional coordinators were selected to serve as network organizers in their areas and stay in touch with the facilitators in our file.

We also began to compile and write articles, information sheets, and other instructional materials. Our small library grew, often through donations by sympathetic authors. Newsletters were regularly assembled, printed, and distributed. We traveled extensively, talking about our ideas and dreams in many workshops, seminars, and lectures and on an occasional radio or television show. We offered five-day and month-long programs on spiritual emergency and discussed the possibility of starting a sanctuary house for people in crisis. Gradually, the ideas and services of the network expanded.

In September 1984 SEN moved to its current location. The project had become too large to handle with our ancient computer, small volunteer staff, and tiny budget. Rita had decided to move on, and our travel schedule forced us to become increasingly less involved. And Dick Price, our support and champion at Esalen, had died. When the Institute for Transpersonal Psychology offered to provide a new home for SEN, we happily accepted. ITP administrator Susanna Davila became our advocate, and first Charles Lonsdale and later Megan Nolan, Nicola Kester, and Jeneane Prevatt became the network coordinators.

Since that time, we have been peripherally involved with SEN as advisers and contributors to its written material. Staff members have expanded and developed many of the activities that were begun at Esalen and have added new services. They have continued the referral listing and telephone line, involving over eleven hundred helpers from many walks of life: psychologists, social workers, psychotherapists, psychiatrists, people who have been through their own spiritual emergencies, physicians, and clergy, to name a few. SEN has expanded its educational program to include regular workshops and lectures on topics related to spiritual emergency and the distribution of relevant articles, bibliographies, and tapes.

The staff has organized a number of invitational conferences for those involved in the field and has made a concerted effort to reach professionals through the promotion of discussion groups, training seminars, conferences, and research projects. The publication of a journal has been added to the regular distribution of the newsletter.

All of this activity takes place in a tiny office at the institute, with a small salaried staff and an impressive number of volunteers. Barely maintained by a budget from random donations and membership fees, the devoted workers handle a large number of calls and help with the multitude of tasks that are involved in maintaining an international network. Because the field of spiritual emergency is so new, it has been difficult for SEN to obtain formal grants, which often require proof of reliability through research projects.

SEN staff members are currently collecting clinical data and case material from the people who contact them for referrals, and they hope to promote international centers that would function like the one in Menlo Park. In spite of their increasingly rich stores of information, they have not been able to encourage active research because of financial restrictions. Plans for the future will, we hope, correct this problem.

SEN is also hoping to enlarge its staff to conduct training for professionals, paraprofessionals, and lay people who want to participate in centers offering twenty-four-hour care. As a way of becoming increasingly available to the public, it also plans to train teams to work with those in spiritual emergencies and their families at home. This, too, will present many opportunities for research.

The staff members of SEN hope to serve as consultants to communities that are interested in learning about coping with spiritual emergencies. They also have plans to focus on using the arts as a means of integrating transformational experiences into daily life and to develop a program for the increasing number of young adults who are, without much support, undergoing spiritual rites of passage.

In these first years of its existence, the Spiritual Emergence Network has accomplished a great deal. It has made important strides in formalizing the concept of spiritual emergence/emergency within the mental-health arena. It has promoted the idea that it is possible for people to undergo a powerful transformation process that, though it can be dramatic, is not pathological. Through education, it has helped professionals and others to differentiate these individuals from those who need medical treatment, and has created an ever-expanding support network. There is much more to do, and all of those involved with SEN believe, as we do, that their work is just beginning.

A VISION FOR A TWENTY-FOUR-HOUR CARE CENTER

Over the years, as we traveled and spoke about crises of transformation, the most frequently heard question during our lectures was: Are there any places that allow clients to go through the experience without traditional psychiatric interventions under the supervision of someone who understands the process?

Although some facilities with such intentions have been initiated in the past, such as John Perry's Diabasis house in San Francisco, they have ultimately closed due to financial problems. This difficulty reflects a lack of cultural understanding of the importance of the transformational journey. Although care at Diabasis costs a fraction of traditional psychiatric hospitalization, no insurance company would pay claims on care given there because such alternative treatment was not recognized by professionals as acceptable and legitimate.

During the time that has passed since then, a great deal has changed. The global crisis, the escalating cost of psychiatric treatment, the resurgence of interest in spirituality, and the simultaneous proliferation of transformational crises has brought us to the point where such sanctuaries may be viable. With consumers increasingly demanding a new understanding and care of individuals experiencing spiritual emergencies, new possibilities for treatment centers are bound to emerge.

We believe that spiritual-emergency centers could be organized in such a way that they would be accepted by the medical establishment and insurance companies as effective alternatives to traditional psychiatric treatment. They could easily develop in the way that birthing centers and hospices did in response to public pressure for a more humane and natural treatment of birth and death. Birth, death, and spiritual transformation are all such innate and prominent aspects of our lives that it seems essential to create special supportive environments for each.

Following is our vision of a twenty-four-hour sanctuary. Since this is a relatively new field, there are aspects of such a model that need to be tested, added to, and changed. Our description is quite general. Operational details would have to be developed according to specific situations.

The philosophy. The concept of a residential spiritual-emergency facility is based on the understanding that the transformational process is to be trusted and supported rather than suppressed and controlled. The clients are not identified as patients and the staff members are not described as experts. Rather, each person is simply seen as a participant at a certain stage in an evolutionary journey. Some have more knowledge, experience, and skills than others, but that may change with time. Staff members are committed to creating a context where the process can unfold naturally.

The setting. Ideally, the sanctuary is located in a natural setting, since people in spiritual emergencies are often very sensitive and attuned to the world around them. If this is not possible, clients and staff need to have some access to grass, trees, beaches, mountains, sunshine, gardens, or other aspects of nature. The location is removed enough from neighboring buildings that the emotional expression so frequently part of a crisis will not be disturbing to others.

The building or buildings are homelike and comfortable, with carpeted common areas for activities and group meetings, bedrooms, and a kitchen. One or two rooms with little or no furniture and cushioned walls and floor are to be used by those who need a safe place during critical stages in their process. Bathtubs or hot tubs are available for those who find comfort and healing in water.

The entire environment is aesthetically pleasing and noninstitutional. The building is painted with the same consideration that we use in painting our homes, and there are always plenty of plants and fresh flowers on the tables. Nourishing, healthy meals are cooked and presented with careful attention to their quality and appearance. And bowls of fresh fruit are always available.

Outside is a beautifully maintained flower and vegetable garden where clients can spend time digging and planting as a way of balancing their complex inner experience. Ideally, there is a swimming pool where individuals can actively express and drain intrusive energies as they arise during their process. Jogging in a nearby park, as well as other vigorous activities, might accomplish the same thing.

The staff. The staff consists of mental-health professionals, para-professionals, and lay people. All members of the staff are personally committed to the general philosophy of encouraging expression rather than suppression. The exact makeup of the staff depends upon the requirements of each situation. However, it is important to have trained facilitators who are willing to support and accompany others through their crises.

A requirement for everyone involved—cooks, administrators, counselors, maintainence people, physicians, and facilitators—is that they have experiential as well as theoretical training. This training may come from their own personal spiritual crises, an experiental method such as the Holotropic Breathwork,™ or various spiritual practices that involve states similar to those encountered during a transformational crisis. Their own experiences, along with a good theoretical foundation, enable them to recognize and understand, from the inside out, the process that they see in others. As a result, they are able to interact with clients in a relaxed, insightful, and supportive way. Ideally, they are each involved in some kind of daily spiritual practice.

A knowledgeable and supportive medical staff is another essential ingredient, since spiritual emergencies often involve physical symptoms that need to be assessed by experts. Problems such as dehydration and lack of nourishment require the supervision of a sympathetic physician. Minor tranquilizers are made available infrequently, not as a form of supressive treatment but in order to assist people in resting after long and intense periods of activity.

The exact roles of staff members depend upon the structure of the center. Because the process of spiritual emergency can be intense, it is helpful as well as healthy for staff members to limit their exposure to clients to a reasonable length of time.

In order to avoid burnout, it may be wise not to have a permanent residential staff; instead, staff members might take turns during shifts. People who are training for work with spiritual emergencies could be incorporated as temporary assistants. Additional assistance and learning might come from individuals who work in the chemical-dependency field.

Services. The general program is based on flexibility, caring, and a willingness to be adventuresome. Although there are many services available, no client receives a prescribed course of treatment. Since the transformation process has its own wisdom, dynamics, and timing, it is impossible to predict its trajectory. However, a general understanding of its nature and possibilities provides a broad frame of reference within which to be creative. In certain stages of their process, clients may go through powerful periods in which they need someone to actively work with them as they face difficult experiences. The appropriate support might range from deep experiential therapy to simple physical contact and the opportunity to talk at length with someone who understands. Sometimes they need to be alone and quiet or involved in creative expression, simple daily activities, or physically demanding exercise.

As they begin to direct their attention back to the world, they become curious about what happened to them, asking for explanations and reassurance. And when the time comes to return home, they want assistance in reentering the ordinary world and interacting with the people in their daily lives. Many of these stages have been discussed in this book; ideas such as these can be expanded during the formation of a treatment program.

In addition to round-the-clock availability of trained facilitators, specific services offered by a spiritual-emergency center might include regular counseling, one-to-one interaction with the staff, Kalff sand play (see appendix III), scheduled sessions of experiential therapy, body work, accupuncture, painting, and clay work. Frequent physical exercise and gardening are also available. Clients and staff have the use of an extensive library of art books, volumes of mythology, religion, and symbolism, and a large collection of photographs and pictures that might offer some clues as to the content of someone's experience. A good selection of videotapes on related subjects is also available.

As well as the primary care offered during a client's stay, sanctuary staff members offer help when he or she returns to the world. They know of several halfway houses that are available for those who need more time in a protected environment. These are staffed with people who are prepared to support, assist, and encourage clients as they reenter relationships, jobs, and a socially demanding world. There, residents live with people who are going through the same process and are able to gain support from the experiences of others. Successful halfway houses in the chemical-dependency arena might provide some guidelines.

The spiritual-emergence center also offers an after-care program for clients in the form of ongoing weekly support groups, individual counseling, experiential therapy, and spiritual practice. Clients also have contact with former residents who come into the sanctuary to volunteer as lay counselors, gardeners, or kitchen help. In this way, they have a chance to meet and talk with others who have traveled a similar path and have successfully integrated many of their experiences into their lives. This kind of contact can provide great hope for someone who may still feel shaky and unsure.

The staff also offers regular programs for family members and friends of people in spiritual emergency. Both while the client is in residence and afterward, family members and friends receive education and counseling related to the dynamics of the transformational process, which may have entered their lives rather suddenly. In this way, they are ultimately more able to support and understand their loved one upon his or her return to the world, as well as to care for themselves.

This dream is far from complete. Perhaps a comprehensive vision will come only with the actual planning and initiation of a spiritual-emergency center, a facility that will then serve as a model for others. And before long, we hope, a whole network of such sanctuaries, as well as halfway houses and support groups, will offer the much-needed understanding that so many people are wishing for.

SPIRITUAL EMERGENCY AND MENTAL-HEALTH PROFESSIONALS

In writing *The Stormy Search for the Self*, we have tried to make its message understandable to a broad audience. At this point, we would like to add some information that might be of interest to those who have training in psychiatry, psychology, and mental-health-related services in general. We have chosen the topics in such a way that they cover the questions most frequently asked by professionals at our lectures and workshops.

Spiritual Emergency and Contemporary Science

Many professionals, even those who are generally sympathetic toward transpersonal psychology and the concept of spiritual emergency, find it difficult to reconcile these concepts with their traditional scientific training. A system of thinking that deliberately discards everything that cannot be weighed and measured does not leave any opening for the recognition of creative cosmic intelligence, spiritual realities, or such entities as transpersonal experiences or the collective unconscious. It is very common in scientific circles to see the transpersonal perspective as something that not only is scientifically unfounded, but is also fundamentally irreconcilable with rigorous thinking. It seems important, therefore, to take a close look at the recent revolutionary developments in Western science and show that the concepts we are suggesting here are not "unscientific" or "irrational." While they are clearly incompatible with traditional Newtonian-Cartesian thinking, they are actually in basic resonance with the revolutionary developments in various disciplines of modern science that are often referred to as the new paradigm.

Let us first look at the traditional paradigm in Western science based on Newtonian physics and its basic assumptions about the nature of reality and human beings.

THE WORLDVIEW OF NEWTONIAN-CARTESIAN SCIENCE

Traditional pre-Einsteinian physics was based on a firm conviction that the universe was material in nature and was composed of fundamental building blocks, or atoms, which were solid and indestructible. The atoms moved according to certain fixed laws in three-dimensional space and in time, which was considered to flow evenly from the past through the present to the future. Newtonian science saw the existence of the universe as the history of evolving matter and the cosmos as a gigantic super-machine that was completely deterministic in its operations. If we could identify and measure all the factors acting in the world in the present moment, we should in principle be able to accurately reconstruct any situation in the past, as well as predict everything in the future. This could not be done in practice owing to the complexity of the world, which prevents us from identifying and measuring all the factors involved.

Newtonian physics was extremely successful as the intellectual force behind the scientific and industrial revolutions. It became the model for scientific endeavors in other areas, and its description of the material world became the mandatory basis for discussing all natural phenomena, including consciousness and human beings. In the worldview created by Newtonian science, life, consciousness, and creative intelligence are seen as accidental byproducts of matter.

Human beings are described as material objects with Newtonian properties, more specifically as highly developed animals and thinking biological machines. The boundaries of the human organism are absolute and coincide with the surface of the skin. In traditional thinking, consciousness and the human psyche are products of neurophysiological processes in the brain and, like this organ, are contained inside the skull. Mental activity is based on information amassed by the sensory organs and stored in the central nervous system. All acquisition of information and communication can occur only in material systems, such as the brain or the physiochemical structure of the genes, and requires the exchange of currently known and measurable energies. Extrasensory communication and access to new information without the mediation of the senses are considered to be impossible.

In addition, the above description of the nature of reality and of human beings has in the past been generally seen not for what it is—a useful model organizing the observations and knowledge available at a certain time in the history of science—but as a definitive and accurate description of reality itself. From a logical point of view, this would be considered a serious confusion of the "map" with the "territory."

The contemporary approach to mental health and disease is a direct result of the generalized application of Newtonian thinking to psychiatric problems. According to this point of view, the central nervous system simply reflects this objectively existing world. All definitions of psychosis emphasize the individual's inability to discriminate between subjective experiences and the world of consensus reality, often referred to as objective reality.

A normally functioning human brain should reflect the universe correctly and accurately. And since traditional science sees the world as actually possessing Newtonian properties, sanity requires that the individual perceive and think about it in those terms. A serious departure from the experience of "objective reality" suggests that some pathological process must have disturbed proper functioning of the brain. Such an individual is seen as suffering from "mental disease."

Since the concepts of objective reality and accurate reality testing are the key factors in determining whether the individual is mentally healthy, the scientific understanding of the nature of reality is absolutely critical in this regard. Therefore, any fundamental change in the scientific worldview has to have far-reaching consequences for the definition of psychosis. In fact, in the course of this century the scientific understanding of reality has undergone dramatic changes, but traditional psychologists and psychiatrists have not yet accepted the inevitable consequences for their disciplines.

THE EMERGING PARADIGM IN WESTERN SCIENCE

Revolutionary developments in a variety of scientific disciplines have now outlined a worldview that is radically different from the Newtonian image of the universe. Some of the most radical changes have occurred in physics, the cornerstone of mechanistic science. With the advent of Einstein's theory of relativity and quantum physics, the traditional concepts of matter, time, and space have been transcended. The physical universe has come to be viewed as a unified web of paradoxical, statistically determined events in which consciousness and creative intelligence play a critical role.

The recognition that the universe is not a mechanical system but an infinitely complex interplay of vibratory phenomena of different types and frequencies prepared the ground for an understanding of reality based on entirely new principles. This approach has become known as holographic, because some of its remarkable features can be demonstrated with the use of optical holograms as conceptual tools. Two scientists who became best known for their contributions to this exciting new way of viewing reality are the physicist David Bohm and the brain researcher Karl Pribram. A comprehensive discussion of the holographic understanding of the universe and the brain would be beyond the scope of this volume; this topic was covered in the book *Beyond the Brain* and other publications, and we have to refer the interested readers to these sources.

An aspect of holographic thinking that is particularly relevant to our discussion is the possibility of an entirely new relationship between the parts and the whole. The information in holographic systems is distributed in such a way that all of it is contained and available in each of its parts. This property can be demonstrated by cutting an optical hologram in many pieces and showing that each of its fragments is capable of reproducing the entire image.

The concept of "distributed information" opens up entirely new perspectives in the understanding of how transpersonal experiences can mediate direct access to information about various aspects of the universe that lie outside the conventionally defined boundaries of the individual. If the individual and the brain are not isolated entities but integral parts of a universe with holographic properties—if they are in some way microcosms of a much larger system—then it is conceivable that they can have direct and immediate access to information outside themselves.

Among some of the other major critics of conventional thinking, we should mention Gregory Bateson, who challenged traditional thinking by demonstrating that all boundaries in the world are illusory and that mind and nature are inseparable. Another fundamental challenge to conventional thinking is the work of the British biologist Rupert Sheldrake. He pointed out that traditional science, in its one-sided pursuit of "energetic causation," has entirely neglected the problem of the origination of form in nature. His concept of morphic resonance suggests that forms in nature and various types of learning are governed by fields that cannot be detected and measured by contemporary science.

Modern discoveries in psychology and psychiatry have not been less startling and radical than those in the natural sciences. Jung's findings concerning the collective unconscious, archetypes, and synchronicity are again undermining the position of mechanistic science, as well as stretching the boundaries of pedestrian common sense. They show the psyche as a universal principle that informs all existence and is inseparable from the material world of consensus reality. And the transpersonal experiences discovered by modern consciousness research have properties that call in question the very foundations of traditonal beliefs about the relationship between consciousness and matter.

The new findings suggest that consciousness is not a product of the human brain; it is mediated by the brain but does not originate there. Modern research has brought forth startling evidence showing that consciousness might be an equal partner of matter, or even supraordinated to it. It is increasingly emerging as a primary attribute of existence that is inextricably woven into the fabric of the universe on all levels.

A NEW IMAGE OF HUMAN BEINGS

The discoveries of the last few decades strongly suggest that the psyche is not limited to postnatal biography and to the Freudian individual unconscious and confirm the perennial truth, found in many mystical traditions, that human beings might be commensurate with all there is. Transpersonal experiences and their extraordinary potential certainly attest to this fact.

The new image of human beings is paradoxical in nature and involves two complementary aspects. In everyday situations involving ordinary states of consciousness, it might seem appropriate to think of people as biological machines. However, in nonordinary states of mind they can also show properties of infinite fields of consciousness—transcending time, space, and linear causality. This is the image that the mystical traditions have described for millenia. Recently it has received unexpected support from thanatology, parapsychology, anthropology, experiential psychotherapies, and psychedelic research, as well as the work with spiritual emergencies.

All the experiences we have in our ordinary state of consciousness systematically confirm the notion that we are Newtonian objects living in a world that has Newtonian properties. Matter is solid, space is three-dimensional, time is linear, and everything is connected by chains of cause and effect. We can call this way of experiencing ourselves and the world the *"hylotropic" mode of consciousness* (literally, "matter-oriented"; from the Greek *hyle* = "matter" and *trepein* = "moving toward"). In the hylotropic state of consciousness we can never experience fully, with all our senses, anything but the present moment and the present location.

This situation is in sharp contrast with the way we experience ourselves and the world in certain nonordinary states of consciousness that occur in deep meditation, hypnosis, experiential psychotherapy, psychedelic sessions, and sometimes spontaneously. Here we are referring to the *"holotropic" mode of consciousness* (literally, "moving toward wholeness"; from the Greek *holos* = "whole" and *trepein*).

In this mode of consciousness, we can experience a wide spectrum of phenomena; some of them are vivid reenactments of past events, others are sequences of death and rebirth, and yet others are various aspects of the transpersonal domain. They give us strong experiential evidence that the world of matter is not solid, that all its boundaries are arbitrary, and that we ourselves are not material bodies but limitless fields of consciousness. They also show the possibility that Newtonian time and space can be transcended and suggest the existence of realities and beings that are not material in nature.

In traditional psychiatry, all holotropic experiences have been interpreted as pathological phenomena, in spite of the fact that the alleged disease process has never been identified; this reflects the fact that the old paradigm did not have an adequate explanation for these experiences and was not able to account for them in any other way. However, careful study of holotropic experiences shows that they are not pathological products of the brain; rather, they reveal extraordinary capacities of the human psyche and important aspects of reality normally hidden from our awareness.

A description of human beings involving a paradox might at first seem strange and unacceptable for science, which demands clear and logical answers. However, it is important to realize that there is a significant precedent; in the 1930s, scientists encountered a paradox in subatomic physics: the so called wave-particle paradox, the fact that light and subatomic matter can manifest themselves in some situations as particles and in others as waves. This is formally expressed in Neils Bohr's complementarity principle, which states that both of these aspects, although seemingly irreconcilable, are two complementary aspects of the same phenomenon. We are now encountering a similar paradox in the sciences that study human beings.

THE DIAGNOSIS OF SPIRITUAL EMERGENCY

Two important and frequently asked questions are how one can diagnose spiritual emergency and how it is possible to differentiate transformational crises from spiritual emergence and from mental illness. To ask these questions seriously, a mental-health professional has to accept the fact that spirituality is a legitimate dimension of existence and that its awakening and development are desirable.

The criteria for distinguishing between spiritual emergence and spiritual emergency are summarized in table 1 (see p. 37). Since there are no sharp boundaries between the two conditions, these criteria have to be considered merely useful general guidelines. The first important cri-

teria are the intensity and depth of the process, its fluidity, and the degree
to which the individual involved can function in everyday life.

Equally important is the attitude to what is happening—whether the
process is seen as exciting and valuable or frightening and overwheming.
And finally, the ability to handle the interface with the rest of the society
is of paramount importance. The degree of discrimination in regard to
the people with whom one chooses to talk about the exeriences and the
language one uses can be a decisive factor in determining whether the
person will be hospitalized.

When the decision has been made that the person has transcended
the boundaries of spiritual emergence and is facing a crisis, diagnostic
considerations come next. We have again summarized in the form of a
table (see table 2 on pp. 254–255) the major criteria for differentiating
spiritual emergencies from strictly medical diseases and from so-called
mental diseases.

The first diagnostic task is to exclude any medical condition detectable
by existing clinical and laboratory techniques that could be responsible
for the perceptual, emotional, and other manifestations involved—such
conditions as encephalitis, meningitis or other infectious diseases, brain
arteriosclerosis, temporal tumor, uremia, and other diseases that are
known to alter consciousness. The psychological symptoms of these organic psychoses are clearly distinguishable from functional psychoses by
means of psychiatric examination and psychological tests. The criteria
for making such distinctions are shown in the first half of table 2.

When the appropriate examinations and tests have excluded the possibility that the problem we are dealing with is organic in nature, the
next task is to find out whether the client fits into the category of spiritual
emergency—in other words, differentiate this state from functional psychoses. There is no way of establishing absolutely clear criteria for dif-
ferentiation between spiritual emergency and psychosis or mental
disease, since such terms themselves lack objective scientific validity. One
should not confuse categories of this kind with such precisely defined
disease entities as diabetes mellitus or pernicious anemia. Functional
psychoses are not diseases in a strictly medical sense and cannot be
identified with the degree of accuracy that is required in medicine when
establishing a differential diagnosis.

The task of deciding whether we are dealing with a spiritual emergency in a particular case means in practical terms that we must assess
whether the client could benefit from the strategies described in this book
or should be treated in traditional ways. The criteria for such a decision
are summarized in the second half of table 2. The content of a typical

TABLE 2. DIFFERENTIATION BETWEEN SPIRITUAL EMERGENCE AND PSYCHIATRIC DISORDERS

Characteristics of the process indicating need for medical approach to the problem	Characteristics of the process suggesting that the strategy for SE might work
Criteria of a Medical Nature	
Clinical examination and laboratory tests detect a physical disease that causes psychological changes	Negative results of clinical examinations and laboratory tests for a physical disease
Clinical examination and laboratory tests detect a disease process of the brain that causes psychological changes (neurological reflexes, cerebrospinal fluid, X ray, etc.)	Negative results of clinical examinations and laboratory tests for pathological process afflicting the brain
Specific psychological tests indicate organic impairment of the brain	Negative results of psychological tests for organic impairment
Impairment of intellect and memory, clouded consciousness, problems with basic orientation (name, time, place), poor coordination	Intellect and memory qualitatively changed but intact, consciousness usually clear, good basic orientation, coordination not seriously impaired
Confusion, disorganization, and defective intellectual functioning interfere with communication and cooperation	Ability to communicate and cooperate (occasional deep involvement in the inner process might be a problem)
Criteria of a Psychological Nature	
Personal history shows serious difficulties in interpersonal relationships since childhood, inability to make friends and have intimate sexual relationships, poor social adjustment, usually long history of psychiatric problems	Adequate pre-episode functioning as evidenced by interpersonal skills, some success in school and vocation, network of friends, and ability to have sexual relationships; no serious psychiatric history

Poorly organized and defined content of the process, unqualified changes of emotions and behavior, unspecific disorganization of psychological functions, lack of meaning of any kind, no indication of direction of development, loosening of associations, incoherence

Sequences of biographical memories, themes of birth and death, transpersonal experiences, possible insight that the process is healing or spiritual in nature, change and development of themes, often definable progression, incidence of true synchronicities (evident to others)

Autistic withdrawal, aggressivity, or controlling and manipulative behavior interferes with a good working relationship and makes cooperation impossible

Ability to relate and cooperate, often even during episodes of dramatic experiences that occur spontaneously or in the course of psychotherapeutic work

Inability to see the process as an intrapsychic affair, confusion between the inner experiences and the outer world, excessive use of projection and blaming, "acting out"

Awareness of the intrapsychic nature of the process, satisfactory ability to distinguish between the inner and the outer, "owning" the process, ability to keep it internalized

Basic mistrust, perception of the world and all people as hostile, delusions of persecution, acoustic hallucinations of enemies ("voices") with a very unpleasant content

Sufficient trust to accept help and cooperate; persecutory delusions and "voices" absent

Violations of basic rules of therapy ("not to hurt oneself or anybody else, not to destroy property"), destructive and self-destructive (suicidal or self-mutilating) impulses and a tendency to act on them without warning

Ability to honor basic rules of therapy, absence of destructive or self-destructive ideas and tendencies, or ability to talk about them and to accept precautionary measures

Behavior endangering health and causing serious concerns (refusal to eat or drink for prolonged periods of time, neglect of basic hygienic rules)

Good cooperation in things related to physical health, basic maintenance, and hygienic rules spiritual emergency is a combination of transpersonal, perinatal, and biographical experiences. It shows a reasonable degree of coherence and likely revolves around one of the themes described in chapter 4 or combines a few of them.

Among the favorable signs are a history of reasonable psychological, sexual, and social adjustment preceding the episode, the ability to consider the possibility that the process might originate in one's own psyche, enough trust to cooperate, and a willingness to honor the basic rules of treatment. Conversely, a lifelong history of serious psychological difficulties and of marginal sexual and social adjustment can generally be seen as suggesting caution. Similarly, a confused and poorly organized content of the experiences, presence of Bleuler's primary symptoms of schizophrenia, strong participation of manic elements, the systematic use of projection, and the presence of persecutory voices and delusions indicate that traditional approaches might be preferable. Strong destructive and self-destructive tendencies and violations of basic rules of treatment are further negative indicators.

In clients who fit the category of spiritual emergency, attempts to use traditional psychiatric labels makes very little sense. However, since professionals with traditional training are used to thinking in those terms and also often have to practice in the context of the established medical system, the labeling issue will be addressed here briefly.

The choices that the official *American Diagnostic and Statistical Manual* (DSM III) gives to mental-health practitioners to describe individuals who are experiencing spiritual emergency are clearly unsatisfactory. They include, by and large, schizophrenic reactions, manic-depressive reactions, and paranoid reactions. Careful analysis of the manifestations of the major types of spiritual emergency shows that they do not fit any of the official categories. Since traditional psychiatry makes no distinction between psychotic reactions and mystical states, not only crises of spiritual opening but also uncomplicated transpersonal experiences often receive a pathological label.

This situation has been justly criticized by transpersonally oriented therapists and researchers. The most outspoken and articulate critic of the present diagnostic practices in regard to mystical states and spiritual emergencies has been David Lukoff, a psychiatrist at the University of California at Los Angeles. He has emphasized the need to clearly distinguish mystical states from psychotic reactions. He feels psychiatry should have, in addition, two categories for conditions in which the mystical and the psychotic overlap: mystical states with psychotic features and psychotic states with mystical features.

Under present circumstances, the use of diagnostic labels obscures the issues and interferes with the healing potential of the process. In addition to its socially stigmatizing and psychologically damaging effects, it creates a false impression that the disorder is a precisely identified disease and serves as a justification for suppressive medication as a scientifically indicated approach.

Therapeutic Techniques and Strategies for Spiritual Emergencies

Nonordinary states of consciousness make it possible for unconscious material with strong emotional charge to emerge into consciousness. This process is an expression of a powerful spontaneous healing potential and should be supported. Under such circumstances, emotional and psychosomatic symptoms are not problems to be combatted but indications of a healing effort by the organism that has to be supported, encouraged, and brought to completion.

As therapists, we have to explain this basic philosophy to our clients and be sure that they understand and accept it before we proceed any further. The next step is to provide a safe environment where the person we are working with will not be disturbed and where we do not have to be concerned about disturbing others by loud noises. Then, if the process is very active, all we have to do, after setting certain rules concerning destructive or self-destructive behavior, is encourage the client to let it unfold and cooperate with what is happening.

In cases involving emergence rather than emergency, or where the crisis of transformation has reached an impasse, it is often necessary or appropriate to use approaches that have an activating effect on the unconscious. These can be different combinations of the experiential therapies developed in the context of humanistic and transpersonal psychology for emotional release, together with body work. We use for this purpose the method of Holotropic Breathwork.™ We originally developed this approach for experiential self-exploration and healing but have found it to be very helpful in situations involving spiritual emergence and emergency as well.

Holotropic Breathwork™ will be discussed at some length, since it is very important for the problem of spiritual development. This method can facilitate powerful transformative experiences and can also accelerate and deepen spiritual emergence in people who are already in this process. In addition, the basic therapeutic strategies used in this work are identical with those that seem to work best with individuals in psychospiritual crises. Thus the training of facilitators for Holotropic Breathwork,™

which combines personal breathing experience with assisting others, is also a very effective training for therapists working with people in spiritual emergencies. And finally, this method can be used with some people in transformational crises as an effective way to overcome impasses or to deepen and accelerate the process. Those who seek more specific information should refer to Stanislav Grof's *The Adventure of Self-Discovery*.

We use the term *holotropic* in two different ways—for the therapeutic technique we have developed and for the mode of consciousness that it induces. The use of the word *holotropic* in relation to therapy suggests that the goal is to overcome inner fragmentation as well as the sense of separation between the individual and the environment. The relationship between wholeness and healing is reflected in the English language, since both words have the same root.

In preparing people for holotropic breathing, we start with a discussion of the types of experiences that can emerge during the process. This is important, since the average Westerner is naive about nonordinary states of consciousness and has many misconceptions and prejudices about some of the experiences that are potentially the most healing. We try to convey a clear message that such phenomena as death-rebirth sequences, archetypal visions, past-incarnation experiences, and states of cosmic unity are absolutely normal and that having them in no way implies pathology.

It is usually emphasized that these experiences occur regularly during this form of self-exploration and that they have already been experienced by many others. The purpose of this part of the preparation is to give the participants permission to accept and trust whatever contents emerge from the depths of the psyche. This message is also extremely important for individuals in transpersonal crisis whose psyche is activated by unknown factors. Most of the difficulties in these states arise from resistance to the process and an unwillingness or inability to cooperate with its healing potential.

Also discussed are the technique of Holotropic Breathwork™, the specifics of the body work, and the basic rules of the procedure. If the work is done in a group—our preferred format—half of the group does the breathing and the other half functions as attendants (or "sitters") who create a safe environment and provide support. In that case, we also give guidelines for sitters. Participants then pair up and decide who will go first. Naturally, people in intense forms of transformation crisis cannot be used as sitters until their process stabilizes.

After this introduction, the holotropic session begins. The people who have chosen to do the breath work are asked to lie down on mattresses. They are guided through a brief relaxation exercise that focuses their attention on the body, mind, and breath. When the breathers are relaxed, we suggest that they increase their rate of breathing and open to the flow of the music that will be played all through the session. We tell them that it is essential to suspend analytical judgment and to allow images, emotions, and physical feelings to emerge, completely uncensored and unimpeded.

The reaction to this combination of accelerated breathing, music, and introspective focus of attention varies from person to person. After a period of about fifteen minutes to half an hour, most of the participants show strong active response. Some experience a buildup of intense emotions, such as sadness, joy, anger, fear, or sexual arousal. The specific form of response depends on the material that is emerging from the unconscious. Others sense a strong increase of body tension and might express it in tremors, spasms, pelvic movements, or dramatic gestures of hands and arms. Very frequently, accompanying visions or memories help to identify the source of these feelings and sensations.

Occasionally, a person completely internalizes the experience, showing very little on the outside. This does not neccessarily mean that he or she is not responding. We have seen many powerful and life-transforming experiences with minimal external expression of emotions or body movement. In each group, there are always several people who respond by becoming progressively more relaxed, feeling permeated by light, and losing their boundaries with the external world. They might move directly into a profound mystical experience of unity without any preceding tension or struggle.

This powerful but peaceful experience directly conflicts with the descriptions of the effects of accelerated breathing found in standard medical handbooks. According to the traditional view, fast breathing always produces dramatic spasms of the hands and feet. This so-called hyperventilation syndrome is seen as a mandatory physiological response to intense breathing and is attributed to changes in the ionized-calcium level of the blood.

Our observations suggest a very different explanation. It seems that the nonordinary state of consciousness induced by holotropic breathing is associated with biochemical changes in the brain that make it possible for the contents of the unconscious to surface, to be consciously experienced, and—if necessary—to be physically expressed. In our bodies and in our psyches we carry imprints of various traumatic events that we have not fully digested and assimilated psychologically. Holotropic breathing makes them available, so that we can fully experience them and release the emotions that are associated with them. The physical tensions and pains that occur in some people during faster breathing are part of the surfacing material, not a simple response to breathing. They tend to disappear when the old traumas are cleared.

Holotropic Breathwork℠ thus represents an extremely effective procedure for reducing stress and tension. The responses of different people to the same situation vary, covering a wide range of physical manifestations and, naturally, an even greater range with regard to psychological content. The possibilities include unfinished biographical issues, a perinatal sequence of psychological death and rebirth, or a transpersonal theme, such as a past-life memory, a mythological motif, or feelings of cosmic unity. In this respect holotropic sessions resemble spiritual emergencies, although of course in the latter case the psyche is stimulated not intentionally but by unknown factors.

Activation of the psyche by faster breathing seems to set into motion spontaneous healing processes that are governed by deep organismic wisdom. Whether or not we understand it at the time, the experiences that emerge are expressions of this healing potential. For this reason, the optimal mental attitude during the holotropic process is one of receptiveness, openness, and willingness to experience with complete trust anything that emerges from the unconscious or superconscious. This yielding and allowing is a stance that is more characteristic of Oriental spiritual disciplines than of Western therapies, where the objective is to work on a specific issue and change it in the desirable direction. In holotropic therapy (and during an episode of spiritual emergency) the most useful strategy is to be fully present, to experience whatever emerges into consciousness, and to surrender to the experience.

Whatever the nature and specific content of the holotropic session, the process seems to have a characteristic trajectory. The intensity of the experiences gradually increases until it reaches a culmination point, where most people who have dealt with some painful issues feel a sense of resolution or even a breakthrough. Their experience opens from darkness into light, tensions are released, pains disappear, and difficult emotions are replaced by a sense of peace and joy. The rest of the session is spent in quiet meditation as they make the transition to everyday consciousness.

At the end of the session, people usually feel completely relaxed and at peace with themselves. We often hear comments such as "I have never been this relaxed in my entire life" and "I have never felt this good." In some, this sense of well-being is more profound: they experience serenity and tranquillity, have visions of soft, radiant light, and feel closely connected with other people, nature, and the universe. Such experiences of cosmic unity are extremely healing and can have lasting beneficial effects.

Many people in holotropic sessions successfully resolve the issues that have emerged through breathing alone and complete the session without needing any external interventions from the sitters or from us. Sometimes, though, the person does have some residual physical or emotional discomfort, such as anger, with pain and tension in the neck and shoulders; sadness, with heaviness in the chest; or excess energy in the arms and hands. These problems indicate that the person has not yet properly completed the experience.

In these cases we use a technique we call "focused body work"; its basic purpose is to bring the problem that underlies the symptom fully into consciousness. This can be done by a combined effort of the person involved and the facilitator. While the breather intentionally accentuates the discomfort, we further reinforce it by external intervention, such as pressure or massage.

The main strategy at this stage is to allow the rest of the body to find its own way to react fully to the situation. The process will automatically find the most effective means of release. However, since the underlying problems can be biographical issues, aspects of biological birth, or anything from the transpersonal realm, the external manifestations can cover an extremely wide range.

We often see intense tremors, body movements, grimaces, complex gestures, or even animal behavior patterns such as crawling, swimming, or clawing. The person may make a variety of sounds—scream, cry and talk like a baby, speak in tongues or in a foreign language, emit animal noises, or sing shamanic chants. It is important to trust the process, since such strange manifestations can often lead to an unexpected resolution of difficult emotional and psychosomatic problems. It is important to continue this work until a satisfactory completion is achieved.

The technique of Holotropic Breathwork™ is extremely simple in comparison with traditional forms of verbal psychotherapy, which emphasize the therapist's understanding of the process, correct and properly timed interpretations, and work with transference—trying to disentagle the distortions in the person's relationship to the therapist that are caused by the emerging unconscious material. It also has a much less technical emphasis than many of the new experiential methods, such as Gestalt therapy, rolfing, and bioenergetics. We simply utilize the spontaneous healing forces that become available in nonordinary states of consciousness and their intrinsic wisdom.

The expertise of the holotropic therapist is not in a profound intellectual understanding of the therapeutic process. This issue is highly problematic anyway, since the theoretical constructs vary widely from school to school. The strength of a holotropic therapist lies in his or her ability to unconditionally encourage and support a dramatic experiential process in another person, even if it involves extreme emotions, unusual physical symptoms, and experiences that are not easily understandable. The emphasis in Holotropic Breathwork™ is not on brilliant insights and interpretations or on standard physical interventions or manipulations. The focused body work follows the energy and facilitates release wherever it is about to happen spontaneously. The same strategy is also extremely useful in situations involving spiritual emergencies.

This capacity to be there for another person, to remain unperturbed no matter what form the process takes, to trust the intrinsic wisdom of the healing forces of the organism, and to support—without judgment and even without intellectual understanding—whatever is happening is the key to effective holotropic work. It can come only from extensive personal experiences of nonordinary states and from repeated exposure to such states in others. This is why the training of holotropic therapists and facilitators for spiritual emergencies always combines working with others on a one-to-one basis, supervised group work, and systematic self-exploration in one's own holotropic sessions.

The term *therapist* is used in holotropic work in its original Greek meaning: "a person assisting in the process of healing." The nonordinary state of consciousness has the remarkable capacity to select and bring into conscious awareness unconscious contents that have a strong emotional charge and are thus psychologically important. In this process, they lose their previous power to disturb the emotional and physical well-being of the person involved. Since healing under these circumstances is spontaneous and elemental, the therapist is not instrumental in the therapeutic process. He or she is a sympathetic coadventurer who can intelligently cooperate with the natural healing forces.

In traditional therapies, the client generally remains in a passive role and relies entirely on the training and skills of the therapist. The therapist's understanding of the problems involved and of the therapeutic process is seen as far superior to that of the client. The general nature of the difficulties is more or less theoretically clear as predicated by the school to which a particular therapist belongs. It is up to the client to catch up with this understanding emotionally and intellectually in the course of therapy. Therapists often have very little awareness of how relative this so-called understanding is; the interpretations vary considerably from one school to another and from therapist to therapist; the lack of agreement in this area is truly astonishing.

In the holotropic model, the client is seen as the real source of healing and is encouraged to realize that and to develop a sense of mastery and independence. In regard to the general understanding of the process, the therapist's theoretical knowledge, specific training, previous personal holotropic sessions, and work with many other clients represent a distinct advantage. However, in understanding the specifics of the problems involved, the client is in many respects ahead of the therapist. In a certain sense, he or she is ultimately the only real expert because of his or her immediate access to the experiential process that provides all the clues. It is the client who discovers the deep roots of symptoms, confronts the unconscious material behind them, works through them, and reports to the therapist his or her observations and insights.

Our experiences with Holotropic Breathwork™ have validated the concept of spiritual emergency both theoretically and practically. They have confirmed that the phenomena that occur spontaneously during transformative crises are normal constituents of the human psyche and not artificial products of some exotic pathological process. The spectrum of holotropic experiences is practically identical with that of spiritual emergencies; the fact that such simple means as an increased rate of breathing can induce them certainly takes away much of their pathological sting. And indirectly, the therapeutic and transformative potential of Holotropic Breathwork™ is in full accord with the assumption that the same is true for most spiritual emergencies.

Many additional therapeutic methods can be of great value in different stages and forms of spiritual emergence and emergency. All of them belong to so-called uncovering therapies—approaches that mediate access to unconscious material and facilitate its integration. They all have the same general goal: to reach a greater self-understanding and to get to the roots of emotional and psychosomatic problems.

Among these methods, Fritz Perls's Gestalt practice can be particularly useful; it can help to focus on the symptoms, explore the underlying unconscious issues, and facilitate completion. Paul Rebillot's unique process, called "the Hero's Journey," a synthesis of Gestalt, psychodrama, music, and ritual, can be extremely helpful in confronting various difficult areas of the psyche in a playful and nonthreatening way. The same is true for various exercises of Roberto Assagioli's psychosynthesis using the method of guided imagery. Dora Kalff's sand-play therapy, based on the principles of Jungian psychology, offers an extraordinary opportunity to concretize the contents of the unconscious by creating complex scenes in a sandbox and making them available for conscious analysis. This remarkable tool should be included in any facility treating psychospiritual crises.

Body work plays an important and integral part in the treatment of transformational crises. We have already described focused body work that is aimed at releasing blocked emotional and physical energies. Bioenergetics and other forms of Reichian and neo-Reichian techniques can be very useful for the same purpose. Rolfing and various forms of massage can be important supplements to therapy, provided the practitioners allow the expression of the emotions that arise in the process. Acupuncture by an experienced practitioner can also be valuable, since it can facilitate the free flow of previously blocked emotions and physical energies.

Artistic expression of various kinds should also be an integral part of any comprehensive treatment program of psychospiritual crises. Like Jungian sand play, painting can play an important role in concretizing unconscious contents and facilitating their conscious integration. Used in a free, expressive way, it is a very powerful therapeutic tool in its own right. Some people find work with clay or other similar materials to be more meaningful and effective. Another significant channel is dancing, particularly spontaneous and creative movements that allow full expression of various dynamic forces in the psyche.

Ideally, the therapy of people in spiritual emergencies should be conducted in a retreat center like the one we have described earlier. Here all these techniques would be available and could be applied with discrimination and sensitivity to the form the process takes, its stage, and its momentary intensity. Depending on circumstances, it could be carried out on an outpatient basis, or the clients could stay overnight if necessary, since expert help would be available around the clock. Such a center would also offer support groups similar to the twelve-step programs.

BIBLIOGRAPHY

Listed below are works related to the problem of spiritual emergency.

Alternative Understanding of Psychotic States

Dabrowski, K. *Positive Disintegration*. Boston: Little, Brown, 1966.

Laing, R. D. *The Divided Self*. Baltimore: Penguin, 1965.

_____. *The Politics of Experience*. New York: Ballantine, 1967.

Mosher, L., and A. Menn. *Soteria: An Alternative to Hospitalization for Schizophrenics*. Vol.1 of *New Directions for Health Services*. San Francisco: Jossey-Bass, 1979.

Rappaport, M., et al. "Are There Schizophrenics for Whom Drugs May Be Unnecessary or Contraindicated?" *International Pharmacopsychiatry* 13 (1978):100.

Silverman, J. "Acute Schizophrenia: Disease or Dis-Ease?" *Psychology Today* 4 (1970):62.

_____. "When Schizophrenia Helps." *Psychology Today* (1971).

Szasz, T. *The Myth of Mental Illness*. New York: Hoeber-Harper, 1961.

Psychological Approaches to Psychotic States

Abraham, K. "A Short History of the Development of the Libido, Viewed in the Light of Mental Disorders." In *Selected Papers of Karl Abraham*. London: Hogarth Press/Institute of Psychoanalysis, 1942.

Arieti, S. *Intepretation of Schizophrenia*. New York: Robert Brunner, 1955.

Bateson, G. "Toward a Theory of Schizophrenia." In *Steps to An Ecology of Mind*. New York: Dutton, 1982.

Freud, S. *Psychoanalytic Notes upon an Autobiographical Account of a Case of Paranoia*. In *The Standard Edition of the Complete Works of Sigmund Freud*, edited by J. Strachey, vol. 12. London: Hogarth Press/Institute of Psychoanalysis, 1958.

Fromm-Reichmann, F.: *Principles of Intensive Psychotherapy*. Chicago: University of Chicago Press, 1950.

Jung, C. G. *The Psychogenesis of Mental Disease*. In *Collected Works*, vol. 3. Bollingen Series XX., Princeton: Princeton University Press, 1972.

Lidz, T. "Schizophrenia and the Family." *Psychiatry* 21 (1958):21.

Malamud, W. "The Application of Psychoanalytic Principles in Interpreting the Psychoses." *Psychoanalytic Review* 16 (1929).

Sullivan, H. S. *Schizophrenia as a Human Process*. New York: Norton, 1962.

Tausk, V. "On the Origin of the Influencing Machine in Schizophrenia." *Psychoanalytic Quarterly* 2 (1933):519–66.

Literature on Consciousness Relevant to Spiritual Emergency

Grof, S. *Beyond the Brain*. Albany, N.Y.: State University of New York Press, 1985.

———. *The Adventure of Self-Discovery*. Albany, N.Y.: State University of New York Press, 1987.

Grof, S., and C. Grof. *Beyond Death*. London: Thames and Hudson, 1980.

Tart, C. *States of Consciousness*. New York: Dutton, 1975.

Walsh, R. and F. Vaughan, eds. *Beyond Ego*. Los Angeles: Jeremy P. Tarcher, 1980.

Wilber, K. *The Spectrum of Consciousness*. Wheaton, Ill.: Theosophical Publishing House, 1977.

———. *The Atman Project: A Transpersonal View of Human Development*. Wheaton, Ill.: Theosophical Publishing House, 1980.

Spiritual Emergency

Assagioli, R. "Self-Realization and Psychological Disturbances." In *Spiritual Emergency: When Personal Transformation Becomes a Crisis*, edited by S. Grof and C. Grof. Los Angeles: Jeremy P. Tarcher, 1989.

Boisen, A. *The Exploration of the Inner World*. New York: Harper, 1962.

Bragdon, E. *A Sourcebook for Helping People in Spiritual Emergency*. Los Altos, Calif.: Lightening Up Press, 1988.

Grof, S., and C. Grof, eds. *Spiritual Emergency: When Personal Transformation Becomes a Crisis.* Los Angeles: Jeremy P. Tarcher, 1989.

Hood, B. L. "Transpersonal Crisis: Understanding Spiritual Emergencies." Ph.D. diss., University of Massachusetts, Boston, 1986.

Lukoff, D. "Diagnosis of Mystical Experiences with Psychotic Features." *Journal of Transpersonal Psychology* 17 (1985):155.

Lukoff, D., and H. Everest. "The Myths of Mental Illness." *Journal of Transpersonal Psychology* 17 (1985):123.

Wilber, K., J. Engler, and D. Brown. *Transformations of Consciousness.* Boston: New Science Library/Shambhala, 1986.

The following are works on specific forms of spiritual emergency.

Shamanism and the Shamanic Crisis

Campbell, J. *The Way of the Animal Powers.* New York: Harper and Row, 1984.

Castaneda, C. *Teachings of Don Juan: A Yaqui Way of Knowledge.* Berkeley: University of California Press, 1968.

———. *A Separate Reality: Further Conversations with Don Juan.* New York: Simon and Schuster, 1971.

Doore, G. *Shaman's Path: Healing, Personal Growth, and Empowerment.* Boston: Shambhala, 1988.

Eliade, M. *Shamanism: The Archaic Techniques of Ecstasy.* New York: Pantheon, 1964.

Halifax, J. *Shamanic Voices: A Survey of Visionary Narratives.* New York: Dutton, 1979.

———. *Shaman: The Wounded Healer.* London: Thames and Hudson, 1982.

Harner, M.: *The Way of the Shaman.* New York: Harper and Row, 1980.

Kalweit, H. *Dreamtime and the Inner Space: The World of the Shamans.* Boston: Shambhala, 1988.

Larsen, S. *The Shaman's Doorway: Opening the Mythic Imagination to Contemporary Consciousness.* San Francisco: Harper and Row, 1976.

Nicolson, S., ed. *Shamanism: An Expanded View of Reality.* Wheaton, Ill.: Theosophical Publishing House, 1987.

Silverman, J. "Shamans and Acute Schizophrenia." *American Anthropologist* 69 (1967):21.

Kundalini Awakening

Jung, C. G. *Psychological Commentary on Kundalini Yoga.* New York: Spring Publications, 1975.

Kripananda, Swami. *Kundalini: The Energy of Transformation.* In *Ancient Wisdom and Modern Science,* edited by S. Grof. Albany, N.Y.: State University of New York Press, 1984.

Krishna, G. *Kundalini: The Evolutionary Energy in Man.* Berkeley: Shambhala, 1970.

_____. *Kundalini for the New Age.* Edited by G. Kieffer. New York: Bantam Books, 1988.

Mookerjee, A. *Kundalini: The Arousal of Inner Energy.* New York: Destiny, 1982.

Muktananda, Swami. *Play of Consciousness.* South Fallsburg, N.Y.: SYDA Foundation, 1974.

_____. *Kundalini: The Secret of Life.* South Fallsburg, N.Y.: SYDA Foundation, 1979.

Sannella, L.: *The Kundalini Experience: Psychosis or Transcendence.* Lower Lake, Calif.: Integral Publishing, 1987.

_____. "The Many Faces of Kundalini." *The Laughing Man Magazine* 4, No. 3 (1983):11–21.

White, J., ed. *Kundalini: Evolution and Enlightenment.* Garden City, N.Y.: Anchor, 1979.

Woodruffe, Sir J. *The Serpent Power.* Madras: Ganesh, 1964.

Peak Experiences

Bucke, R. *Cosmic Consciousness.* New York: Dutton, 1923.

James, W. *Varieties of Religious Experience.* New York: Collier, 1961.

Laski, M. *Ecstasy: A Study of Some Secular and Religious Experiences.* New York: Greenwood, 1968.

Maslow, A. *Toward a Psychology of Being.* Princeton: Van Nostrand, 1962.

_____. *Religions, Values, and Peak Experiences.* Cleveland: Ohio State University Press, 1964.

Underhill, E. *Mysticism: A Study in the Nature and Development of Man's Spiritual Consciousness.* New York: Meridian, 1955.

Mythology, Jungian Writings, and John Perry's Work

Campbell, J. *The Masks of God*. New York: Viking, 1968.

_____. *The Hero with a Thousand Faces*. Cleveland: World Publishing, 1970.

_____. *Myths to Live By*. New York: Bantam, 1972.

_____. *The Mythic Image*. Princeton: Princeton University Press, 1974.

_____. *The Inner Reaches of Outer Space: Metaphor as Myth and as Religion*. New York: Alfred van der Marck, 1986.

Campbell, J., and B. Moyers. *The Power of Myth*. New York: Doubleday, 1988.

Jung, C. G. *Collected Works*. Bollingen Series XX. Princeton: Princeton University Press, 1960.

_____. *Synchronicity: An Acausal Connecting Principle*. In *Collected Works*, vol. 8. Bollingen Series XX. Princeton: Princeton University Press, 1980.

Perry, J. W. *The Self in Psychotic Process*. Berkeley: University of California Press, 1953.

_____. *Lord of the Four Quarters*. New York: Braziller, 1966.

_____. *The Far Side of Madness*. Englewood Cliffs, N.J.: Prentice-Hall, 1974.

_____. *Roots of Renewal in Myth and Madness*. San Francisco: Jossey-Bass, 1976.

Past-Life Experiences and Karma

Bache, C. "Lifecycles: Reincarnation and the Web of Life." Paragon Press, in press.

Cranston, W. and C. Williams. *Reincarnation: A New Horizon in Science, Religion, and Society*. New York: Julian Press, 1984.

Kelsey, D. and J. Grant. *Many Lifetimes*. Garden City, N.Y.: Doubleday, 1967.

Lati Rinbochay and J. Hopkins. *Death, Intermediate State, and Rebirth in Tibetan Buddhism*. Valois, N.Y.: Snow Lion Press, 1979.

Netherton, N.: *Past Lives Therapy*. New York: William Morrow, 1978.

Prajnananda, Swami. "The Mystery of Karma." In *Ancient Wisdom and*

Modern Science, edited by S. Grof. Albany, N.Y.: State University of New York Press, 1984.

Stevenson, I. *Twenty Cases Suggestive of Reincarnation*. Charlottesville, Va.: University of Virginia Press, 1966.

_____. *Unlearned Language*. Charlottesville, Va.: University of Virginia Press, 1984.

Wambach, H.: *Reliving Past Lives: The Evidence Under Hypnosis*. New York: Bantam, 1978.

Whitton, J. and J. Fisher. *Life Between Life*. Garden City, N.Y.: Doubleday, 1986.

Woolger, R. *Other Lives, Other Selves*. New York: Bantam, 1988.

Psychic Opening

Greeley, A. *The Sociology of the Paranormal*. Beverly Hills, Calif.: Sage, 1975.

Hastings, A. "A Counseling Approach to Parapsychological Experience." *Journal of Transpersonal Psychology* 15 (1983):143.

Jung, C. G. *Synchronicity: An Acausal Connecting Principle*. In *Collected Works*, vol. 8. Bollingen Series XX. Princeton: Princeton University Press, 1980.

Krippner, S. *The Song of the Siren: A Parapsychological Odyssey*, New York: Harper and Row, 1977.

_____. *Human Possibilities*. Garden City, N.Y.: Anchor/Doubleday, 1980.

Monroe, R. *Journeys Out of the Body*. New York: Doubleday, 1971.

_____. *Far Journeys*. Garden City, N.Y.: Doubleday, 1985.

Peat, D. *Synchronicity: The Bridge between Matter and Mind*. New York: Bantam 1987.

Progoff, I. *Jung, Synchronicity, and Human Destiny: Non-Causal Dimensions of Human Experience*. New York: Julian Press, 1973.

Targ, R., and H. Puthoff. *Mind Reach: Scientists Look at Psychic Ability*. New York: Delta, 1977.

Targ, R., and K. Harary. *The Mind Race*. New York: Villard, 1984.

Tart, C. "Out-of-the-Body Experiences." In *Psychic Explorations*, edited by E. Mitchell and J. White. New York: Putnam, 1974.

_____. *Learning to Use Extrasensory Perception*. Chicago: University of Chicago Press, 1975.

_____. *PSI: Scientific Studies of the Psychic Realm*. New York: Dutton, 1977.

Channeling

Hastings, A. *Tongues of Men and Angels*. New York: Holt, Rinehart & Winston, 1990.

Kautz, W., and M. Branon. *Channeling: The Intuitive Connection*. San Francisco: Harper and Row, 1987.

Klimo, J. *Channeling: Investigations on Receiving Information from Paranormal Sources*. Los Angeles: Jeremy P. Tarcher, 1987.

Experiences of UFO Encounters and Extraterrestrial Contacts

Jung, C. G. *Flying Saucers: A Modern Myth of Things Seen in the Skies*. In *Collected Works*, vol. 10. Bollingen Series XX. Princeton: Princeton University Press, 1964.

Thompson, K. "The UFO Experience as a Crisis of Transformation." In *Spiritual Emergency: When Personal Transformation Becomes a Crisis*, edited by S. Grof and C. Grof. Los Angeles: Jeremy P. Tarcher, 1989.

Thompson, K., ed. "Angels, Aliens, and Archetypes." Parts 1, 2. *Re-Vision Journal* 11, nos. 3, 4 (1989).

Vallée, J. *UFOs in Space: Anatomy of a Phenomenon*. New York: Ballantine, 1965.

_____. *Dimensions: A Casebook of Alien Contact*. New York: Contemporary Books, 1988.

Near-Death Experiences

Gallup, G. *Adventures in Immortality*. New York: McGraw-Hill, 1982.

Greyson, B. and C. P. Flynn. *The Near-Death Experience: Problems, Prospects, Perspectives*. Springfield, Ill.: Charles C. Thomas Publishers, 1984.

Moody, R. *Life after Life*. Atlanta: Mockingbird, 1975.

Noyes, R. "Dying and Mystical Consciousness." *Journal of Thanatology* 1 (1971):25.

_____. "The Experience of Dying." *Psychiatry* 35 (1972):174.

Osis, K. et al. *Deathbed Observations of Physicians and Nurses*. New York: Parapsychology Foundation, 1961.

Ring, K.: *Life at Death*. New York: Coward, McCann and Geoghegan, 1980.

————. *Heading Toward Omega*. New York: William Morrow, 1984.

Sabom, M.: *Recollections of Death*. New York: Simon and Schuster, 1982.

Possession States

Allison, R. *Minds in Many Pieces*. New York: Rawson and Wade, 1980.

Dusen, W. van. *The Natural Depth in Man*. New York: Harper and Row, 1972.

————. *The Presence of Other Worlds: The Teachings of Emanuel Swedenborg*. New York: Harper and Row, 1974.

Addiction as Spiritual Emergency

Alcoholics Anonymous. New York: Alcoholics Anonymous World Services, 1976.

As Bill Sees It. New York: Alcoholics Anonymous World Services, 1976.

Bateson, G. "The Cybernetics of 'Self': A Theory of Alcoholism." In *Steps to An Ecology of Mind*. New York: Dutton, 1972.

Grof, S., ed. "Mystical Quest, Attachment, and Addiction." *Re-Vision Journal* 10 (2):1987.

Pass It On. New York: Alcoholics Anonymous World Services, 1984.

Seymour, R. B., and D. E. Smith. *Drugfree*. New York: Facts on File, 1987.

Small, J. *Awakening in Time: From Co-Dependency to Co-Creation*. New York: Bantam, in press.

Twelve Steps and Twelve Traditions. New York: Alcoholics Anonymous World Services, 1953.

Personal Accounts of Spiritual Emergency

Armstrong, A. "The Challenges of Psychic Opening: A Personal Story." In *Spiritual Emergency: When Personal Transformation Becomes a Crisis*, edited by S. Grof and C. Grof. Los Angeles: Jeremy P. Tarcher, 1989.

Courtois, F. *An Experience of Enlightenment*, Wheaton, Ill.: Theosophical Publishing House, 1986.

Hakuin. "Yasenkanna." In *The Tiger's Cave*, edited and translated by Trevor Leggett. London: Routledge and Kegan Paul, 1977.

Steinfeld, N. "Surviving the Chaos of Something Extraordinary." *Shaman's Drum* 4 (1986):22.

Tweedie, I. *The Chasm of Fire: A Woman's Experience of Liberation through the Teaching of a Sufi Master*. The Old Brewery, Tisbury, Wiltshire: Element Books, 1979.

Therapies Useful in Spiritual Emergencies

Assagioli, R. *Psychosynthesis*. New York: Penguin, 1976.

Cassou, M. *The Painting Experience*. Videotape. Can be obtained from Michell Cassou, The Painting Experience, 2101 20th Ave., San Francisco, CA 94116.

Garfield, P. *Creative Dreaming*. New York: Ballantine, 1974.

Grof, S. *The Adventure of Self-Discovery*. Albany, N.Y.: State University of New York Press, 1988.

Hannah, B. *Encounters with the Soul: Active Imagination*. As developed by C. G. Jung, Sigo Press, Santa Monica, Calif., 1981.

Kalff, D. *Sandplay: Mirror of a Child's Psyche*. San Francisco: Hendra and Howard, 1971.

Mindell, A. *Dreambody: The Body's Role in Revealing Itself*. Santa Monica, Calif.: Sigo Press, 1982.

_____. *Working with the Dreambody*. London and New York: Routledge and Kegan Paul, 1985.

Perls, F. *The Gestalt Approach and Eye-Witness to Therapy*. New York: Bantam, 1976.

Ram Dass and P. Gorman. *How Can I Help?* New York: Knopf, 1985.

Singer, J. *Boundaries of the Soul: The Practice of Jung's Psychology*. Garden City, N.Y.: Anchor/Doubleday, 1972.

Small, J. *Becoming Naturally Therapeutic*. Austin, Tex.: Eupsychian Press, 1981.

_____. *Transformers: The Therapists of the Future*. Marina del Rey, Calif.: DeVorss, 1982.

Vaughan, F. *The Inward Arc: Healing and Wholeness in Psychotherapy and Spirituality*. Boston and London: New Science Library/Shambhala, 1985.

Spiritual Emergence and the Global Crisis

Aurobindo, Sri. *The Mind of Light.* New York: Dutton, 1971.

Friedman, W. "Toward a Psychology of Peace: A Study in Global Psychosynthesis." In *Readings in Psychosynthesis: Theory, Process, and Practice,* edited by J. Weiser and T. Yeoman. Toronto: Department of Applied Psychology/Ontario Institute for Studies in Education, 1985.

Grof, S., ed. *Human Survival and Consciousness Evolution.* Albany, N.Y.: State University of New York Press, 1988.

Grosso, M. *The Final Choice.* Walpole, N.H.: Stillpoint, 1985.

Perry, J. W. *The Heart of History: Individuality in Evolution.* Albany, N.Y.: State University of New York Press, 1987.

Russell, P. *The Global Brain,* Los Angeles: Jeremy P. Tarcher, 1983.

Teilhard de Chardin, P. *The Phenomenon of Man.* New York: Harper and Row, 1959.

Walsh, R. *Staying Alive: The Psychology of Human Survival.* Boulder, Colo.: Shambhala, 1984.

Wilber, K. *Up from Eden: A Transpersonal View of Human Evolution.* Garden City, N.Y.: Doubleday/Anchor, 1981.